Coursebook

Iwonna Dubicka
Margaret O'Keeffe
Bob Dignen
Mike Hogan
Lizzie Wright

Business Partner

B1+

Contents

UNIT 1 > ORGANISATION p.7
Videos: 1.1 A news organisation 1.3 Managing first meetings

1.1 > A news organisation	1.2 > Innovative organisations	1.3 > Communication skills: Managing first meetings	1.4 > Business skills: Small talk in first meetings	1.5 > Writing: Emails – Organising information	Business workshop > 1 Office space (p.88)
Video: A news organisation **Vocabulary:** Roles and responsibilities **Pronunciation:** → Word stress (p.114) **Project:** Showing someone around a department	**Listening:** Flat and tall organisations **Grammar:** Future forms: Present Simple, Present Continuous and be going to **Writing:** An email about future plans and arrangements	**Video:** Managing first meetings **Functional language:** Greetings, introductions and goodbyes **Pronunciation:** → Intonation and politeness (p.114) **Task:** Making introductions and contacts at an event	**Listening:** Interview with a communication coach; Small talk between colleagues **Functional language:** Asking and answering questions in first meetings **Task:** Meet a visitor and manage small talk	**Model text:** Invitation to an induction day **Functional language:** Ordering information in an email **Grammar:** Present Simple and Continuous **Task:** Write a reply to a work-related invitation	**Listening:** Employee views on their workspace **Reading:** Millennial-friendly workspaces **Task:** Design a new office space

Review p.104

UNIT 2 > BRANDS p.17
Videos: 2.1 A luxury brand 2.3 Teamwork

2.1 > The life of luxury	2.2 > Asian brands go west	2.3 > Communication skills: Supporting teamwork	2.4 > Business skills: Making a presentation	2.5 > Writing: Formal and semi-formal emails	Business workshop > 2 Kloze-Zone (p.90)
Video: A luxury brand **Vocabulary:** Marketing and brands **Pronunciation:** → Stress in compound nouns (p.114) **Project:** Research and discuss an advertising campaign	**Reading:** Chinese combine holidays with luxury shopping **Grammar:** Connectors **Pronunciation:** → Connectors: intonation and pausing (p.114) **Speaking:** Discussing brands using connectors	**Video:** Teamwork **Functional language:** Giving and responding to advice **Task:** Asking for and giving advice	**Listening:** Different ways to open a presentation **Functional language:** Signposting in presentations **Task:** Prepare and give a presentation	**Model text:** Invitation to a corporate event **Functional language:** Writing, accepting and declining an invitation **Grammar:** Verbs + -ing vs. infinitive **Task:** Write a formal reply to an invitation	**Listening:** Customer and staff feedback on a clothing store **Task:** Brainstorm a brand awareness campaign **Writing:** An email summary of the campaign

Review p.105

UNIT 3 > JOB HUNTING p.27
Videos: 3.1 Applying for an internship 3.3 Demonstrating active listening

3.1 > A job search	3.2 > Job interview questions	3.3 > Communication skills: Listening actively	3.4 > Business skills: Interviews	3.5 > Writing: Covering letters	Business workshop > 3 Social media manager required (p.92)
Video: Applying for an internship **Vocabulary:** Getting a job **Pronunciation:** → Stress in derived words (p.115) **Project:** Plan and write a job advertisement	**Listening:** Interview questions and answers **Grammar:** Indirect questions **Pronunciation:** → Voice range and intonation in indirect questions (p.115) **Speaking:** A job interview	**Video:** Demonstrating active listening **Functional language:** Active listening **Task:** The listening/distraction game	**Listening:** Two job interviews **Functional language:** Useful phrases for candidates **Task:** Create a job and interview for it	**Model text:** Covering letter **Functional language:** Useful phrases for covering letters **Grammar:** Past Simple and Present Perfect **Task:** Write a covering letter	**Listening:** Three video CVs; First interviews **Reading:** Analysis of three CVs and covering letters **Task:** Conduct a second interview

Review p.106

UNIT 4 > BUSINESS STRATEGY p.37
Videos: 4.1 A food company's strategy for growth 4.3 Problem-solving styles

4.1 > Food industry strategies	4.2 > PEST analysis	4.3 > Communication skills: Solving problems	4.4 > Business skills: Problem-solving meetings	4.5 > Writing: Reporting reasons and results	Business workshop > 4 Supermarket wars (p.94)
Video: A food company's strategy for growth **Vocabulary:** Business strategy collocations and word building **Project:** Investigate a food brand's attitude to health	**Listening:** A lecture on PEST analysis **Grammar:** Modal verbs: obligation, prohibition, necessity, recommendation **Writing:** A short PEST analysis of a company or organisation	**Video:** Problem-solving styles **Functional language:** Offering and asking for help **Pronunciation:** → /iː/, /ɪ/, /eɪ/ and /aɪ/ (p.115) **Task:** Offering and asking for help in work and social situations	**Listening:** A problem-solving team meeting **Functional language:** Leading and participating in problem-solving meetings **Pronunciation:** → Intonation in 'OK' (p.115) **Task:** Take part in a problem-solving meeting	**Model text:** Report extract **Functional language:** Reporting problems, reasons and results **Grammar:** Comparison **Task:** Write a short report outlining problems, reasons and results	**Reading:** Profiles of competing supermarket chains **Task:** Select the best strategies for growth **Listening:** Compare your strategies with a business news report

Review p.107

UNIT 5 > LOGISTICS p.47
Videos: 5.1 Amazon: the logistics of e-commerce 5.3 Collaborating on a project

5.1 > E-commerce	5.2 > Driverless technology	5.3 > Communication skills: Collaborating	5.4 > Business skills: Negotiating	5.5 > Writing: Letter of complaint	Business workshop > 5 Robots wanted for warehouse (p.96)
Video: Amazon: the logistics of e-commerce **Vocabulary:** Logistics and word building **Pronunciation:** → Pausing and stress in presentations (p.116) **Project:** Debate the use of drones	**Reading:** Lorries lead cars in the technology race **Grammar:** Passive forms **Pronunciation:** → Auxiliary verbs in passives (p.116) **Speaking:** Describe a process	**Video:** Collaborating on a project **Functional language:** Agreeing and disagreeing **Task:** A meeting to discuss controversial proposals	**Listening:** Negotiating new terms and conditions **Functional language:** Negotiating **Task:** Negotiate a new deal	**Model text:** Letter of complaint **Functional language:** Useful phrases for letters of complaint **Grammar:** Linking **Task:** Write a letter of complaint	**Listening:** Criteria for choosing a supplier; Teleconferences with suppliers **Task:** Negotiate and select a supplier **Writing:** A formal email confirming the result of the negotiation

Review p.108

UNIT 6 > ENTREPRENEURS p.57
Videos: 6.1 The world's first ethical smartphone 6.3 Influencing styles: push and pull

6.1 > Fairphone	6.2 > Young entrepreneurs	6.3 > Communication skills: Influencing	6.4 > Business skills: Presenting facts and figures	6.5 > Writing: Summarising	Business workshop > 6 Doable crowdfunding (p.98)
Video: The world's first ethical smartphone **Vocabulary:** Running a business **Pronunciation:** → Consonant-vowel linking (p.116) **Project:** Brainstorm and present new business ideas	**Reading:** Leaving Harvard to start a business **Grammar:** Reported speech **Speaking:** Talk to a journalist about your start-up **Writing:** An email/article based on the interview	**Video:** Influencing styles: push and pull **Functional language:** Dealing with objections **Task:** Influencing others to overcome objections	**Listening:** A presentation based on visual data **Functional language:** Presenting visual information **Pronunciation:** → Intonation and discourse marking in presentations (p.116) **Task:** A presentation to an investor	**Model text:** Summary of a business talk **Functional language:** Summarising **Grammar:** Order of information in sentences **Task:** Listen to a talk and write a summary	**Listening:** Three crowdfunding pitches **Speaking:** Decide which crowdfunding project to back **Task:** Prepare and deliver a crowdfunding pitch

Review p.109

UNIT 7 > WORKING ABROAD p.67
Videos: 7.1 Working abroad 7.3 Decision-making styles

7.1 > Global work cultures	7.2 > Cultural anecdotes	7.3 > Communication skills: Decision-making	7.4 > Business skills: Relationship-building	7.5 > Writing: Making recommendations	Business workshop > 7 Cross-cultural consultants (p.100)
Video: Working abroad **Vocabulary:** Working abroad: Adjectives, prefixes, opposites **Project:** Research a different work or study culture	**Listening:** Working in other cultures **Grammar:** Past tenses: Past Simple, Past Continuous and Past Perfect Simple **Pronunciation:** → Phrasing and intonation in past sentences (p.117) **Speaking:** Tell an anecdote **Writing:** An anecdote	**Video:** Decision-making styles **Pronunciation:** → Strong or weak? (p.117) **Functional language:** Expressing preferences **Task:** Discuss preferences and reach agreement	**Listening:** Conversations at a networking event **Functional language:** Keeping a conversation going **Task:** Meeting new people at an induction day	**Model text:** Report giving suggestions, advice and recommendations **Functional language:** Formal/neutral/informal language for recommendations **Grammar:** First and second conditional **Task:** Write a report giving suggestions, advice and recommendations	**Reading:** Blog posts on cultural awareness **Listening:** Interviews with staff about working internationally **Task:** Prepare and present recommendations for working in your culture **Writing:** A formal email confirming the outcome of the presentations

Review p.110

UNIT 8 > LEADERSHIP p.77
Videos: 8.1 Safari Vet School 8.3 Positive and developmental feedback

8.1 > Learning to lead	8.2 > Neuroleadership	8.3 > Communication skills: Giving and receiving feedback	8.4 > Business skills: Leading meetings	8.5 > Writing: Informing of a decision	Business workshop > 8 Talent management (p.102)
Video: Safari Vet School **Pronunciation:** → Glottal stops (p.117) **Vocabulary:** Leadership **Project:** Discuss and write about a great leader	**Reading:** Business leaders need neuroscience **Grammar:** Relative clauses **Pronunciation:** → Phrasing and intonation in relative clauses (p.117) **Speaking:** Truth or lie game using relative clauses	**Video:** Positive and developmental feedback **Functional language:** Giving and responding to feedback **Task:** Give and respond to developmental feedback	**Listening:** Managing a team meeting **Functional language:** Leading and managing meetings **Task:** Lead a mini-meeting	**Model text:** Email about decisions made by Board of Directors **Functional language:** Formal and semi-formal language for decisions **Grammar:** Reduced relative clauses **Task:** Write a formal email to inform staff of decisions made	**Listening:** Three employees talking about their training needs **Reading:** Profiles of training courses **Task:** Design a development plan for an employee **Writing:** An email to justify a training course

Review p.111

Pronunciation p.112 Grammar reference p.118 Additional material p.126 Videoscripts p.138 Audioscripts p.146 Glossary p.154

Introduction for learners

Why... Business Partner?

Our research talking to teachers and learners proved a few very obvious points.
1 People study business English in order to communicate more effectively in their workplace or to find a job in an international environment.
2 To achieve these goals, you need to improve your knowledge of English language as it is used in the workplace, but also develop key skills for the international workplace.
3 People studying business English have different priorities and amounts of study time. You therefore need a flexible course which you can adapt to suit your needs.

Business Partner has been developed to meet these needs by offering a flexible course, focused on delivering a balance of language and skills training that you can immediately use to improve your performance in your workplace, studies or job search.

Why... skills training?

Language is only one aspect of successful communication. Effective communication also requires an understanding of different business situations and an awareness of different communication styles, especially when working across cultures.

In *Business Partner* we refer to 'Communication skills' and 'Business skills'. Every unit has a lesson on these two areas.
- 'Communication skills' (Lesson 3) means the soft skills you need to work effectively with people whose personality and culture may be different from your own. This includes teamwork, decision-making and influencing skills.
- 'Business skills' (Lesson 4) means the practical skills you need in different business situations, such as skills for taking part in meetings, presentations and negotiations.

Why... authentic content?

In order to reflect the real world as closely as possible, *Business Partner* content is based on authentic videos and articles from leading media organisations such as the BBC and the Financial Times. These offer a wealth of international business information as well as real examples of British, U.S. and non-native speaker English.

Why... video content?

We all use video more and more to communicate and to find out about the world. This is reflected in *Business Partner*, which has two videos in every unit:
- an authentic video package in Lesson 1, based on real-life video clips and interviews suitable for your level of English.
- a dramatised communication skills video in Lesson 3 (see p.6 for more information).

Why... flexible content?

This course has been developed so that you can adapt it to your own needs. Each unit and lesson works independently, so you can focus on the topics, lessons or skills which are most relevant to you and skip those which don't feel relevant to your needs right now.

You can then use the extra activities and additional materials in MyEnglishLab to work in more depth on the aspects that are important to you.

What's in the units?

Lesson outcome and self-assessment
Each lesson starts with a lesson outcome and ends with a short Self-assessment section. The aim is to encourage you to think about the progress that you have made in relation to the lesson outcomes. More detailed self-assessment tasks and suggestions for extra practice are available in MyEnglishLab.

Vocabulary
The main topic vocabulary set is presented and practised in Lesson 1 of each unit, building on vocabulary from the authentic video. You will get lots of opportunities to use the vocabulary in discussions and group tasks.

Functional language
Functional language (such as giving advice, summarising, dealing with objections) gives you the capability to operate in real workplace situations in English. Three functional language sets are presented and practised in every unit: in Lessons 3, 4 and 5. You will practise the language in group speaking and writing tasks.

 In MyEnglishLab you will also find a Functional language bank so that you can quickly refer to lists of useful language when preparing for a business situation, such as a meeting, presentation or interview.

Grammar
The approach to grammar is flexible depending on whether you want to devote a significant amount of time to grammar or to focus on the consolidation of grammar only when you need to.
- There is one main grammar point in each unit, presented and practised in Lesson 2.
- There is a link from Lesson 5 to an optional second grammar point in MyEnglishLab – with short video presentations and interactive practice.

Both grammar points are supported by the Grammar reference section at the back of the coursebook (p.118). This provides a summary of meaning and form, with notes on usage or exceptions, and business English examples.

Listening and video
The course offers a wide variety of listening activities (based on both video and audio recordings) to help you develop your comprehension skills and to hear target language in context. All of the video and audio material is available in MyEnglishLab and includes a range of British, U.S. and non-native speaker English. Lessons 1 and 3 are based on video (as described above). In four of the eight units, Lesson 2 is based on audio. In all units, you also work with significant audio recordings in Lesson 4 and the Business workshop.

Reading
You will read authentic texts and articles from a variety of sources, particularly the Financial Times. Every unit has a main reading text with comprehension tasks. This appears either in Lesson 2 or in the Business workshop.

 In MyEnglishLab, you will also find a Reading bank which offers a longer reading text for every unit with comprehension activities.

Speaking
Collaborative speaking tasks appear at the end of Lessons 1, 3, 4 and the Business workshop in every unit. These tasks encourage you to use the target language and, where relevant, the target skill of the lesson. There are lots of opportunities to personalise these tasks to suit your own situation.

Writing
- Lesson 5 in every unit provides a model text and practice in a business writing skill. The course covers a wide range of genres such as reports, proposals, note-taking and emails, and for different purposes, including formal and informal communication, summarising, invitations, replies and project updates.
- There are also short writing tasks in Lesson 2 which provide controlled practice of the target grammar.

 In MyEnglishLab, you will find a Writing bank which provides models of different types of business writing and useful phrases appropriate to your level of English.

Pronunciation
Two pronunciation points are presented and practised in every unit. Pronunciation points are linked to the content of the unit – usually to a video/audio presentation or to a grammar point. The pronunciation presentations and activities are at the back of the coursebook (p.112), with signposts from the relevant lessons. This section also includes an introduction to pronunciation with British and U.S. phonetic charts.

Reviews
There is a one-page review for each unit at the back of the coursebook (p.104). The review recycles and revises the key vocabulary, grammar and functional language presented in the unit.

Signposts, cross-references and the Pearson English Portal

T **Signposts for teachers** in each lesson indicate that there are extra activities in the Portal which can be printed or displayed on-screen. These activities can be used to extend a lesson or to focus in more depth on a particular section.

L **Signposts for learners** indicate that there are additional interactive activities in MyEnglishLab.

 page 000
Cross-references refer to the Pronunciation bank and Grammar reference pages.

Pearson English Portal

Access to the Pearson English Portal is given through a code printed on the inside front cover of this book.

The code will give you access to:

Interactive eBook: a digital version of the coursebook including interactive activities, all class video clips and all class audio recordings.

Online Practice on MyEnglishLab: a self-study interactive workbook with instant feedback and automatic gradebook. Teachers can assign workbook activities as homework.

Digital Resources: including downloadable coursebook resources, all video clips, all audio recordings.

The **Global Scale of English (GSE)** is a standardised, granular scale from 10 to 90 which measures English language proficiency. The GSE Learning Objectives for Professional English are aligned with the Common European Framework of Reference (CEFR). Unlike the CEFR, which describes proficiency in terms of broad levels, the Global Scale of English identifies what a learner can do at each point on a more granular scale—and within a CEFR level. The scale is designed to motivate learners by demonstrating incremental progress in their language ability. The Global Scale of English forms the backbone for Pearson English course material and assessment.

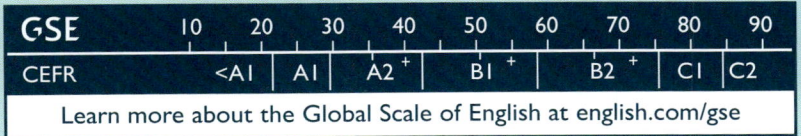

COMMUNICATION SKILLS
Video introduction

Introduction

The Communication skills videos (in Lesson 3 of each unit) is to introduce you to the skills needed to interact successfully in international teams, with people who may have different communication styles due to culture or personality.

In each Communication skills lesson, you will:

1. watch a setup video which introduces the main characters and challenge of the lesson;
2. watch the main character approach the situation in two different ways (Options A and B);
3. answer questions about each approach before watching the conclusion.

There is a storyline running through the eight units, with the main characters appearing in different situations. Each clip, however, can be watched separately and each lesson done independently without the need to watch the preceding video clips.

Communication skills video storyline

PRO-Manage is a global company providing project management training qualifications. It is active in the USA, Germany and the UK, and it is the market leader in each country. An international project team has just been created. The team has to launch their online project management courses for universities and corporate clients, in two important new countries: Japan and Mexico.

The overall project manager (PM) is Matt Farnham, Head of UK Operations. Throughout the eight units of the book, we watch Matt and his team as they face challenges at different stages in the project lifecycle. Matt supports Kenji to manage the launch in Japan and Paula to launch in Mexico. Stefanie, from Germany, is the main technical expert.

In addition to the practical project challenges, the people in the team experience challenges as they learn to work with each other.

Characters

Matt Farnham (British) Head of UK Operations, overall PM (units: 1, 2, 3, 4, 5, 6, 8)

Stefanie Hatke (German) Head of the German office, the company's main technical expert, she is supporting the project team (units: 1, 2, 5, 7, 8)

James Toomey (British) Part of the UK design team (unit 3)

Alistair Fraser (British) Part of the UK design team (units: 3, 4)

Paula Rodriguez (Mexican) PM for the Mexico launch (units: 2, 3, 6, 7, 8)

Dan King (American) U.S.-based PM with technical expertise, working on programming for the Mexico part of the project (unit 2)

Kenji Kobayashi (Japanese) PM for the Japan launch (units: 4, 8)

Jack Collins (Australian) UK-based PM and friend of Matt's (unit 4)

Raj Kumar (Indian) PM for IT supplier in India which is building the platform for the online courses (unit 5)

Susan Jones (American) and Pedro Sanchez (Mexican) Potential clients from Mexico (units: 6, 7)

Video context by unit

1 Managing first meetings
Video synopsis: Matt and Stefanie meet for the first time in London. They have different expectations of the meeting.

2 Teamwork
Video synopsis: The key team members hold their first team conference call. A personality clash develops between Stefanie and Dan.

3 Demonstrating active listening
Video synopsis: Paula visits the London office. Matt talks to her about feedback he has received from her previous manager.

4 Problem solving
Video synopsis: Kenji visits the London office. Matt talks to him about issues with the schedule in Japan.

5 Collaborating on a project
Video synopsis: Matt has a video call with Raj to discuss rising costs and technical issues.

6 Influencing styles
Video synopsis: Paula and Matt present the PRO-Manage courses to potential Mexican clients.

7 Decision-making styles
Video synopsis: Paula and Stefanie discuss implementation details with the potential Mexican clients.

8 Giving and responding to feedback
Video synopsis: At the end of the project, Matt holds a feedback meeting with the team.

Organisation 1

'The best place to work is a place where you can be your best.'
Rosalene Glickman, Ph.D., executive coach

Unit overview

1.1 A news organisation
Lesson outcome: Learners can use vocabulary related to a range of job roles and responsibilities within a company or organisation.

Video: A news organisation
Vocabulary: Roles and responsibilities
Project: Showing someone around a department or campus

1.2 Innovative organisations
Lesson outcome: Learners can use a range of future forms to talk about intentions, plans, arrangements and predictions.

Listening: Two company profiles: flat and tall organisations
Grammar: Future forms: Present Simple, Present Continuous and be going to
Writing: An email about future plans and arrangements

1.3 Communication skills: Managing first meetings
Lesson outcome: Learners are aware of different ways to manage first meetings and can use a range of phrases for greetings, introductions and goodbyes.

Video: Managing first meetings
Functional language: Greetings, introductions and goodbyes
Task: Making introductions and contacts at an event

1.4 Business skills: Small talk in first meetings
Lesson outcome: Learners can use a range of questions and responses to make small talk in first meetings.

Listening: Interview with a communication coach; Small talk between colleagues
Functional language: Asking and answering questions in first meetings
Task: Meet a visitor and manage small talk during a first meeting

1.5 Writing: Emails – Organising information
Lesson outcome: Learners can organise information in a work-related email and write a reply to a work invitation.

Model text: Invitation to an induction day
Functional language: Ordering information in an email
Grammar: Present Simple and Present Continuous
Task: Write a reply to a work-related invitation

Business workshop 1: p.88 | **Review 1:** p.104 | **Pronunciation:** 1.1 Word stress 1.3 Intonation and politeness p.114 | **Grammar reference:** p.118

1.1 A news organisation

Lesson outcome: Learners can use vocabulary related to a range of job roles and responsibilities within a company or organisation.

Lead-in

1 Discuss these questions.
1 These are some typical departments in a company. What do you think each one does? Use some of the key words and phrases in the second box to help you.

| finance   human resources   marketing   operations   production   sales |

| brand image   cash flow   customer service   health and safety   invoicing |
| manufacturing   pricing   promotion   quality control   recruitment   supply chain |

2 Can you name any other departments?
3 Which departments do you think do the most important work? Why?

VIDEO

2A Would you like to work for a news organisation? What do you imagine it is like?

B In what ways do you think working for a news organisation is:
a stressful?   b glamorous?   c interesting?

3A ▶ 1.1.1 Watch the video and match the five speakers with the jobs.

| Director of Human Resources   Finance Supervisor   News Editor |
| Programme Director   News Reporter |

Arti Lukha

Nick Thatcher

John Roberts

Melanie Tansey

Ray Snelling

1 _____   2 _____   3 _____   4 _____   5 _____

B Which of these people probably work closely together on a daily basis?

4 Watch the video again and complete the information. Use one word in each gap.
1 It is important that individuals and teams understand their _____ and responsibilities.
2 Staff [in the newsroom] are responsible for _____ the teams gathering* news globally.
3 Arti gives a(n) _____ the task of covering a news story.
4 Nick works with a camera _____ to make sure they are getting the right pictures.
5 John's role is to lead the production _____ .
6 He describes his job as similar to the _____ of an orchestra.
7 The HR director has several strategic and _____ priorities.
8 Ray says it's important to make sure the _____ come in on time.

Teacher's resources: extra activities

5 Work in pairs or small groups. What do you think each person likes most and least about their job?

Vocabulary

Roles and responsibilities

6 What do the words in the box mean? Complete the extracts from the video using the words and phrases in the box.

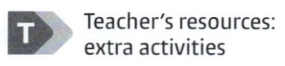
involves   lead   make sure   running

1 My job _____ newsgathering for a major news organisation.
2 My role as Programme Director is to _____ the production team.
3 I'm responsible for _____ the human resources team.
4 We need to _____ we're getting cash in.

*gather: get things from different places and put them together in one place

1.1 A news organisation

7 Look at some expressions people use to talk about their jobs. Complete the expressions in bold using the prepositions in the box.

after   for   of   of   of   to   with   with

1 I **report** _____ the IT Director.
2 I'm the **Head** _____ Sales.
3 I **work closely** _____ the Head of Marketing.
4 I **look** _____ the company website.
5 I **take care** _____ the export documentation.
6 I'm **responsible** _____ coordinating the production team.
7 I'm **in charge** _____ the research and development team.
8 I **coordinate** _____ all departments to ensure customer satisfaction.

8 Read how two more people at the news organisation describe their jobs. Complete the texts using words from Exercises 6 and 7. Use one word in each gap.

My name's Frances Mullan. I'm the Head of Marketing. I ¹_____ a small team of two marketing managers and a video producer. Our work ²_____ a variety of marketing strategies to promote the business, including events, social media and printed advertising. I'm in ³_____ of attracting new customers, retaining existing customers and positioning the business as innovative and creative. I ⁴_____ directly to the Head of Strategy and Development.

My name's Donovan Parsons. I'm a camera operator and I take ⁵_____ of the camera equipment. I'm ⁶_____ for interpreting what the director wants to happen and putting it on screen. I ⁷_____ closely with other technical departments, such as lighting and sound. My duties also include supervising the work of the camera assistant. We're in a live television environment so we have to make ⁸_____ we can do the job under pressure.

9 Work in pairs. How would you describe your own job, a job you would like to have in the future, or a job in the box? Use some of the vocabulary from Exercises 6 and 7.

actor   hotel manager   journalist   personal shopper   photographer   sports trainer

Teacher's resources: extra activities

→ page 114   See Pronunciation bank: Word stress

PROJECT: Showing someone around

10A Work in pairs or small groups. Imagine that you are going to show a new member of staff around the organisation where you work or a new/overseas student around the campus of the place where you study.
- Decide which departments/areas you would take the new employee/student to and why.
- Which key people would you introduce your new employee/student to?
- How would you briefly describe the roles and responsibilities of three people you meet?

B Roleplay the introductions with the new employee/student. What would be some good questions to ask the three people about their roles and responsibilities?

Self-assessment

- How successfully have you achieved the lesson outcome? Give yourself a score from 0 (I need more practice) to 5 (I know this well).
- Go to My Self-assessment in MyEnglishLab to reflect on what you have learnt.

1.2 Innovative organisations

Lesson outcome — Learners can use a range of future forms to talk about intentions, plans, arrangements and predictions.

Lead-in

Tall organisation

Flat organisation

1 Look at the tall and flat organisational structures. What do you think are some advantages and disadvantages of each?

2A Match the words and phrases in the box with the definitions.

> bureaucracy   centralised   decentralised   hierarchy   innovative   promotion

1 a move to a more important job in a company or organisation
2 new, different and better than before
3 a system of organisation in which people are divided into levels of importance
4 a complicated official system that has a lot of rules and processes
5 organised the control of an organisation so that everything is done or decided in one place
6 moved parts of an organisation, etc. from a central place to several different smaller ones

B Work in pairs. Can you use any of the words in Exercise 2A to talk about the organisational structures in Exercise 1? Compare your ideas with the information on page 126.

Listening

W. L. GORE
CEO: Terri Kelly
Sector: Manufacturing
Number of staff: Over 10,000

ZAPPOS
CEO: Tony Hsieh
Sector: Online shoe and clothing sales
Number of staff: Over 1,500

3 Look at the two company profiles: W. L. Gore and Zappos. Do you think they are likely to have flat or tall structures? Why?

4 🔊 1.01 Listen to the radio discussion with Janet Wood, an organisation consultant. Check your answers in Exercise 3.

5 Listen again and decide if these sentences are *true* (T) or *false* (F). Correct the incorrect sentences.
1 Organisations with tall structures can change and innovate fast.
2 Bob and Genevieve Gore started their company in the 1960s.
3 Employees voted to decide who should be the CEO of Gore.
4 'Holacracy®' is a system without traditional managers.
5 All the functions at Zappos are now done by teams.
6 The transition at Zappos will take a few months to complete.

6 Choose the correct option. Listen to the discussion again if necessary.
1 Janet Wood seems
   a critical of hierarchies.
   b positive about hierarchies.
   c sceptical about flat structures.
2 Which statement about W. L. Gore is true?
   a Employees work in teams of 30.
   b Staff are called associates.
   c Nobody in the company has a job title.
3 Which statement about Zappos is true?
   a The company started two years ago.
   b Staff work in about 500 teams called circles.
   c The lead link of a circle decides what everyone does.
4 What do W. L. Gore and Zappos have in common?
   a Senior executives are elected by the employees.
   b Any member of staff can start a new project team.
   c Staff decide their own roles in a team.

Teacher's resources: extra activities

7 Work in pairs. How would you feel about working in a flatter organisation with few or no managers?

1.2 Innovative organisations

Grammar Future forms: Present Simple, Present Continuous and *be going to*

1 You decide what you **are going to contribute** to the team.

2 Zappos **has** a training session next week.

3 **I'm flying** to Las Vegas tomorrow.

4 I'm sure that **'s going to be** a very interesting experience.

8A Look at these extracts from the discussion. Which one is:
- a a personal intention?
- b a plan/arrangement?
- c a prediction?
- d a scheduled event?

B Which verb form is used in each example in Exercise 8A?

→ **page 118** See Grammar reference: Future forms

9 Decide which is the best option in each sentence and explain your choice. There may be more than one possible answer.

1 What time _____ the first flight _____ on Sundays?
  a does … leave   b is … leaving   c is … going to leave

2 When I get more free time, I _____ a gym.
  a join   b am joining   c am going to join

3 He can't remember what time he _____ the client tomorrow.
  a visits   b is visiting   c is going to visit

4 I _____ to her email until later today.
  a don't reply   b am not replying   c am not going to reply

5 We _____ some friends after work this evening.
  a meet   b are meeting   c are going to meet

6 Susan hasn't studied all year. She _____ her final exams next week.
  a fails   b is failing   c is going to fail

7 The conference _____ until 10 o'clock but let's get there early.
  a doesn't start   b isn't starting   c isn't going to start

8 There's a lot of traffic. _____ in time to catch the train?
  a Do we arrive   b Are we arriving   c Are we going to arrive

10A Complete the conversation with appropriate future forms, using contractions where possible. There may be more than one possible answer.

A: Hi, Juliana. What time ¹_____ (the department meeting / start) tomorrow?
B: At 10 o'clock as usual, but I think I ²_____ (be) about fifteen minutes late. I have a dentist's appointment.
A: ³_____ (you/be) able to talk after your trip to the dentist's?
B: Yes, it's just a check-up. In fact, I ⁴_____ (give) a presentation on the company restructuring.
A: I'm sure that ⁵_____ (be) interesting. Is it true we ⁶_____ (move) to offices outside the city?
B: I ⁷_____ (not tell) you anything before the meeting. You know that.
A: Well, I ⁸_____ (sit) right at the front. I don't want to miss anything.

T Teacher's resources: extra activities

B ◁ 1.02 Listen to the conversation in Exercise 10A. Which future forms do the speakers use in each case? Why do you think this is?

Writing **11** Write an email to a friend or colleague about a real or imaginary trip you have planned for work or pleasure. Write 100–120 words.
- Say when and where you are going and how you are travelling there.
- Say where you are staying.
- Mention your predictions for the weather.
- Talk about your intentions and arrangements for the visit.

Self-assessment
- How successfully have you achieved the lesson outcome? Give yourself a score from 0 (I need more practice) to 5 (I know this well).
- Go to My Self-assessment in MyEnglishLab to reflect on what you have learnt.

1.3 COMMUNICATION SKILLS
Managing first meetings

Lesson outcome Learners are aware of different ways to manage first meetings and can use a range of phrases for greetings, introductions and goodbyes.

Lead-in **1** Work in pairs and discuss the questions.
1. When you meet someone for the first time, what do you usually do and say to be polite?
2. Across cultures, there are many ways of being polite in first meetings, e.g. some people shake hands, some people kiss, etc. How many different ways to be polite can you think of?
3. Is it more polite to invest time to build relationships with small talk first and then focus on the work or task, or is it better to focus directly on the task, and build a relationship later? Why?

VIDEO **2A** ▶ 1.3.1 Watch as Matt and Stefanie prepare to meet each other in London.
1. Where do they work? 2. What is their usual job? 3. What is their project role?

B Watch the video again. Mark which qualities Matt (M) and Stefanie (S) use to describe themselves and their own communication style. Which words do the other speakers use to describe Stefanie? You do not need to use all the words.

| efficient flexible work-focused rude informal friendly polite quiet |
| professional organised open effective |

C Overall, do you think Matt and Stefanie will work well together? Why?

3A In small groups, discuss which is the best communication style (option A or B) for Matt to use in his first meeting with Stefanie. Give reasons for your answers. As a class, decide which video to watch first.

Option A – Focus on the relationship first: Be polite by meeting Stefanie in an informal way and focusing on the relationship first before getting down to business.

Option B – Focus on work first: Be polite by meeting Stefanie in a formal way and focusing the conversation quickly onto work topics.

B Watch the videos in the sequence the class has decided, and answer the questions for each video.

Option A ▶ 1.3.2
1. How does Matt introduce himself?
2. How does he begin the visit and why do you think he does this?
3. Overall, how successful do you think the meeting is? Why?

Option B ▶ 1.3.3
1. How does Matt introduce himself?
2. What two reasons does Matt give for discussing business immediately?
3. Overall, how successful do you think the meeting is? Why?

4 In pairs, discuss the questions and agree what you can learn from Matt's experiences.
1. What did Matt do to be polite in each video?
2. What happened as a result?

5 ▶ 1.3.4 Watch the Conclusions section of the video.
1. Compare what is said with your answers in Exercise 4.
2. Note down the three main learning points which are described.
3. Decide how far you agree with these points. Why?

Reflection **6** Think about the following questions. Then discuss your answers with a partner.
1. Which communication style (relationship-focused or work-focused) do you prefer when meeting people for the first time? Why?
2. What is one advantage and one possible disadvantage of your own personal style?

1.3 Communication skills: Managing first meetings

Functional language

Greetings, introductions and goodbyes

7 Complete the table with these phrases from the video.

1 OK, so we need to leave it there.
2 [Good/Great/Lovely/Nice] to finally meet you in person.
3 Do you know [the design guys]?
4 [Guys,] this is Stefanie.
5 Sorry to [be in a rush like this / rush off so soon].
6 [Good/Great/Lovely/Nice] to see you again.
7 Thank you for coming and have a [safe trip / good weekend]!
8 So, first time in London?

Meeting and greeting	Introducing people	Saying goodbye
How's it going?	Let's go and [say hello to …]	Excuse me. [I must take this call.]
[Did you have a] good trip?	I'd like to introduce you to …	_____
Can I get you [a coffee]?	Have you met [Miran] before? She works for / works with / runs …	_____
_____	_____	_____
_____	_____	

8A Look at the conversation between Suzanne Jones and her visitor. Match what Suzanne says (1–5) with the responses (a–e).

1 Hello, I'm Suzanne Jones, Head of Planning.
2 How's it going?
3 Everything's fine. Good trip?
4 It's always the same. Can I get you anything to drink?
5 Let's go and meet the rest of the team.

a No thanks. I'm fine.
b Hi, Suzanne. Nice to finally meet you in person.
c Great! Can't wait!
d Not bad, not bad. How about you?
e A bit of a delay on the underground today.

B Work in pairs. Use phrases from Exercises 7 and 8A to write your own dialogue between a host and business visitor. Then roleplay your dialogue.

C Work with another pair. Hosts: introduce your visitor to the other pair. Visitors: respond. One person should say goodbye to the group, giving a reason.

T Teacher's resources: extra activities

→ page 114 See Pronunciation bank: Intonation and politeness

TASK

9A Work in pairs. Choose an industry from the list and invent your roles. Think about your job titles, company name and geographical location.

| architecture | fashion | movies | music |
| toy makers | video games | | |

B You are at a large public event. Introduce yourself and your colleague to other people. If you find someone who could be a useful contact, make a note of their name. If not, say goodbye politely and move on.

C At the end, tell the class how many useful contacts you made. Why did you think these people could be useful?

D In your pairs, discuss which phrases you used from Exercise 7 and what you found difficult.

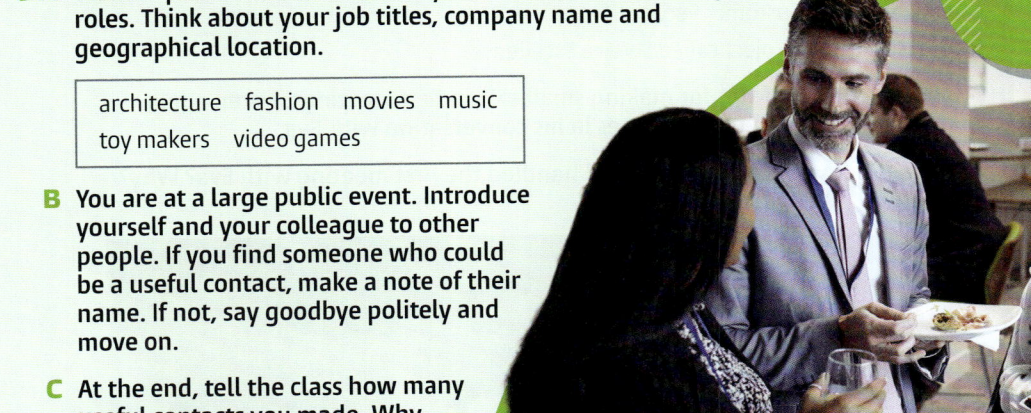

Self-assessment

- How successfully have you achieved the lesson outcome? Give yourself a score from 0 (I need more practice) to 5 (I know this well).
- Go to My Self-assessment in MyEnglishLab to reflect on what you have learnt.

1.4 BUSINESS SKILLS
Small talk in first meetings

Lesson outcome — Learners can use a range of questions and responses to make small talk in first meetings.

Lead-in

1 Work in pairs and discuss the following questions.
1 What is 'small talk'? How important is it during first meetings?
2 What questions would you normally ask when meeting someone for the first time?
3 Are there any problems with asking questions in a first meeting? Why?

Listening

2A 🔊 1.03 Listen to a short interview with Angela Dawson, a communication coach based in New York, about how to use small talk and manage first meetings. Then answer the questions.
1 Why is managing first meetings in international business often difficult?
2 What is the value of asking questions?
3 Which types of question are most effective? Why?
4 What should you ask questions about?

B Listen again and answer the questions.
1 What two things does Angela say about silence?
2 Why does she say that some questions don't matter?
3 What is the relationship between asking questions and building trust?

C In pairs, discuss these questions about Angela's ideas.
1 How far do you agree with Angela's ideas about asking questions? Why?
2 At the end of the interview, Angela talks about the need to find something in common: *When you and the other person have similar interests, the conversation often goes better*. Do you agree? Why / Why not?
3 What other things should you do, in your opinion, to make a conversation go well?

3A 🔊 1.04 Paul Robson works for a London-based international company. He is welcoming Eva Neumann, a colleague from another office of his company. Listen and decide if these sentences are *true* (T) or *false* (F).
1 Eva travelled directly from the airport to the meeting.
2 This is Eva's first visit to London.
3 Eva works full time in Geneva.
4 Paul is head of Customer Service.
5 Eva is leading a project called Service Excellence.

B Look at the list of tips for making small talk in first meetings. Listen again and tick (✓) which tips Paul uses in his conversation with Eva.

C How effectively do you think Paul handled the first meeting with Eva? Why?

Tips for small talk in first meetings

a Give a clear and positive welcome. ✓
b Offer to take the other person's coat. ☐
c Ask about their journey to the office. ☐
d Offer them a drink. ☐
e Check if their hotel is OK. ☐
f Offer help to organise a taxi. ☐
g Ask if it's their first time in the city. ☐
h Suggest going for dinner later in the evening. ☐
i Ask where the other person works. ☐
j Check when they joined the company. ☐
k Make a positive comment about working with them. ☐

14

1.4 Business skills: Small talk in first meetings

Functional language

Asking and answering questions in first meetings

4A Complete the questions from the recording in Exercise 3A with the words in the box. If necessary, use the audioscript on page 146 to help you.

time   join   have   free   offer   take   work   report

1 Offer help/ hospitality	Can I [1]_____ your [coat/bag]? Can I [2]_____ you [something to drink / a coffee / a glass of water]? Can I order you a taxi?
2 Journey	Did you [3]_____ a good [flight/journey/trip]?
3 Experience	Is it your first [4]_____ [in the London office / at the conference]?
4 Place of work	Where do you [5]_____ exactly? Where are you based? Are you in the [Zurich] office at the moment?
5 Time with company	When did you [6]_____ the company?
6 Colleagues	Do you [7]_____ to [Paul Blaettner]? Do you work with [Davide in the Mexico office]?
7 Socialising	Are you [8]_____ for [lunch today / dinner this evening]?

B Match the answers (a–g) with the topics (1–7) in Exercise 4A.

a I'm actually based in Warsaw at the moment.
b About five years ago.
c Sorry, I'm meeting a friend today. Are you free tomorrow?
d Yes, I do. Do you know him?
e That would be great, thanks.
f Actually, I had a delay at the airport.
g No, I was here last month, actually.

Teacher's resources: extra activities

> TASK

5A Work in groups of three. Roleplay meeting a visitor and managing small talk during a first meeting. There are three scenarios. Each person will take the roles of host, observer and visitor once.

Host: You are welcoming a member of the project team to the London office, meeting in reception and moving to your office.

Visitor: You are visiting the London office.

Observer: You will observe and give feedback after the roleplay.

Student A: Look at your three role cards on page 126.
Student B: Look at your three role cards on page 128.
Student C: Look at your three role cards on page 137.

B Take a few minutes to prepare, then roleplay your meetings.

C When you have finished, listen to the observer's feedback and discuss how easy or difficult it is to manage a first meeting. Share your group's ideas with the class.

Self-assessment

- How successfully have you achieved the lesson outcome? Give yourself a score from 0 (I need more practice) to 5 (I know this well).
- Go to My Self-assessment in MyEnglishLab to reflect on what you have learnt.

1.5 WRITING
Emails – Organising information

Lesson outcome: Learners can organise information in a work-related email and write a reply to a work invitation.

Lead-in

1 Read the email about an induction day. Complete it with the phrases in the box and add capital letters where necessary. Then compare in pairs.

> after   all the best   dear Jill   feel free to call me if you have any questions
> firstly   just a quick email to let you know   then

---

1 _____ ,

2 _____ that we are organising an induction day for you on Thursday or Friday next week.

3 _____ , Mike Evans, the Production Supervisor, plans to show you around the factory at 8 a.m. 4_____ , at 10 a.m. Anna Hargreave, who is responsible for Marketing, would like to introduce you to her team and explain the new projects they are working on. I think you'll find it very interesting.

5 _____ that you'll have lunch with the finance team in the staff canteen. In the afternoon Davina Porter, who deals with customer service, feels that it's a good idea for you to accompany her on a visit to some of our most important clients.

Let me know which day is best for you and 6_____ or need any help.

7 _____

Greg

Functional language

2A Look at the email again. Write the words and phrases from Exercise 1 in the correct place in the table.

Greeting/Opening	
Reason for writing	
Ordering information	
Concluding email	
Closing	

B Write these words and phrases in the correct place in the table in Exercise 2A.

> Dear Sir/Madam,   I'm writing to inform you that …   Finally,   Good morning Jacques   Yours,
> Further to our conversation, I confirm that …   Hope to hear from you soon.   Kind regards,
> Hello/Hi George   I look forward to hearing from you.   Thank you for your email.   Thirdly,
> Please do not hesitate to contact me if you have any questions.   Regards,   Yours sincerely,

→ **page 118** See Grammar reference: Present Simple and Continuous

T Teacher's resources: extra activities

L The email contains examples of the Present Simple and Present Continuous. Go to MyEnglishLab for optional grammar work.

TASK

3A Work in pairs. Look at page 126 and discuss the best order to put the information in.

B Write a reply to Greg's email in around 80 words. Thank him and confirm which day you can attend and why you cannot attend on the other day.

C Exchange emails with your partner. How many of the words and phrases in Exercises 2A and 2B did your partner use? Did your partner use different phrases from you?

Self-assessment
- How successfully have you achieved the lesson outcome? Give yourself a score from 0 (I need more practice) to 5 (I know this well).
- Go to My Self-assessment in MyEnglishLab to reflect on what you have learnt.

Brands

> 'We use brands to project who we want to be in the world, how we want people to perceive us and how we want to feel about ourselves.'
>
> Debbie Millman, U.S. designer and brand strategist

Unit overview

2.1 The life of luxury
Lesson outcome: Learners can use a range of vocabulary related to marketing and brands.

Video: A luxury brand
Vocabulary: Marketing and brands
Project: Research and discuss an advertising campaign

2.2 Asian brands go west
Lesson outcome: Learners can use a range of connectors to link ideas in sentences.

Reading: Chinese combine holidays abroad with luxury shopping
Grammar: Connectors to link, add and contrast ideas
Speaking: Discussing brands using connectors

2.3 Communication skills: Supporting teamwork
Lesson outcome: Learners are aware of different ways to support team colleagues and can use a range of phrases for giving and responding to advice.

Video: Teamwork
Functional language: Giving and responding to advice
Task: Asking for and giving advice

2.4 Business skills: Making a presentation
Lesson outcome: Learners are aware of techniques for beginning a presentation and can use a range of signposting phrases to structure a presentation and highlight main ideas.

Listening: Different ways to open a presentation
Functional language: Signposting in presentations
Task: Prepare and give a presentation

2.5 Writing: Formal and semi-formal emails
Lesson outcome: Learners can distinguish between formal and semi-formal emails and write a reply to a formal invitation.

Model text: Invitation to a corporate event
Functional language: Writing, accepting and declining an invitation
Grammar: Verbs + -ing vs. infinitive
Task: Write a formal reply to an invitation

Business workshop 2: p.90
Review 2: p.105
Pronunciation: 2.1 Stess in compound nouns and noun phrases
2.2 Connectors: intonation and pausing   p.114
Grammar reference: p.119

2.1 The life of luxury

Lesson outcome — Learners can use a range of vocabulary related to marketing and brands.

Lead-in

1 Discuss these questions.
1 What kinds of product do you associate with luxury brands?
2 Have you ever bought anything from a luxury brand? What was it?
3 Some people think that spending large amounts of money on luxury brands is crazy. Do you agree? Why? / Why not?

VIDEO

2 ▶ 2.1.1 Watch the video about the luxury jewellery brand, Bulgari. How did Bulgari extend the brand? What area did they move into?

3 Watch the video again and answer the questions.
1 What is the best way to extend a luxury brand?
2 When and where was Bulgari founded?
3 What kinds of products did Bulgari sell at the end of the '90s?
4 Where was its first hotel? What is next to it?
5 How old is the building?
6 What is special about Bulgari's London hotel?
7 According to Peter York, what is the problem with over-extending a brand?
8 How many hotels has Bulgari launched so far?

4 Watch the last part of the video again (2:55–4:24). Who says what? Peter York or Silvio Ursini?
1 At the end, if you overdo it, your brand is devalued.
2 Do something only if you have something to say.
3 If you say 'Let's copy the competitors', for me the customer ultimately will read between the lines and punish you.
4 I think the brands which are most careful have the longest future.

5 Work in pairs or small groups. Discuss these questions.
1 Think of a company that copied its competitors. What happened? Did customers stay loyal to the original brand? Think of an example for each of these categories.

| a soft drink   a mobile phone   an item of clothing |

2 Can you think of any other categories?

Teacher's resources: extra activities

Teacher's resources: alternative video and extra activities

Vocabulary — **Marketing and brands**

6 Complete the sentences from the video using the words and phrases in the box.

| bad history   base of clients   brands   cautious approach   core business   devalued   fast growth   further afield   stretching   ultra-luxury   venture into |

1 So what's the best way to extend a luxury brand? ... _____ the brand.
2 One company that has taken a(n) _____ to expansion is Bulgari.
3 To pave the way for growth we needed to speak to a broader and aspirational _____ .
4 After fragrances, the company began to look _____ .
5 And this idea of doing a very small collection of _____ hotels came about.
6 Experts agree that care and control are vital when moving beyond the _____ .
7 There's a lot of _____ about brand extensions. ... If you overdo it, your brand is _____ .
8 I think the _____ which are most careful have the longest future.
9 This slow and steady process is not for everyone, particularly for businesses looking for _____ .
10 'OK, let's _____ this business, and what are we gonna do? Let's copy the competitors'.

2.1 The life of luxury

7 Match the words in the box with the definitions.

> awareness   brand stretching   customer engagement   image
> interactive marketing   logo   loyalty   product placement

1 advertising by placing an item in a television programme or film
2 using internet history to target customers
3 extending a brand to include other types of products
4 consumer interest
5 knowledge or understanding
6 a recognisable design or official sign on a product
7 buying the same brand regularly
8 general opinion people have of a product

8 Work in pairs. Discuss these questions.

1 Name three well-known people who lead 'a life of luxury'.
2 If you had a month's salary to spend, which luxury product(s) would you buy?
3 Name some brands that use product placement in TV programmes. What other ways are there of increasing brand awareness or encouraging customer loyalty?
4 If you had to stretch a well-known brand, how would you expand it? What new products or services could you offer?

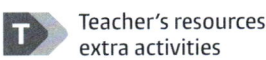
Teacher's resources: extra activities

→ **page 114** See Pronunciation bank: Stress in compound nouns and noun phrases

PROJECT: Research an advertising campaign

9A Work in pairs. Research an advertising campaign to discuss with your classmates. Follow these steps.

- Choose an example of a newspaper/magazine/online/TV advertisement for a luxury brand.
- Make notes on the brand image. Use the ideas on page 135 to help you.
- Survey your classmates: ask questions and get their reaction to the advert, e.g. Are people aware of the brand? How does it make them feel?

B When you have finished your analysis and survey, work with another pair. Exchange your findings about your advertising campaigns. Which one is the most effective? Why?

Self-assessment
- How successfully have you achieved the lesson outcome? Give yourself a score from 0 (I need more practice) to 5 (I know this well).
- Go to My Self-assessment in MyEnglishLab to reflect on what you have learnt.

2.2 Asian brands go west

Lesson outcome — Learners can use a range of connectors to link ideas in sentences.

Lead-in

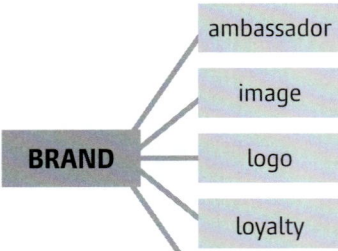

1 Work in pairs or small groups.

1 Think of two global brands for each of these sectors.

| accessories | cars | fashion | jewellery | fragrances | technology |

2 Do you know which country each brand is originally from?
3 Choose one brand to focus on. Why do you think it is so successful? What qualities do you associate with it?

2 Look at the collocations in the diagram and check new words in your dictionary. Then talk about the brand you chose in Exercise 1.

1 Describe the brand logo, brand image and brand personality for your chosen brand.
2 Does it have a brand ambassador? If so, who?
3 Do you think the company has created brand loyalty? Describe the target market.

Reading

3 Read the article quickly. How many brands are mentioned? Do you know what kind of companies they are?

FT

Chinese combine European and U.S. breaks with spending trips

1 <u>Recently</u>, Asian brands, like fine jewellery brand Qeelin, have started to appear in U.S. shops. This unusual move is a sign of the ambitions of Asian luxury companies.

5 <u>Previously</u>, the global luxury industry moved only in one direction: from west to east. <u>Then</u> European and U.S. brands bought up prime retail sites in Asian megacities as a 10 new generation of Asian customers were attracted to owning products made by companies that were more than a century old.

15 <u>In recent years, however</u>, Chinese customers have started to combine holidays abroad with shopping 20 expeditions, and Chinese brands have begun to follow the money. Luxury research institute Hurun reports that France – home to labels <u>such as</u> 25 Chanel and Louis Vuitton – has emerged as the top holiday destination for wealthy Chinese millennials. Other popular destinations include London, San Francisco and New York, <u>as well as</u> Japan and South Korea.

30 The fine jewellery sector is leading this global expansion. Chow Tai Fook, the biggest jeweller in the world, says Chinese outbound tourism was behind its expansion into Southeast Asian countries, such as South Korea and Taiwan. Over 2,000 of its 35 stores are in mainland China, <u>but</u> those overseas are increasingly important. <u>While</u> the group prefers to run large-scale advertising and marketing campaigns to deliver a consistent brand image, there are 40 regional adaptations. <u>Earlier this year, for example</u>, members of Taiwanese boyband SpeXial were asked to 45 help publicise a store opening in Taiwan.

Some Asian brands are expanding after being bought by larger 50 groups. Recent examples include Qeelin and Shang Xia, a luxury label <u>now</u> operated by French luxury group Hermès. Qeelin began selling its products in the USA, 55 a strong market when it comes to luxury, partly to meet demand from the local Chinese community.

Building a brand overseas takes time. This is particularly true when it comes to establishing iconic 60 designs that are as recognisable around the world as a Chanel handbag. You don't build luxury brands overnight.

2.2 Asian brands go west

4 Read the article again and decide if these sentences are *true* (T) or *false* (F).
1 In recent years, Asian luxury companies have started to expand into the West.
2 Chinese millennials like to go shopping for luxury brands when they go abroad.
3 The jeweller Chow Tai Fook has recently opened over 2,000 stores in South Korea and Taiwan.
4 Asian brands are adapting their marketing plans for stores according to the region.
5 SpeXial is an all-male music group from Taiwan.
6 A French luxury group has been bought by Qeelin and Shang Xia.
7 Luxury products are popular with the Chinese community in the USA.
8 The writer thinks that the new Asian brands will soon become as successful as Western brands like Chanel.

Grammar Connectors

5 Look at the underlined words and phrases in the article, which show how different ideas are connected to one another. Write the words and phrases in the correct place in this table.

Adding ideas	Contrasting ideas	Referring to time	Giving examples	Sequencing
		Recently		

➡ **page 119** See Grammar reference: Connectors
➡ **page 114** See Pronunciation bank: Connectors: intonation and pausing

6 Choose the correct option in italics to complete the sentences.
1 *However / Although* the global luxury industry previously moved only in one direction, Chinese customers now go on shopping trips in the West.
2 Examples of luxury goods that are popular in Asia include, *for instance, / as well as* handbags and watches.
3 For Asian buyers, part of the attraction of having a luxury handbag or scarf is that the brand is more than a century old. France is famous for its luxury brands, *first of all / such as* Chanel, Louis Vuitton and Hermès.
4 Hermès, *first of all / recently*, started as a horse harness business in Paris in 1837, and is *now / previously* a champion of traditional French craftsmanship and high-quality manufacturing.
5 So, where are wealthy Chinese millennials going? *To start with / Then*, France is the top holiday destination.
6 *However / Although*, other popular shopping destinations *also / in addition* include London and New York, *as well as / also* Japan, Malaysia and South Korea.

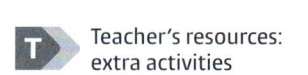

7 Add the new connectors in the box to the table in Exercise 5.

| also   although   first of all   in addition   to start with   for instance |

Speaking

8A Complete the questions with suitable connectors.
1 _____ they are expensive, do you like to buy designer labels?
2 When it comes to luxury goods, _____ clothing, jewellery or shoes, what's the most expensive item you have ever bought?
3 Which brands are popular with your generation _____ your parents' generation?
4 Which brands have become more popular _____ in your country or region?
5 Why do some people like to buy luxury goods and designer brands _____ others prefer simpler and cheaper products?

B In pairs or small groups, ask and answer the questions in Exercise 8A.

Self-assessment
- How successfully have you achieved the lesson outcome? Give yourself a score from 0 (I need more practice) to 5 (I know this well).
- Go to My Self-assessment in MyEnglishLab to reflect on what you have learnt.

2.3 COMMUNICATION SKILLS
Supporting teamwork

Lesson outcome Learners are aware of different ways to support team colleagues and can use a range of phrases for giving and responding to advice.

Lead-in **1** Work in pairs and discuss the questions.
1 Think about different teams and groups you are or have been part of. What challenges do groups or teams have which can make them less effective?
2 How useful and/or problematic is it to have people in a group or team who are very different to each other? Why?
3 Who do you prefer to work with – people who are similar to you or very different? Why?

VIDEO **2** ▶ 2.3.1 Matt has organised a conference call to plan how the team will work together to deliver online project management courses on time in Mexico. Watch the call and note down what each person sees as a priority or project success.

Matt: _____ Dan: _____
Stefanie: _____ Paula: _____

3 Watch the video again.
1 How well do you think Matt leads the meeting? Why?
2 How does Stefanie feel about working with Dan? Why?

4A In small groups, discuss what Matt should advise Stefanie to do at the beginning of the project: focus on working with Paula or with Dan. Give reasons for your answers. As a class, decide which video to watch first.
Option A – Advise Stefanie to work mainly with Paula and the Mexico part of the project.
Option B – Advise Stefanie to work mainly with Dan and the U.S. part of the project.

B Watch the two videos in the sequence the class has decided, and answer the questions for each video.

Option A ▶ 2.3.2
1 Why does Matt advise Stefanie to work with Paula at the start of the project?
2 How far does she agree or disagree? Why?
3 What does Stefanie now think about Dan's first idea that quality is a priority?
4 Overall, how effectively does Matt advise and support Stefanie?

Option B ▶ 2.3.3
1 Why does Matt advise Stefanie to work with Dan at the start of the project?
2 How far does she agree or disagree? Why?
3 What is Stefanie's experience of working with Dan on the project?
4 Overall, how effectively does Matt advise and support Stefanie?

C In pairs, discuss the questions and agree what you can learn from Matt and Stefanie's project team experiences.
1 What advice did Matt give Stefanie in each video about working with Dan?
2 What choice did Stefanie make in each video about working with Dan? What happened as a result?
3 What can we learn from these experiences about offering advice and support to colleagues in international teams?

5 ▶ 2.3.4 Watch the Conclusions section of the video. Compare what is said with your answers in Exercise 4C Question 3. Note down the three main learning points about working in international teams. How far do you agree with this? Why?

Reflection **6** Think again about a team or group you are or have been part of. Look at the questions and discuss your answers with a partner.
1 How effective is the team or group? Why?
2 What advice and/or support would help the team to be even more effective?
3 What advice (one idea) would you give yourself about how to support the team better?

2.3 Communication skills: Supporting teamwork

Functional language

Giving and responding to advice

7A Look at these phrases for giving advice from the video. Match the beginnings of the phrases (1–7) with the endings (a–g).

1. Quality **should**
2. Why don't you
3. Maybe it would be
4. Have you tried
5. You need to
6. Don't be
7. I think it's important

a. **talking** to him?
b. **better** (for you) **to** just **focus** on Mexico.
c. **be** your number one priority.
d. (for you) **to work** with Dan.
e. just **try**?
f. **afraid to ask** his advice where you need it.
g. **be able to** keep in touch with Dan yourself.

B Look at the words in bold in the phrases in Exercise 7A. Which phrases for giving advice are followed by:

a *to* + infinitive?   b infinitive?   c verb + *-ing*?

8A Which five phrases in exercise 7A are stronger / more direct ways to give advice? Is this similar or different in your language?

B Who would you expect to give you strong advice?

> an expert   a colleague   your boss   your best friend   your mother
> someone you don't know very well   someone you've just met

9A Work in pairs. Take turns to explain the problems below and give each other advice. Respond using the phrases in the box.

1. I haven't taken any time off work in the last six months.
2. I'm worried that I might fail my driving test.
3. I don't know how to use Excel very well.
4. I really have too much to do at work.

> That's a good/great idea!   Yes, maybe I should (do that).
> That sounds like a good/great idea.   Yes, but (I don't think) …   OK, I'll think about it.

B Write short dialogues based on your conversations.

Teacher's resources: extra activities

TASK

10A Work in groups of three and read the situations on page 126. Take turns to ask for and give advice. Remember to respond to the advice you receive.

B Think of another situation (real or invented) you could ask your colleagues advice on.

C When you have discussed all the situations, compare the best advice with another group. Who preferred to use stronger advice structures? When? Why?

Self-assessment

- How successfully have you achieved the lesson outcome? Give yourself a score from 0 (I need more practice) to 5 (I know this well).
- Go to My Self-assessment in MyEnglishLab to reflect on what you have learnt.

2.4 BUSINESS SKILLS
Making a presentation

Lesson outcome — Learners are aware of techniques for beginning a presentation and can use a range of signposting phrases to structure a presentation and highlight main ideas.

Lead-in **1A** In which of these situations have you given and/or attended a talk or presentation? What went well and what didn't? Do you like presenting? Why / Why not?
- An informal presentation to colleagues at work or college/university
- A presentation to (business) customers
- A conference presentation
- A speech at a wedding or other event

B Work in pairs. Read the blog extract on how to begin a presentation. Discuss which ideas you agree with, and why. Can you add any of your own ideas to the list?

THE PERFECT START
Things to do (and not to do) when opening a presentation

Making a presentation in a foreign language is for many people one of the most terrifying things they have to do at work. Here are some standard techniques to help you make a confident and effective start, with a few tips on what not to do, too!

DO
- Begin with a warm welcome – thank the audience for coming
- State your name and job title (or say what you do)
- Confirm the objective of the presentation
- Explain the structure of the presentation
- Say how long you will talk for
- Let the audience know when to ask questions – during or at the end of the presentation
- Move smoothly to the first point in the presentation

DON'T
- Apologise for your English (be confident and focus on expressing your ideas)
- Worry about making mistakes (people want to listen to your ideas, not your grammar)
- Rush things (take your time and give your audience time to understand the information)

Listening **2A** 🔊 2.01 Listen to three speakers starting a presentation to visitors to their organisation. Which 'dos' and 'don'ts' in Exercise 1B does each speaker use?

B Now look at three more unusual ways to start a presentation. What do you think is the value of using these techniques?
- Open with questions
- Begin by telling the audience about a conversation you had recently
- Start with a personal story

C 🔊 2.02 Listen to three more presentation openings and decide which unusual technique in Exercise 2B each speaker uses.

D How effective do you think these alternative techniques were, and why? Would you be comfortable using them? Why / Why not?

3A 🔊 2.03 Listen to the first speaker continuing his presentation and introducing his company. Note down the information he gives about the following.

COMPANY PROFILE
When established: _____
Main strength: _____
Size of workforce: _____
Countries of operation: _____
Plan for growth: _____

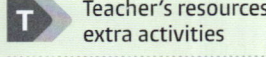
Teacher's resources: extra activities

B How did the speaker react to the question? Do you think this is a good way to react to questions? Why / Why not?

2.4 Business skills: Making a presentation

Functional language

Signposting in presentations

4 Complete the signposting phrases from the presentations in Exercises 2 and 3 using the words in the box. If necessary, use the audioscripts on pages 146–147 to help you.

| begin   close   feel   hand   make   said   take   today |

Beginning the presentation	To start, I'd like to [share a story with you]. What I want to do ¹_____ is [to give you a short introduction to the company]. Let's ²_____ with [the most important part of the company].
Sequencing	Firstly, …; Secondly, …; And finally, …
Highlighting important information	There are three important points I want to ³_____ . This is also important because [we want to stay personal].
Referring to visuals	So, if you can ⁴_____ a look at this slide, …
Referring to different sections of the presentation	As I ⁵_____ earlier, … I'll say more about that later.
Inviting questions	If you have any questions, ⁶_____ free to [interrupt / ask me at the end].
Dealing with questions	Great question. Really good question.
Closing	So, I'll ⁷_____ there. Thank you very much for listening. And I'll ⁸_____ over to [Paul].

Teacher's resources: extra activities

> **TASK**

5A Prepare a short presentation on one of the topics in the box. Write a plan using the notes below and the phrases in Exercise 4.
- Decide which technique to use at the beginning.
- Structure the presentation clearly into two or three sections.
- Link the sections as you speak.
- Highlight important information in each section.
- Invite questions at the end.

Possible presentation topics:
- your job
- your organisation
- a product you love/hate
- a place you visited
- a hobby
- your own idea

B Work in small groups. Take turns to give your presentations and answer questions. When you are listening, note down:
- three things which the presenter does well.
- one thing which the presenter might do better next time.

C When everyone has given their presentation, share your feedback and decide on the most effective presentation. What do you find most problematic when making a presentation? How could you deal with this problem?

Self-assessment
- How successfully have you achieved the lesson outcome? Give yourself a score from 0 (I need more practice) to 5 (I know this well).
- Go to My Self-assessment in MyEnglishLab to reflect on what you have learnt.

25

2.5 WRITING
Formal and semi-formal emails

Lesson outcome — Learners can distinguish between formal and semi-formal emails and write a reply to a formal invitation.

Lead-in

1 Read the formal email invitation to a corporate event. Choose the most formal phrases in italics. Then compare in pairs. The other phrases are correct, but are semi-formal.

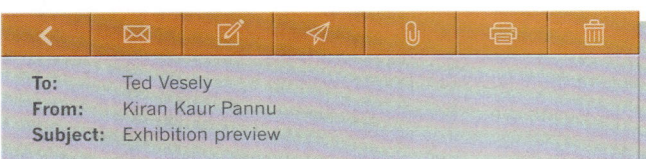

To: Ted Vesely
From: Kiran Kaur Pannu
Subject: Exhibition preview

¹*Hello Ted / Dear Mr Vesely*

I remember discussing modern art with you last month and, as a valued customer, ²*I want / I'd like* to invite you to a preview of the new Street Art Exhibition at the National Gallery of Modern Art which C&P Marketing have decided to sponsor.

Our preview event ³*will be held / is* on Tuesday 22nd November at 7.30 p.m. on the top floor of the NGMA. Drinks and refreshments will be ⁴*provided / there*.

In addition, we are ⁵*delighted to announce / pleased to tell you* that the artist Karla Lansing has agreed to talk to us about the impact of street art in marketing today. Ms Lansing has ⁶*collaborated / worked* with our team on several marketing campaigns to be launched in the new year.

⁷*Could you please let me know if you can come / Please confirm your attendance* by Friday 11th November and, if you are able to join us, please remember to bring this invitation with you to gain admittance to the venue.

⁸*We look forward / Looking forward* to seeing you at this event.

⁹*Best wishes / Kind regards*

Kiran Kaur Pannu

Events Manger, C&P Marketing

Functional language

2 Decide if each phrase in the table below is *formal* (F) or *semi-formal* (SF).

Inviting
I'd like to invite you to …
I'm writing to invite you to …
We are delighted to invite you to …
It would be great if you could come …

Accepting
Many thanks for the invitation.
Thanks for inviting me.
I'd (would) be delighted to accept your invitation/offer.
Although Mr … is unable to attend, … will be happy to take his place.

Declining
I'm sorry but I won't be able to come.
I'm afraid (that) I will be unable to attend.
I'd love to come but …
I'm afraid I can't make it.
Unfortunately, I have already made other arrangements.

Closing
We (very much) look forward to seeing you.
We are looking forward to seeing you.
Looking forward to seeing you soon!
Best wishes
Kind regards
All the best

 Teacher's resources: extra activities

 The email contains examples of verbs + -ing and verbs + infinitive. Go to MyEnglishLab for optional grammar work.

 page 119 See Grammar reference: Verbs + -ing vs. infinitive

TASK

3A Work in pairs. Read the reply to the invitation in Exercise 1 on page 127. Rewrite the email to make it more formal.

B Write your own formal reply of about 80 words accepting the invitation in Exercise 1.

C Exchange emails with your partner. Which formal expressions in Exercise 2 did your partner use? How many were the same as the ones you used?

Self-assessment
- How successfully have you achieved the lesson outcome? Give yourself a score from 0 (I need more practice) to 5 (I know this well).
- Go to My Self-assessment in MyEnglishLab to reflect on what you have learnt.

Job-hunting 3

> Getting a job is a job in itself.

Unit overview

| 3.1 | **A job search**
Lesson outcome: Learners can use vocabulary related to applying for and getting a job. | **Video:** Applying for an internship
Vocabulary: Getting a job
Project: Plan and write a job advertisement |

| 3.2 | **Job interview questions**
Lesson outcome: Learners can use a range of direct and indirect questions for job interviews. | **Listening:** Interview questions and answers
Grammar: Indirect questions
Speaking: A job interview |

| 3.3 | **Communication skills:** Listening actively
Lesson outcome: Learners are aware of different ways to listen actively and can use phrases for a range of active listening techniques. | **Video:** Demonstrating active listening
Functional language: Active listening
Task: The listening/distraction game |

| 3.4 | **Business skills:** Interviews
Lesson outcome: Learners can use a range of questions and phrases for different stages of a job interview. | **Listening:** Two job interviews
Functional language: Useful phrases for candidates
Task: Create a job and interview for it |

| 3.5 | **Writing:** Covering letters
Lesson outcome: Learners can write a covering letter addressing specific information mentioned in a job advertisement. | **Model text:** Covering letter
Functional language: Useful phrases for covering letters
Grammar: Past Simple and Present Perfect
Task: Write a covering letter |

Business workshop 3: p.92 | **Review 3:** p.106 | **Pronunciation:** 3.1 Stress in derived words / 3.2 Voice range and intonation in indirect questions p.115 | **Grammar reference:** p.120

27

3.1 A job search

Lesson outcome — Learners can use vocabulary related to applying for and getting a job.

Lead-in

1 Discuss these questions.
1 Have you ever written a CV? If so, when was the last time you updated it? How long is it?
2 In some countries including a photo on a CV is a requirement. Is this true in your country? What do you think of this idea?
3 Have you ever applied for a job/internship? If so, when? What happened?
4 Have you ever received advice from a careers coach? What did they say?

VIDEO

2  Watch the video about Esther, a jobseeker who's applying for an internship. What are the three rules for writing a CV?

3 Watch the video again and answer the questions.
1 What does entrepreneur James Caan think Esther isn't very good at?
2 What mistake does Esther make in her CV?
3 What are examples of soft skills? What are examples of hard skills?
4 According to expert John Lees, what <u>shouldn't</u> you put under 'interests' in your CV?
5 Complete what Esther has written: 'I would very much appreciate the _____ of an interview to find out more about the _____ and to demonstrate how I believe I can be of _____ to your company.'
6 How many interviews has Esther had so far?
7 What do you think the expression 'Getting a job is a job in itself' mean?

4 Watch the video again from 2:30 to 2:56 and complete what the expert, John Lees, says about Rule 3.

'Graduate CVs make the same ¹_____ over and over again. They use clichéd ²_____. So everyone says "I'm a(n) ³_____, I'm a(n) ⁴_____, I'm highly ⁵_____." And if you use the same language as everyone else, all that shows is that you are exactly the same as every other ⁶_____ .'

5 Work in pairs or small groups. Discuss these questions.
1 What could you say at a job interview to make yourself 'stand out from the crowd' and give a good impression?
2 Think of three positive characteristics and three skills you have, or things that you are (very) good at. Compare your answers with your partner or group.

 Teacher's resources: extra activities

Vocabulary — **Getting a job**

6 Match the words and phrases from the video with the synonyms and definitions.

1 character
2 employer
3 CV
4 jobseeker
5 internship
6 cliché
7 gain (*formal*), e.g. experience
8 be of value to
9 apply for
10 sort out
11 come across well
12 stand out from

a someone who is looking for a job
b when a student or graduate works for a short time to get experience
c get or obtain
d be important or useful
e be very easy to see or notice
f successfully deal with a problem or difficult situation
g curriculum vitae (or *résumé* in U.S. English)
h personality
i be easy to understand or know how to communicate effectively
j a person or company that pays people to work for them
k make a formal, usually written, request, especially for a job or university place
l an idea that is used so much that it isn't effective, or it doesn't have much meaning any longer

28

3.1 A job search

7 Choose the correct option in italics to complete the job advertisement.

SALES INTERNS NEEDED FOR IMMEDIATE START

Do you have a degree in business studies or sports education?
Are you [1]*competition / competitive*?
Are you looking for an internship with a dynamic, international [2]*employer / employee*?

At Surfing Technologies we need graduates who are highly [3]*motivated / motivation*, organised and [4]*communication / communicative*. You must be prepared to learn quickly about the latest trends in surfing and you will be [5]*responsible / responsibility* for selling to key clients.

Surfing Technologies are based in Sydney and we have a proven track record in offering our successful [6]*internships / interns* an exciting career in sales with opportunities to travel around the world. This [7]*positioning / position* is for 3–6 months. No previous experience is required and working hours are [8]*flexibility / flexible*.

If you think you have the necessary [9]*skillful / skills* and are [10]*passion / passionate* about surfing, please send your CV with a covering letter to our Head of [11]*Recruitment / Recruiter* at hr@surftechnologies.au. Successful candidates will be called for an [12]*interview / interviewer*. We would love to hear from you!

8 Discuss these questions with a partner.

I don't have much experience in job-seeking.
1 How difficult is it for young people to find work in your country?
2 What are some of the things that can go wrong in job interviews?
3 What kind of internship or job position would you like to apply for in the future?

I have some experience in job-seeking.
1 What kind of skills does your organisation look for when recruiting?
2 Have you ever interviewed someone for a job position? How did you choose the right candidate?
3 How does the recruitment process work in your company or organisation?

 Teacher's resources: extra activities

→ **page 115** See Pronunciation bank: Stress in derived words

PROJECT: Write a job advertisement

9A Work in pairs. Imagine you work in HR. Write a job advertisement for an internship or job position in your company or organisation. If you don't work, write one for a position you would like to apply for. Write 120–150 words. Follow these steps.
- Before you write, look online for similar job advertisements.
- When you write the advertisement, use the job advert in Exercise 7 to help you.
- Consider these points:
  - the kind of candidate you are looking for
  - a description of duties and responsibilities for the role
  - the length of the internship, if relevant
  - opportunities for promotion
  - if any previous experience is required
  - working hours and pay, if relevant

B When you have finished, work with another pair and read each other's job advertisement. Would you apply for the position? Why? / Why not?

Self-assessment

- How successfully have you achieved the lesson outcome? Give yourself a score from 0 (I need more practice) to 5 (I know this well).
- Go to My Self-assessment in MyEnglishLab to reflect on what you have learnt.

3.2 Job interview questions

Lesson outcome — Learners can use a range of direct and indirect questions for job interviews.

Lead-in 1 Work in pairs. If you had a job interview next week, how would you prepare for it?

2 Look at the photos (a–d). What do you think about the candidate's body language in each photo? Is it positive or negative? Give reasons for your answers.

Listening 1 3 Complete the task with a partner.

> *I don't have much experience in going for interviews.*
> Look at the questions on page 127. Decide with your partner if the questions are appropriate or inappropriate/irrelevant for a job interview.

> *I have some experience in going for interviews.*
> Write five typical job interview questions. Compare your questions with another pair.

4 🔊 3.01 A candidate has applied for a job as a chemical engineer at a company that works in waste water management. Listen to eight questions from his job interview. Did you have similar questions in Exercise 3?

5 Put the words in the correct order to make questions. Then listen again and check your answers.
1 are weaknesses What your strengths and?
2 moment you Are at working the?
3 as a you long worked engineer How have chemical?
4 you have any experience in technologies green Do?
5 us you would for Why like work to?
6 first at your work would What day do you on?
7 certificates Do have you your you original with?
8 years' you Where see do in five yourself time?

Grammar **Indirect questions**

6A 🔊 3.02 Listen to some more interview questions and complete what the interviewer says. Contractions count as one word.
1 _____ _____ _____ _____ _____ your greatest weakness is?
2 _____ _____ _____ _____ _____ your work experience?
3 _____ _____ _____ _____ _____ a time when you showed leadership skills?
4 _____ _____ _____ _____ _____ you've ever done any voluntary work.
5 _____ _____ _____ _____ _____ you would add value to our company?
6 _____ _____ _____ _____ _____ you are prepared to travel for the job.
7 _____ _____ _____ _____ _____ I should contact for a reference.

B What kinds of questions are these? How are they different from the questions in Exercise 5?

→ page 120 See Grammar reference: Direct and indirect questions

→ page 115 See Pronunciation bank: Voice range and intonation in indirect questions

3.2 Job interview questions

7 Correct the errors in the word order in these direct and indirect questions.

Direct: Why would you ~~would~~ like to work for us?
Indirect: I'd like to know why you would ~~you~~ like to work for us.

1. Direct: What your greatest strength is?
   Indirect: Can you tell me what is your greatest strength?
2. Direct: You have ever managed a team?
   Indirect: I'd like to know if have you ever managed a team.
3. Direct: Who your previous employer was?
   Indirect: I'd like to know who was your previous employer.
4. Direct: Do you enjoy what about working in teams?
   Indirect: You could tell me what you enjoy about working in teams?
5. Direct: When the last time was you solved a problem successfully?
   Indirect: Could you tell me when about a time you solved a problem successfully?

Teacher's resources: extra activities

Listening 2

8 🔊 3.03 Listen to the candidate answering the questions in Exercise 6A. Does he answer the questions effectively? Write *good* (G), *OK*, or *poor* (P) for each of the interviewer's main questions.

1 __ 2 __ 3 __ 4 __ 5 __ 6 __ 7 __

9 Listen to the interview again. How does the candidate start answering each question? Match the expressions (a–i) with the interview questions (1–7). One of the replies uses more than one phrase.

a As I said before, …
b Let me think now …
c I'll need to check and get back to you.
d I'm afraid I don't have much experience, but I …
e I'm not sure, but my friends tell me …
f Sorry, I didn't catch that.
g Sure. I was responsible for …
h That's a difficult question.
i Yes, of course.

1 __ 2 __ 3 __ 4 __ 5 __ , __ and __ 6 __ 7 __

10 Match the expressions from Exercise 9 (a–i) with the strategies (A–F) for dealing with questions. What other ways are there for dealing with difficult questions?

A Being honest __
B Answering positively __ , __
C Buying time __ , __ , __
D Repeating yourself __
E Asking for repetition __
F Expressing uncertainty __

Teacher's resources: extra activities

Speaking

11A Read the job advertisement on page 127. What questions do you think you might be asked in an interview for the position? Write at least five questions and include some indirect questions.

B Think about how a candidate could answer the questions effectively. How would *you* answer the questions? Then write five questions to ask the interviewer, e.g. about the team, working hours, training, opportunities for promotion, salary and holidays, etc.

12 Roleplay the interview. When you have finished, swap roles.

Interviewer: Nice to meet you. Did you find us easily? First, I'd like to ask you about …
Candidate: Nice to meet you, too. Thank you for inviting me to an interview …

Self-assessment

- How successfully have you achieved the lesson outcome? Give yourself a score from 0 (I need more practice) to 5 (I know this well).
- Go to My Self-assessment in MyEnglishLab to reflect on what you have learnt.

3.3 COMMUNICATION SKILLS
Listening actively

Lesson outcome — Learners are aware of different ways to listen actively and can use phrases for a range of active listening techniques.

Lead-in **1A** Work in pairs and discuss the statements. Which one do you agree with more?
1 'In business, it's better to act neutrally and not show your feelings.'
2 'It's better not to hide your feelings when talking about work-related topics.'

B What are the advantages and disadvantages of each approach?

VIDEO **2A** ▶ 3.3.1 Watch the videos of Paula and Matt before they meet each other.

1 How does Paula describe herself?
2 How did Matt sound to Paula? How does he actually feel?
3 What does Matt need to talk to Paula about?

B Do you think their meeting will go well? Why / Why not?

3A In small groups, discuss which is the best approach (Option A or B) for Matt to take in his first meeting with Paula. As a class, decide which video to watch first.

Option A – Talk about the facts he has heard and try to get to the bottom of them.
Option B – Listen to Paula's perspective and discuss how they can best work together.

B Watch the two videos in the sequence the class has decided, and answer the questions for each video.

Option A ▶ 3.3.2 1 Watch the video and tick (✔) the points Matt focuses on.
a Paula missed her deadline on her last project.
b She thought her project manager (Julio) was incompetent.
c The project was late.
d Her project manager didn't want to listen to her.
e She disagreed with her project manager.

2 How does Paula respond to Matt's questions? How does she feel at the end of the discussion? Why?
3 What could Matt have done to improve the outcome of the discussion?

Option B ▶ 3.3.3 1 How does Matt manage the conversation and what effect does this have on the outcome?
2 Complete Matt's questions using the words in the box. Watch again to check your answers.

| describe | important |
| mean | rushed | say |

a 'Julio's incompetent. Totally incompetent.'
'OK, why don't you tell me a bit more? You _____ he's incompetent. How would you _____ a competent manager?'
b 'A good manager should support their team and listen to their team.'
'… So it's _____ for you, as a team member, to be involved in decision-making, right?'
c 'I wanted to take extra time to make sure we weren't rushing a complicated project.'
'Why did you have concerns about the project being _____ ?'
d 'There were too many things that all had to happen at the same time.'
'What do you _____ by "too many things"? Do you think you might have managed a bit better if there had been greater planning or more support, for example?'

4 Discuss what lessons you have learnt about listening actively and adapting your style to focus on facts and maintain positive relationships at the same time.

5 ▶ 3.3.4 Watch the Conclusions section of the video and note down the four tips for successful active listening. How far do you agree with these tips? Why?

Reflection **6** Think about the following questions. Then discuss your answers with a partner.
1 Do you often ask questions when talking to others?
2 In discussions, do you often begin sentences with *I think* … and *We should* … ?
3 What is one advantage and one possible disadvantage of your style?
4 Decide on one thing *you* can do to listen more actively and successfully in the future.

3.3 Communication skills: Listening actively

Functional language

Active listening

7 Use the seven phrases from the video (a–g) to complete the gaps in the table (1–7).

a OK, why don't you tell me [a bit more]?
b OK, that's [useful to think about / interesting to know].
c So, it's important for you [to be involved …], right?
d Why did you [have concerns about …]?
e What do you mean by ['too many things']?
f No, that's not what [I said].
g How would you [describe a competent manager]?

Clarifying/Exploring	1 _____ 2 _____ 3 _____
Summarising/Paraphrasing	4 _____ So, you [had a disagreement with your manager].
Checking understanding	5 _____ Sorry, I don't understand [what you said about …]. I'm not clear about [how it happened].
Correcting	6 _____ Sorry, that's not what [I meant].
Giving feedback	7 _____ I can see you are [unhappy/frustrated/angry].

8A Work in pairs. How would you respond to the speaker in these situations? Use one or two phrases from Exercise 7 to reply to each speaker.

1 Dinner's going to be a bit late I'm afraid.
2 She can be difficult to work with sometimes.
3 I refused the invitation to give a presentation.
4 He says he hates travelling for work.
5 This new accounting system is driving me crazy.
6 But you said you wanted a new challenge.

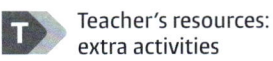
Teacher's resources: extra activities

B Choose one situation in Exercise 8A and write a short dialogue using at least three phrases from Exercise 7.

> **TASK**

9A Work in groups of three and play the listening/distraction game. On your own, prepare to tell the members of your group about one of the following topics:
- a favourite free-time activity.
- a memorable day in your life or career.
- the area where you live or work (location, building, facilities).

B Take turns to talk about your topics for two minutes.
- When one of your colleagues is telling their story, listen actively and use phrases from Exercise 7 to get as much information as possible.
- When the other colleague is talking, make a detailed list of all the things you have to do today, or look at your phone and read your messages.

C Report back to your group members. How many facts do you remember from the story you really focused on? How many facts do you remember from the other story?

D Give your group members feedback on how well he/she listened actively. Did he/she:
- use clarifying and exploring phrases?
- summarise or paraphrase what you said?
- check that he/she understood you correctly?
- give you feedback?

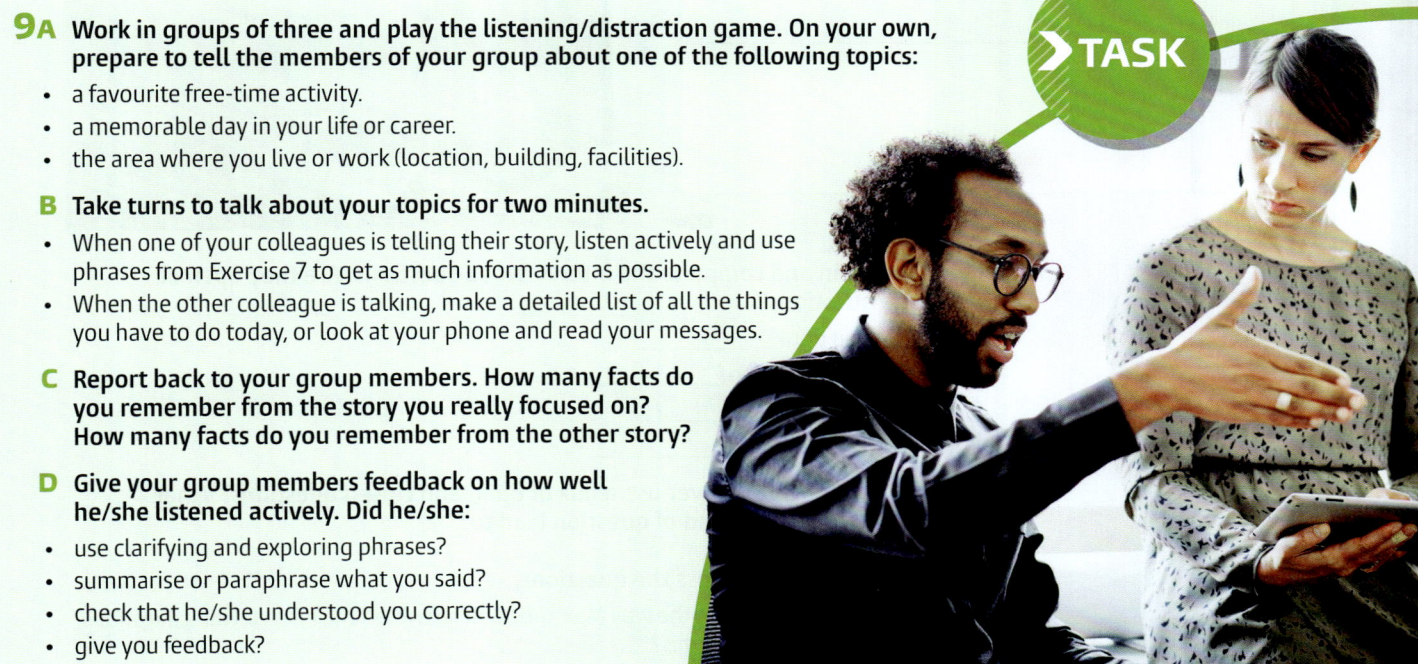

Self-assessment
- How successfully have you achieved the lesson outcome? Give yourself a score from 0 (I need more practice) to 5 (I know this well).
- Go to My Self-assessment in MyEnglishLab to reflect on what you have learnt.

3.4 BUSINESS SKILLS
Interviews

Lesson outcome: Learners can use a range of questions and phrases for different stages of a job interview.

Lead-in **1** Work in pairs and discuss the questions.
1 Why do organisations hold interviews?
2 Have you been to an interview in the past, e.g. for a job, internship, or study place?
3 What went well? What didn't go well?
4 What did you learn? How can you improve?

Listening **2A** Work in small groups and discuss the pairs of tips for preparing for an interview. Which tip in each pair do you agree with?
1 a Prepare answers to possible questions.
  b Improvise answers to questions you are asked.
2 a There's no need to ask any questions. Just focus on getting the job.
  b Interviews are two-way: prepare questions to ask.
3 a Telling small lies is OK in interviews if it helps you get the job.
  b Never tell lies – it's cheating the interviewer and yourself. You might end up with responsibilities you can't manage.
4 a Give long, detailed answers to all questions.
  b Give short, concise answers where possible.

B What other tips can you think of for preparing and answering interview questions?

3A 🔊 3.04 Listen to two different interviews for the same job. Note down the positive and negative points about the skills and experience of the candidates, Max and John.

	Positive	Negative
1 Max		
2 John		

B Listen again and complete the interviewer's questions. Are they open or closed questions?
1 Why do you think _____ ?
2 Have you ever worked _____ ?
3 Do you have a _____ ?
4 Can you tell me about _____ ?

C Why does the interviewer use a mix of open and closed questions? What response does each kind of question lead to?

4 Work in pairs and discuss the questions.
1 What was different about the way Max and John answered the interviewer's questions? What can you learn from this?
2 John hasn't worked in a regional sales team before, but lists his transferable skills. Which relevant skills does he say he has?
3 How does Sue help John feel comfortable at the beginning of the second interview?
4 Who is more suitable for the job, Max or John?

3.4 Business skills: Interviews

Functional language
Useful phrases for candidates

5A Complete the phrases from the recording in Exercise 3A. If necessary, use the audioscript on page 147 to help you.

A	Beginning the interview	Thank you for your time today.
B	Dealing with questions	That's a good [1]_____ .
		It's good you [2]_____ .
C	Asking questions about the role/organisation	Could you tell me what a normal [3]_____?
D	Ending the interview	So, what are the next [4]_____?
		When can I expect to [5]_____?

B Match the phrases below (1–8) with the categories (A–D) in the table in Exercise 5A.
1 Could you tell me more about [the mentoring programme]?
2 Can I speak to some of the people I would be working with?
3 I'm looking forward to talking to you about this role.
4 There are two ways to answer your question.
5 I look forward to hearing from you.
6 I haven't had that exact experience. However, …
7 Thank you very much for taking the time to talk to me today.
8 It's nice to meet you.

 Teacher's resources: extra activities

1 Marketing Executive
Role Description: Managing the company's social media strategy
Necessary Skills: Strong digital skills and ability to work independently and spontaneously
Qualifications: Relevant marketing certificate or degree
Salary: £17,000–£22,000 depending on experience

2 Project Planning Coordinator
Role Description: Supporting the product design project team
Necessary Skills: Good organisational and communication skills
Qualifications: Office administration and technical qualification will be a benefit
Salary: €24,000–€28,000

TASK

6A Work in pairs. Read the information below and create a job that you will interview each other for. Alternatively, use one of the job advertisements on this page.

> A local company is recruiting for a specific role. Decide on:
> - the job title and role description.
> - the necessary skills.
> - the necessary qualifications.
> - details of the salary.

B Decide who will be the interviewer and who will be the interviewee. Read your role cards: interviewers turn to page 126, interviewees turn to page 127.

C When you are ready, roleplay the interview.
- Make notes during the interview and give each other feedback so that you can improve each time you practise.
- Reflect on what went well, what didn't go well, and how you can improve next time.

D Change roles and roleplay the interview again with the same job or a different one.

Self-assessment
- How successfully have you achieved the lesson outcome? Give yourself a score from 0 (I need more practice) to 5 (I know this well).
- Go to My Self-assessment in MyEnglishLab to reflect on what you have learnt.

3.5 WRITING
Covering letters

Lesson outcome: Learners can write a covering letter addressing specific information mentioned in a job advertisement.

Lead-in

1 Read the covering letter. It accompanies a CV for an application for the Sales Intern post on page 127. Proofread the letter and find nine more language mistakes. Think about spelling, grammar and missing words. Then compare in pairs.

Dear Ms Saunders

Re: Position of Sales Intern

attached
Please find ~~attach~~ my CV in response to the above vacancy as advertised on your website.

I have just completed a sports education degrees and am looking for a chance to work for a dynamic interntional company like Surfing Technologies. As a keen and experience surfer, I organised a surfing team at university and last year we have won a national competition.

I have spent last three summer holidays working for a local surfing company, where my communication skills helped me to increasing their sales significant. In addition, the flexible working hours enabled me to complete the ASI Surfing Instructor Level 2 course last year. Due to my passion for surfing, I have always kept up-to-date with current trends and feel that I would be suitable fit for your company.

I would very much appreciate the opportunity of an interview to find out more about the position and to demonstrate how I can be of value to your company.

I look forward to hear from you.

Yours sincerely

Gemma Sinclair

Functional language

2 Complete the table using the words and phrases in the box.

| advertised allow asset confident considered |
| degree enclosed exceeding experience grateful |
| have been vacancy |

Paragraph 1
Please find my CV ¹_____ .
I'm writing to apply for the ²_____ of manager as ³_____ in *The Times*.
I'd like to be ⁴_____ for the post of manager.

Paragraph 2
I ⁵_____ working as a manager for 10 years.
I have a(n) ⁶_____ in maths.
I have six years' ⁷_____ in sales.
I have proved to be a capable manager often ⁸_____ performance targets set.

Paragraph 3
I am ⁹_____ (that) my skills will make me a strong salesperson.
My skills will ¹⁰_____ me to …
I feel (that) my experience will be a valuable ¹¹_____ to your company.

Last paragraph
I would be ¹²_____ to have the opportunity of an interview.
I would very much appreciate the opportunity of an interview.

T Teacher's resources: extra activities

L The covering letter contains examples of the Past Simple and Present Perfect. Go to MyEnglishLab for optional grammar work.

→ **page 120** See Grammar reference: Past Simple and Present Perfect

3A Work in pairs. Read the job advert on page 130. Discuss ways in which you could improve the covering letter which has been written in response to it.

B Write your own covering letter in around 180 words.

C Exchange letters with your partner. Which functional language phrases did your partner use that were different from the ones you used?

Self-assessment
- How successfully have you achieved the lesson outcome? Give yourself a score from 0 (I need more practice) to 5 (I know this well).
- Go to My Self-assessment in MyEnglishLab to reflect on what you have learnt.

Business strategy   4

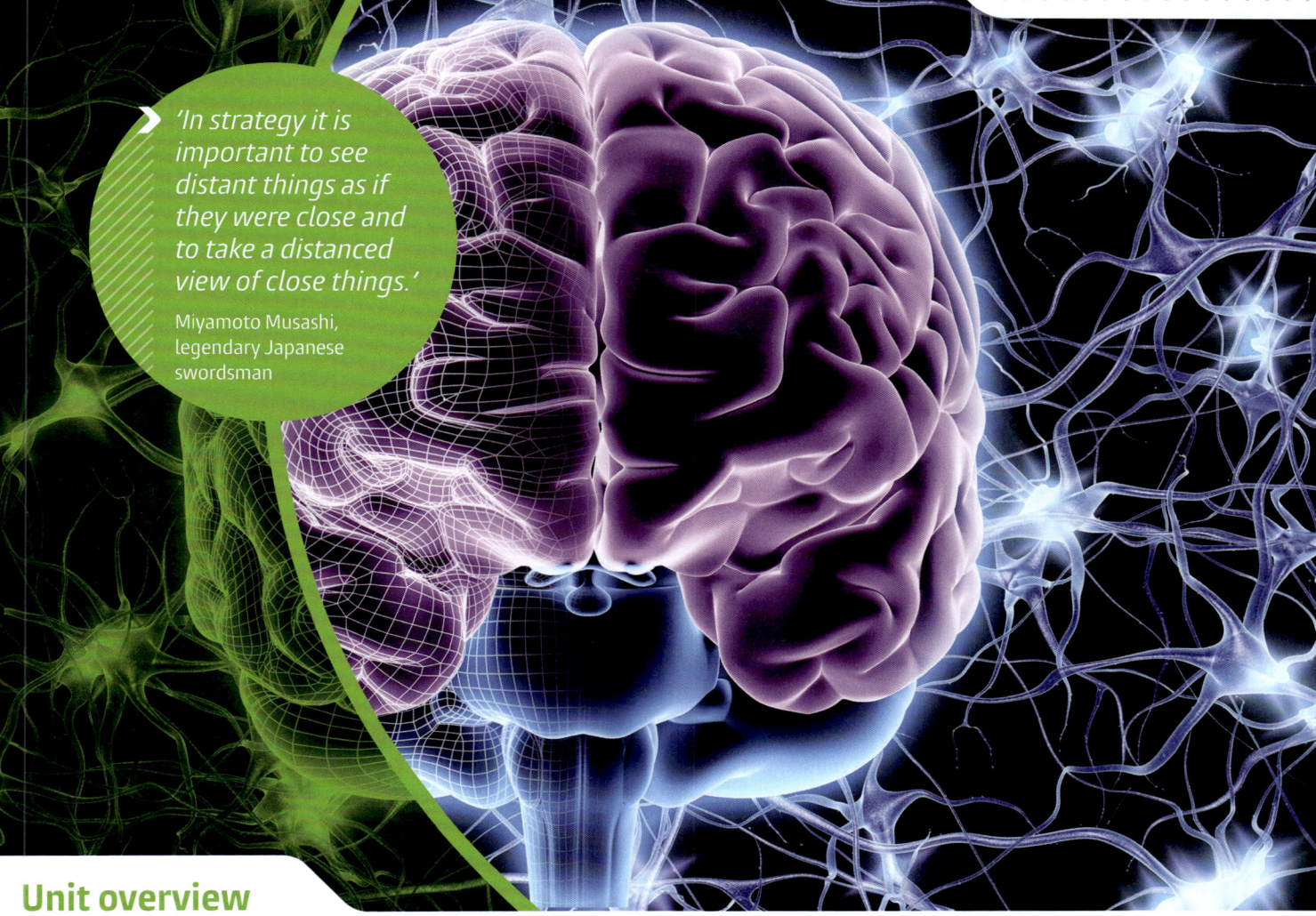

'In strategy it is important to see distant things as if they were close and to take a distanced view of close things.'

Miyamoto Musashi, legendary Japanese swordsman

Unit overview

4.1 Food industry strategies
Lesson outcome: Learners can use common verbs, nouns and adjectives related to business and business strategy.

Video: A food company's strategy for growth
Vocabulary: Business strategy collocations and word building
Project: Investigate a food brand's attitude to health

4.2 PEST analysis
Lesson outcome: Learners can use a range of modal verbs to talk about obligation, prohibition, necessity and recommendation.

Listening: A lecture on business strategy: PEST analysis
Grammar: Modal verbs
Writing: Write a short PEST analysis of a company or organisation

4.3 Communication skills: Solving problems
Lesson outcome: Learners are aware of different ways to deal with problems and can use a range of phrases for offering and asking for help.

Video: Direct and indirect approaches to solving problems
Functional language: Offering and asking for help
Task: Offering, asking for and responding to help in work and social situations

4.4 Business skills: Problem-solving meetings
Lesson outcome: Learners are aware of techniques to use in problem-solving meetings and can use a range of phrases for leading and participating in meetings.

Listening: A problem-solving team meeting
Functional language: Leading and participating in problem-solving meetings
Task: Take part in a problem-solving meeting

4.5 Writing: Reporting reasons and results
Lesson outcome: Learners can report reasons and results using suitable linking phrases.

Model text: Report extract describing problems, reasons and results
Functional language: Reporting problems, reasons and results
Grammar: Comparison
Task: Write a short business report outlining problems, reasons and results

Business workshop 4: p.94 | **Review 4** p.107 | **Pronunciation:** 4.3 /iː/, /ɪ/, /eɪ/ and /aɪ/ 4.4 Intonation in 'OK' p.115 | **Grammar reference:** p.121

4.1 Food industry strategies

Lesson outcome: Learners can use common verbs, nouns and adjectives related to business and business strategy.

Lead-in

1 Discuss these questions.
1 Think of some famous food brands. What products do they make?
2 What trends have you noticed in the food industry in your country? Use some of the words in the box in your discussion.

> famous food brands   food prices   health issues   organic food
> ready meals   supermarket chains

VIDEO

2 ▶ 4.1.1   Watch the video. Which food companies are mentioned and what is the relationship between them?

3 Watch the video again and complete the information. Use a maximum of four words in each gap.
1 In the first decade of the 21st century Kraft's performance _____ .
2 It was seeing _____ processed food and drinks decline.
3 The second issue was Kraft relied too heavily on _____ .
4 The company's third problem was its _____ .
5 Cadbury had a 200-year history. Its products were well established _____ .
6 Because it became a bigger company Kraft essentially _____ .
7 Heinz's development of new product lines met _____ .
8 One immediate result was that the Kraft Heinz's share price _____ .

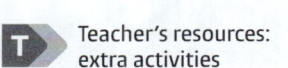

4 Work in pairs or small groups. Discuss these questions.
1 Can you suggest other food companies that would be suitable partners for Kraft?
2 Is consolidation in the food manufacturing industry inevitable? Why / Why not?

Teacher's resources: extra activities

Vocabulary   Business strategy collocations

5 Choose a word from each box to complete the phrases from the video.

> emerging   major   product   profit   takeover

> bid   lines   margin   markets   player

1 The Kraft Heinz company based in the USA is a(n) _____ in the food industry.
2 … the _____ – the amount of money it was making from every unit of sales – had been squeezed …
3 … it was missing opportunities in fast-growing _____ around the world.
4 It started with a(n) _____ for the chocolate maker Cadbury.
5 Heinz was considered more innovative in its development of new _____ …

6 Match verbs 1–4 with nouns a–d and verbs 5–8 with nouns e–h to make collocations from the video.

1 develop   a opportunities   5 make   e costs
2 tackle   b strategies   6 come up with   f a profit / money
3 take   c problems   7 solve   g a plan
4 miss   d risks   8 cut   h problems

38

4.1 Food industry strategies

Word building – verbs, nouns and adjectives

7 Complete the table with the correct word forms.

Verb	Noun	Adjective
acquire	1 _____	
2 _____	competition	competing, 3 _____
develop	4 _____	developing, 5 _____
6 _____	expansion	7 _____, expansive, expanded
8 _____	failure	failing
grow	9 _____	growing
innovate	10 _____	11 _____
12 _____	merger	
perform	13 _____	
14 _____	profit	profitable
risk	risk	15 _____
succeed	16 _____	17 _____
18 _____	takeover	

8 Complete the pairs of questions with the correct form of the word in capitals. Then discuss the questions with a partner.

COMPETE
1 In what ways is _____ good or bad for business?
2 Which supermarket chains offer the most _____ prices in your country?

GROW
3 Can you name two countries with fast-_____ emerging markets?
4 Which industries are experiencing most _____ in your country?

SUCCESS
5 Can you name any _____ businesspeople in your country?
6 What are some qualities you need to _____ in running a business?

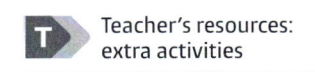

T Teacher's resources: extra activities

PROJECT: Attitudes to health

9A Work in pairs or small groups. Look at the news headlines. Why do you think the food giants are losing market share?

> Big food and drinks companies in health drive to keep market share

> World Health Organization new warning about rising obesity

> Young consumers turn to smaller organic brands

B Choose a large or small food brand and find out what it is doing about health. Think about additives, ingredients, labelling and product lines. Visit the company's website and see what, if anything, they are doing in this area.

C When you have finished your investigation, work with another pair or group and exchange your findings.

Self-assessment

- How successfully have you achieved the lesson outcome? Give yourself a score from 0 (I need more practice) to 5 (I know this well).
- Go to My Self-assessment in MyEnglishLab to reflect on what you have learnt.

4.2 PEST analysis

Lesson outcome Learners can use a range of modal verbs to talk about obligation, prohibition, necessity and recommendation.

Lead-in **1A** Look at these situations when you might need to develop a strategy. Choose one and briefly discuss your strategy in pairs.

1 You are sixteen years old and dream of studying medicine at university.
2 You don't have much money and you want to get a driving licence.
3 You are a member of a sports team. There is a match against your main rivals next week.
4 It's 1 January and you plan to get fit and healthy this year.

B Can you think of any other everyday situations when you have to develop a strategy?

strategy /ˈstrætɪdʒi/ plural **strategies** [C] a plan or series of plans for achieving an aim, especially success in business or the best way for an organisation to develop in the future

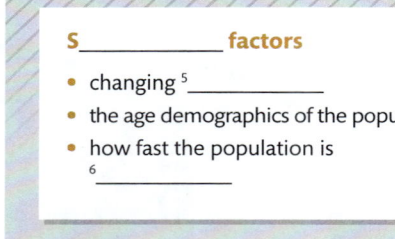

2 Look at the dictionary definition of 'strategy'. What types of organisations (a–d) do you think need strategies? Give reasons for your answers.

a only large multinationals
b only small and medium enterprises
c government organisations
d all types of organisations, e.g. an amateur sports club, a music band, etc.

Listening **3A** 🔊 4.01 Look at the diagram below. What do you think PEST means? Listen to the first part of a lecture on business strategy and complete only the four headings in the diagram.

P_____ factors
- the ^{1}_____ of governments
- the ^{2}_____ laws in each country
- corporate taxes

E_____ factors
- a(n) ^{3}_____ affects demand
- high inflation affects costs and prices
- exchange rates affect ^{4}_____

PEST Analysis

S_____ factors
- changing ^{5}_____
- the age demographics of the population
- how fast the population is ^{6}_____

T_____ factors
- uses of emerging technologies, e.g. automation on ^{7}_____
- the internet and online shopping
- the ^{8}_____ revolution

B Listen again and answer the questions.
1 What do the four factors have in common?
2 How can PEST analysis be extended to include two more factors?

4A 🔊 4.02 Listen to the second part of the lecture and complete the speaker's examples (1–8) in the diagram. Use a maximum of three words in each gap.

B Can you add one more example to each category?

5A 🔊 4.03 In the third part of the lecture, the speaker will talk about what happens after a company collects data. In which order do you think the speaker will mention these tasks? Listen and check.

a Come up with a strategy to deal with risks.
b Identify any business opportunities.
c Prioritise the most relevant factors.
d Identify any significant risks to the business.

Teacher's resources: extra activities

B Listen again. What were the examples of an opportunity and a risk?

4.2 PEST analysis

Grammar **Modal verbs**

6 Match the bold phrases (1–5) from the lecture with the meanings (a–d). One of the meanings is used twice.

1 You **don't have to** take notes ...
2 ... **should** the company develop new product lines?
3 ... managers **have to** go beyond analysis into action.
4 A company **mustn't** miss any opportunities ...
5 ... the company **must** come up with a strategy.

a It is necessary <u>not</u> to do this, or it isn't allowed.
b It is a good idea to do this.
c It's necessary to do this
d It's not necessary to do this.

→ **page 121** See Grammar reference: Modal verbs

7 Look at the first sentence in each pair. Complete the second sentence with a suitable modal verb so that the meaning does not change.

1 It's a legal requirement to pay 32 percent corporate tax in this country.
Companies _____ pay 32 percent corporate tax in this country.
2 In a PEST analysis it's not necessary to look at all factors, just the most relevant ones.
In a PEST analysis you _____ look at all factors, just the most relevant ones.
3 Experts recommend all businesses have a social media strategy.
All businesses _____ have a social media strategy, according to experts.
4 It's not a good idea to leave strategic planning to senior managers only.
Companies _____ leave strategic planning to senior managers only.
5 I strongly recommend we evaluate emerging technologies more closely.
We _____ evaluate emerging technologies more closely.
6 In the future, companies will be obliged to change business plans more frequently.
In the future, companies _____ change business plans more frequently.

8 Complete the conversation about workplace rules and regulations using suitable modal verbs. There may be more than one possible answer.

A: Paula, as it's your first day, I'll tell you about company policy. Firstly, everyone ¹_____ clear their desktops at the end of the day.
B: Where do I ²_____ leave everything?
A: Locked inside your desk. Also, you ³_____ go into the R&D area without a white lab coat. You'll always ⁴_____ show your ID badge to get into the building. My advice is you ⁵_____ leave it in your bag so you don't forget it. And staff ⁶_____ never use personal emails for work.
B: Of course, I understand.
A: It's not essential but you ⁷_____ read the company policies when you can. By the way, we have a badminton team in the local league. Would you be interested? No rush, you ⁸_____ decide right now.

9 Work in pairs. Discuss these questions.

1 How much corporate tax do companies have to pay in your country?
2 What are some of the written and unwritten rules where you work or study?
3 What recommendations would you give to a new person at your organisation?

T Teacher's resources: extra activities

Writing **10** Work in pairs or small groups and write a short PEST analysis of a company or organisation you know well. See page 129 for an example. Include the following:

- **Introduction:** Include a brief description of the company/organisation.
- **Visual:** Use a similar graphic to the one in Exercise 3A. Write two significant factors affecting the company/organisation under each category.
- **Conclusion:** Decide which of the factors already listed are most relevant and any action the company/organisation needs to take or continue taking to make the most of opportunities and deal with any threats.

Self-assessment
- How successfully have you achieved the lesson outcome? Give yourself a score from 0 (I need more practice) to 5 (I know this well).
- Go to My Self-assessment in MyEnglishLab to reflect on what you have learnt.

4.3 COMMUNICATION SKILLS
Solving problems

Lesson outcome — Learners are aware of different ways to deal with problems and can use a range of phrases for offering and asking for help.

Lead-in 1 It is common to classify communication styles as *direct* or *indirect*. A person's communication style may depend on their culture. In pairs, read the text and discuss the questions.

> In **direct** cultures, people often focus on facts, and give clear opinions. They want to communicate with honesty and will argue strongly for their ideas, and against the ideas of others.

> In **indirect** cultures, the focus is more on feelings. People do not like to argue against other people's ideas, and may say they agree to show respect for the other person. They also try to avoid making things difficult for others.

1 Think of one potential advantage and disadvantage of communicating directly, and one potential advantage and disadvantage of communicating indirectly.
2 How would you classify the communication style of your own national culture? Do you like this style? Why?

VIDEO 2A ▶ 4.3.1 Watch as Matt prepares for a progress meeting with Kenji about the Japan side of the project.
1 In general, how happy is Matt with the progress of the Japanese side of the project. Why?
2 Note down the challenges Kenji has in managing the Japanese side of the project.
3 What advice does Matt get from Jack, his colleague, on how to handle Kenji?
4 Why is Matt unsure about following this advice?

B Do you agree that project leaders need to push people hard to make projects work? Why / Why not?

3A In small groups, discuss which is the best communication style (option A or B) for Matt to manage his meeting with Kenji. Give reasons for your answers. As a class, decide which video to watch first.

Option A Matt takes Jack's advice to communicate directly with Kenji and confront him about the problems with his side of the project. He demands that Kenji delivers on time and imposes a way forward.

Option B Matt follows his instincts to be supportive and communicate indirectly with Kenji. He asks questions to clarify the reasons for project delay and involves Kenji in deciding a way to get his side of the project back on track.

Option A ▶ 4.3.2
Option B ▶ 4.3.3

B Watch the videos in the sequence the class has decided and answer the same questions for each video.
1 How many weeks has the project now been delayed, according to Matt?
2 How does Kenji respond to Matt when he raises the problem? What is Matt's reaction to this explanation?
3 What is the solution which is agreed? Who suggests it?
4 Overall, how successful is Matt's communication style? Why?

4 In pairs, discuss the questions and agree what you can learn from Matt's experiences.
1 What did Matt do to communicate in a direct way, and in an indirect way, with Kenji?
2 What happened as a result?
3 Which style – direct or indirect – is the more effective way to communicate in such situations? Why?

5 ▶ 4.3.4 Watch the Conclusions section of the video and compare what is said with your answers in Exercise 4. Note down three main learning points. How far do you agree with these points? Why?

Reflection 6 Think about the following questions. Then discuss your answers with a partner.
1 Which communication style, direct or indirect, do you prefer to use? Why?
2 What are one advantage and one possible disadvantage of your own personal style?

4.3 Communication skills: Solving problems

Functional language

Offering and asking for help

7 Look at these extracts from the video. Which phrases in bold are a) offering help, and b) responding to an offer of help?
1. **I think** [we] **can manage**.
2. **I'd like to help**. Is there any further support from our side which can help?
3. Maybe Stefanie, is she available? [Her expertise] **would be very** [helpful].
4. **I can** [ask her to travel to Japan].
5. **Yes, that would be** [good].
6. **Thanks for** [the support Matt,] **I appreciate it**.

8A Decide if these phrases in bold are a) offering help, b) responding to an offer of help, or c) asking for help.
1. **Is there anything I can do** [to help]?
2. **Could you** [help me, please]?
3. **Would you like me to** [help you out]?
4. **Let me** [give you a hand with that].
5. **No thanks, I'm** [fine/OK].
6. **Need a hand** [with finishing that / to move that]?
7. **Thanks for offering but** [I'll be fine/OK].
8. **Would you mind** [helping me with this]?

B Which two offers in Exercise 8A sound informal?

9A How could you offer help or support to the people in these situations? Use phrases from Exercises 7 and 8A to offer help.
1. This new printer looks complicated.
2. Is it just me or is it hot in the office today?
3. Where did I leave my notes from the meeting?
4. I've got so much work today; I'll have to skip lunch.

B Work in pairs. Read your offers of help to each other and respond to the offers.

> **Teacher's resources: extra activities**

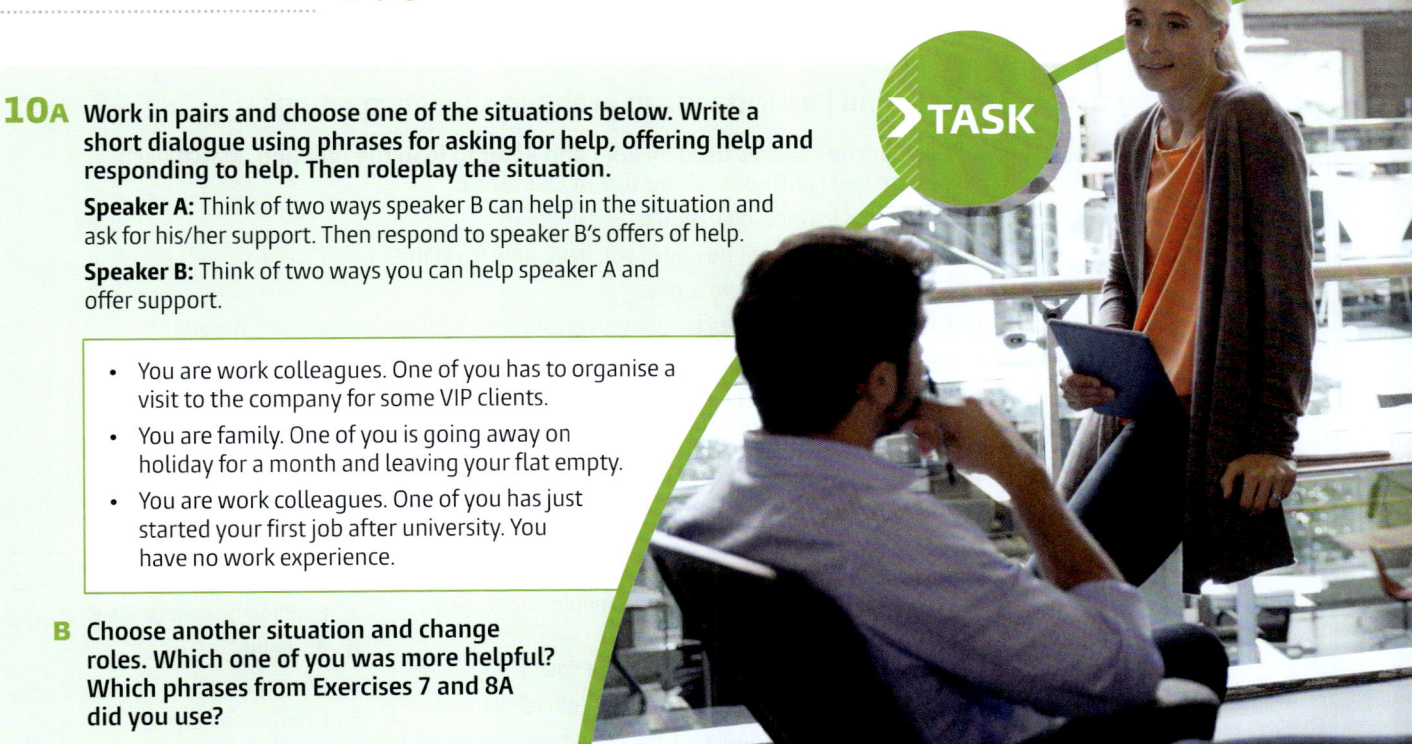

➔ **page 115** See Pronunciation bank: /iː/, /ɪ/, /eɪ/ and /aɪ/

> TASK

10A Work in pairs and choose one of the situations below. Write a short dialogue using phrases for asking for help, offering help and responding to help. Then roleplay the situation.

Speaker A: Think of two ways speaker B can help in the situation and ask for his/her support. Then respond to speaker B's offers of help.

Speaker B: Think of two ways you can help speaker A and offer support.

- You are work colleagues. One of you has to organise a visit to the company for some VIP clients.
- You are family. One of you is going away on holiday for a month and leaving your flat empty.
- You are work colleagues. One of you has just started your first job after university. You have no work experience.

B Choose another situation and change roles. Which one of you was more helpful? Which phrases from Exercises 7 and 8A did you use?

Self-assessment

- How successfully have you achieved the lesson outcome? Give yourself a score from 0 (I need more practice) to 5 (I know this well).
- Go to My Self-assessment in MyEnglishLab to reflect on what you have learnt.

4.4 BUSINESS SKILLS
Problem-solving meetings

Lesson outcome — Learners are aware of techniques to use in problem-solving meetings and can use a range of phrases for leading and participating in meetings.

Lead-in

1 Work in pairs and read the tips below. Decide which of the two ideas in each pair is more important. Then decide which two are the most important overall.

Six tips for leading effective problem-solving meetings

Begin with energy
- **#1** Build positive energy at the beginning (e.g. ask one person to briefly talk about a recent success).
- **#2** Explain what the problem is in a few words. Make clear what will happen if it's not solved. This focuses people on the need to find solutions urgently.

Discuss with creativity
- **#3** Ask for new and creative ideas.
- **#4** Give positive feedback on *all* ideas. This can support creative thinking.

End with commitment
- **#5** Make sure the final decision is agreed and understood by everyone.
- **#6** Take time to confirm who will do what and by when. This builds commitment and makes sure things are done.

Listening

2A 🔊 4.04 Listen to Roel Jansen, who works as Head of Sales for a furniture company in the Netherlands. He has called a meeting with his sales team to discuss an urgent problem. Answer the questions.

1. What is the problem?
2. What could happen if the problem is not solved?
3. Which three possible solutions are suggested by team members?

B 🔊 4.05 Listen to the end of the meeting and answer the questions.

1. What is the decision?
2. Who has to do what, and by when?
3. When will the problem be solved?

C How many of the six tips in Exercise 1 were used by Roel's team during their meeting? How effective do you think the discussion was? Why?

➔ **page 115** See Pronunciation bank: Intonation in 'OK'

Functional language

Leading and participating in problem-solving meetings

3A Look at the phrases used by Roel and Peter to lead the meeting. Match each phrase (a–f) with one of the tips in Exercise 1.

a. I think that's a nice idea; [simple and doable].
b. Shall I take this on, or do any of you have time to do this?
c. Great to see you all here today.
d. OK, then I think we need to look at [recruitment as the quick solution]. Agreed?
e. What else can we do?
f. The real problem is [a lack of language competence here in the company, which we need to solve or we will lose potential customers].

B Now look at these sentences (1–9). Match the sentences with the categories (a–f) for participating in problem-solving meetings.

1. Just building on Roel's idea, I think [it's easier to hire someone than train them ...].
2. Would it be possible to [train our people here to use different languages]?
3. If we do that, it will just [increase our costs].
4. Can you explain again what the problem is, exactly?
5. To pick up on what Roel said, why don't we [hire people with the right skills]?
6. Why do you think this is such a problem?
7. I think that makes a lot of sense.
8. I'm happy to take that on.
9. How about [using a call centre]?

a. Clarifying the problem __ , __
b. Suggesting a solution __ , __
c. Building on others' ideas __ , __
d. Agreeing __
e. Disagreeing __
f. Offering to help __

4.4 Business skills: Problem-solving meetings

4 In pairs, discuss a problem using the steps below. Choose one of these ideas or a problem of your own.
- You can't decide where to go on holiday next year.
- There's no time to do sport during the week.

Student A:
Explain the problem → Re-state the problem → Build on Student B's idea → Ask for more ideas → Disagree → Agree and decide solution

Student B:
Clarify the problem → Suggest a solution → Agree → Suggest another solution → Suggest another solution → Offer to help

Teacher's resources: extra activities

TASK

5A Work in small groups and read the information.

Professional context
You work in the Learning and Development Department of a university with thousands of overseas students. Some senior management and academic staff (ten people) need to improve their English language skills. You have made a list of recommendations (see below). The costs represent the price of training all ten managers equally over a one-year period. You have a budget of €65,000.

English training options	Cost (€)
Access to online self-learning portal (1 year)	15,000
Group (10 per group) in-company training: 2 hours per week for 48 weeks	34,000
Individual training in the UK or USA: 2 weeks per year	47,000
30-minute weekly email contact with a language teacher	20,000
Telephone lessons: 2 hours per week for 40 weeks	29,000
Establish a self-access centre with a range of audio and video materials	32,000
Create an English-language management newsletter	5,000
Individual videoconference language training: 1 hour per week for 48 weeks	30,000

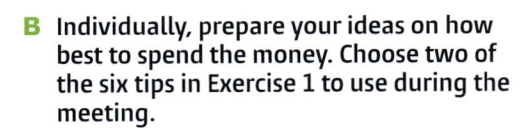

B Individually, prepare your ideas on how best to spend the money. Choose two of the six tips in Exercise 1 to use during the meeting.

C In groups, hold a meeting to discuss the problem and the options to solve it. Decide who will lead the meeting. Then decide how to spend your €65,000 budget.

D After your meeting, discuss what went well and what was difficult. Discuss which of the six tips people used in the meeting, and if/how they helped to find a solution to the problem. Then share your ideas with the class.

Self-assessment
- How successfully have you achieved the lesson outcome? Give yourself a score from 0 (I need more practice) to 5 (I know this well).
- Go to My Self-assessment in MyEnglishLab to reflect on what you have learnt.

4.5 WRITING
Reporting reasons and results

Lesson outcome — Learners can report reasons and results using suitable linking phrases.

Lead-in 1 Decide if each of the underlined words and phrases in the report introduces a reason or a result. Then compare in pairs.

Report on current problems

The supermarket group has faced several problems over the last year. This report aims to outline the main problem areas and reasons for them.

MAIN PROBLEMS & REASONS

- **Out-of-town stores**
  Last year sales decreased significantly in these stores. This seems to be mainly ¹<u>because of</u> changes in consumer habits, as people try to use their cars less often. ²<u>As a result</u>, customers do not want to travel long distances to shop, even if prices are much lower, and prefer to visit smaller localised shops.

- **Customer service**
  Last year self-service checkouts were introduced and staff numbers were cut in the stores. This ³<u>has led to</u> very negative customer feedback. We carried out a survey last month ⁴<u>in order to</u> find out what the problems were. Firstly, customers complain that now there are not as many staff members as before to help them. Secondly, the self-service checkouts often go wrong so that customers have to wait longer and longer. ⁵<u>Therefore</u>, many customers give this as a reason for leaving our stores.

- **Competition**
  A new discount chain arrived in the market last year, offering a more limited range of products at very low prices ⁶<u>so</u> this has also had a big impact on sales.

Functional language 2 Complete the sentences in the table using the words and phrases in the box.

| as a result of   because   due   has led   has resulted in   in order to   resulting in   so |

Problem	Reason	Result
Sales have fallen	¹_____ there was a new competitor,	²_____ fewer customers are buying from us.
Profits are down	³_____ the economic depression,	⁴_____ the need to come up with a strategy to improve them.
Customer complaints have increased	⁵_____ to the installation of self-service checkouts	and this ⁶_____ to the return of staffed checkouts.
Fewer people visit out-of-town stores	⁷_____ save fuel,	which ⁸_____ lower sales.

→ **page 121** See Grammar reference: Comparison

T Teacher's resources: extra activities

L The report contains examples of comparatives. Go to MyEnglishLab for optional grammar work.

TASK

3A Work in pairs. Brainstorm possible reasons for the following problems: customers unhappy, staff unhappy, sales falling.

B Look at the table on page 130 and use the information to write a report extract of about 180 words outlining problems in a mobile phone company and giving details of the reasons and results.

C Exchange reports with your partner. Did your partner use many of the phrases in Exercise 2? Which phrases did your partner use that were different from yours?

Self-assessment
- How successfully have you achieved the lesson outcome? Give yourself a score from 0 (I need more practice) to 5 (I know this well).
- Go to My Self-assessment in MyEnglishLab to reflect on what you have learnt.

Logistics

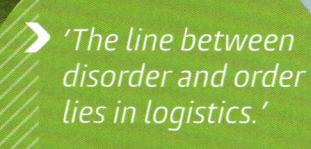

> 5

'The line between disorder and order lies in logistics.'

Sun Tzu, Chinese general and military strategist, 544–496 BC

Unit overview

5.1 E-commerce
Lesson outcome: Learners can use vocabulary related to logistics and the delivery of goods.

Video: Amazon: the logistics of e-commerce
Vocabulary: Logistics
Project: Debate the use of drones for delivering medicines

5.2 Driverless technology
Lesson outcome: Learners can use passive forms in a range of past, present and future tenses to describe processes.

Reading: Self-driving lorries
Grammar: Passive forms
Speaking: Describe a process

5.3 Communication skills: Collaborating
Lesson outcome: Learners are aware of different ways to collaborate with other people and can use a range of phrases for agreeing and disagreeing.

Video: Collaborating on a project
Functional language: Agreeing and disagreeing
Task: A meeting to discuss controversial proposals

5.4 Business skills: Negotiating
Lesson outcome: Learners are aware of the stages in a typical negotiation and can use a range of phrases for each stage of the negotiation process.

Listening: Negotiating new terms and conditions
Functional language: Negotiating
Task: Negotiate a new deal

5.5 Writing: Letter of complaint
Lesson outcome: Learners can write a letter or email of complaint with supporting details.

Model text: Letter of complaint
Functional language: Useful phrases for letters of complaint
Grammar: Linking
Task: Write a letter of complaint

| Business workshop 5: p.96 | Review 5: p.108 | Pronunciation: 5.1 Pausing and stress in presentations 5.2 Auxiliary verbs in passives   p.116 | Grammar reference: p.122 |

5.1 E-commerce

Lesson outcome Learners can use vocabulary related to logistics and the delivery of goods.

Lead-in

1 Discuss these questions.
1 How often do you send parcels or packages? Who do you usually send them to? How do you send them?
2 When was the last time you received a parcel or package at home or at work? What was it? How was it delivered? Give examples of specific brands and items, e.g. books, food.
3 Why do you think e-tailers like Amazon are successful?

VIDEO

2 ▶ 5.1.1 Watch the video about e-commerce and logistics. How many people are interviewed? What are two new ways of delivering packages?

3 Watch the video again and decide if these sentences are *true* (T) or *false* (F). Correct the incorrect sentences.
1 One day Amazon dispatched 1.2 million items and last year a truck left the warehouse every 2 minutes 40 seconds.
2 The packing process is still done by hand to make sure items are not damaged in transit.
3 Goods may be delivered by the national post office or by courier companies.
4 There are now robots that drive trucks and are controlled using a mobile app.
5 Amazon says that in the near future goods will be delivered by drone in half an hour.
6 Airline pilots are worried about issues such as convenience and speed.

4 Watch the middle part of the video again (1:48–3:06). Complete the sentences.
1 Consumers enjoy the _____ of having goods delivered to their homes. But of course customers are not always _____ _____ to receive their package. … Packages can be _____ inside and the customer can _____ _____ _____ at any time by entering a(n) _____ number.
2 This _____ has been _____ to deliver packages. Customers can arrange to collect their _____ from the _____ via a mobile _____ .
3 Some companies are also considering using _____ to transport goods to customers. This _____ is being _____ by the postal service in Finland. …
4 In the future, customers could _____ goods and they would be _____ by _____ in as _____ as thirty minutes.

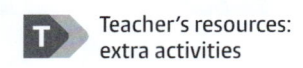

Teacher's resources: extra activities

5 Work in pairs or small groups. Discuss these questions.
1 Do consumers prefer to buy online instead of shopping in physical stores in your country? Why? / Why not?
2 What are the implications of online shopping for a) retailers, b) distributors and c) consumers?
3 How would you feel about having your goods delivered by a robot or drone?
4 What are some of the logistical problems with delivering goods? How do you think technology will help companies with some of these issues?

Vocabulary Logistics

6 Look at these groups of words taken from and related to the video. Which is the odd one out? Give reasons for your answers.
1 deliver   items   collect
2 goods   packages   transport
3 postal service   collection locker   courier company
4 couriers   robots   drones
5 damaged   packed   broken
6 properly   badly   correctly
7 pick up   receive   congestion
8 congested   balanced   crowded

48

5.1 E-commerce

Word building – verbs, things and people

7 Complete the table with the correct word forms.

Verb	Noun – thing	Noun – person
automate	automation	–
collect	1 _____	collector
2 _____	delivery	–
distribute	distribution	3 _____
fulfil	4 _____	–
–	5 _____	logistician
6 _____	manufacturing	manufacturer
7 _____	8 _____	operator
pack	10 _____ ,	packer
9 _____	11 _____	packager
12 _____	product/production	13 _____
retail for/at	14 _____	retailer
15 _____	supply	16 _____
transport	17 _____ (Br. Eng.), 18 _____ (Am. Eng.)	transporter

8 Look at the questions and decide if the words in bold are correct. Change them as necessary and then discuss the questions with a partner.

1 How feasible or safe is it for items to be **delivery** by drone where you live/work? Consider different kinds of **good**, such as books, clothes, toys, electronic equipment, office equipment, food and drink.
2 What are the advantages and disadvantages of **manufacturers** using robotics (robot technology) in warehouses?
3 If drones become a popular method of delivering goods to customers, how will **supplies** and **distributes** need to adapt their **operations**?

Teacher's resources: extra activities

→ **page 116** See Pronunciation bank: Pausing and stress in presentations

PROJECT: The drone debate

9A Work in small groups. Imagine drones were banned in your country two years ago, although neighbouring countries use drone delivery for professional purposes. Debate the following statement, using the steps below.

'We propose using drones for delivering medicines and medical supplies to patients.'

Group A: You work for the health service in your region and are FOR DRONES. Make recommendations for medicines and medical supplies to be delivered by drone for certain people in certain areas.

Group B: You work for the government and are AGAINST DRONES. Make recommendations for why medicines and medical supplies should <u>never</u> be delivered by drone.

- Prepare arguments for or against delivery by drones. Give reasons and examples. Consider these points:

  convenience   cost   delivery locations
  licences for operators   public safety
  solutions for customers/patients   speed of delivery

- Prepare any counter arguments you anticipate the other team will make.

  Student A: *Our supplies will be delivered much more quickly by drone. This way we'll avoid delays for very sick patients, or for patients living in remote areas.*

  Student B: *Delivery by drone might be faster than delivery by road, but drones will cause traffic congestion and accidents, especially in busy cities.*

B Debate in groups or as a class. Then vote individually for or against the proposal.

Self-assessment

- How successfully have you achieved the lesson outcome? Give yourself a score from 0 (I need more practice) to 5 (I know this well).
- Go to My Self-assessment in MyEnglishLab to reflect on what you have learnt.

5.2 Driverless technology

Lesson outcome — Learners can use passive forms in a range of past, present and future tenses to describe processes.

Lead-in

1 Work in pairs. Look at and discuss the picture. How is this possible? Use some of the vocabulary in the box.

| commercial vehicles | drivers | logistics systems | long-haul | manufacturers |
| new technologies | pedals | self-driving systems | steering wheel | truck operators |

2 Discuss these questions.
1 How carefully do lorries drive on motorways in your country? How could technology help them?
2 What are some of the problems for long-distance or long-haul drivers of commercial vehicles?
3 How would you define logistics?

Reading

3 Read the article quickly. How many automotive companies are mentioned in the article? Which ones?

4 Read the article again and answer the questions.
1 Why are software companies taking an interest in buses and lorries?
2 What words are used in the text instead of 'buses' and 'lorries'?
3 What was the focus of the IAA commercial vehicles show?
4 Why is self-driving technology easier to develop in buses and lorries than in cars?
5 Find two ways self-driving technology will benefit the automotive sector.
6 How will the work of lorry drivers change in the future?
7 What is special about Mercedes-Benz's new delivery van?
8 What will happen to commercial vehicles in the near future?

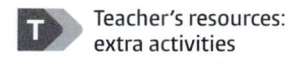

Teacher's resources: extra activities

5 Work in pairs. What other changes do you think there might be in the way goods are transported in the next ten years?

FT

Lorries lead cars in the technology race

Silicon Valley is just waking up to technology opportunities in buses and lorries, which are ahead of passenger cars in self-driving systems. Martin Lundstedt of Volvo, the Swedish bus and lorry maker, said software companies were taking an interest in both long-haul freight and public transport, as technology developed in these areas will be used in passenger cars.

'Four years ago, nobody was talking about transportation, logistics systems and new technologies,' said Mr Lundstedt at the IAA commercial vehicles show in Hanover. 'But now the focus is on logistics and efficiency.'

Volvo says self-driving technology in buses and lorries is easier compared to cars partly because these commercial vehicles can be tested in closed areas far away from humans. Mr Lundstedt said the technology that has been used in lorries to improve predictive cruise control systems will be deployed in other areas, including self-driving cars.

German car parts maker ZF said lorries were likely to see big advances in self-driving technology because investments can significantly reduce truck operators' costs. ZF has already designed a self-driving lorry where the driver can step down and rest while the truck is unloaded, and then loaded again.

With self-driving technology, drivers can be given new tasks to plan routes or process shipping documents. 'Truckers of the future will be more like logistics managers,' said Markus Hein at Bosch, the world's largest automotive supplier by revenue.

At the IAA show, Daimler, the world's biggest manufacturer of commercial vehicles, was showing a battery-powered delivery van that was made by its Mercedes-Benz subsidiary that has neither pedals nor steering wheel, and relies on a joystick controller. It is equipped with drones to be used for the last mile of deliveries.

'In the next 10 years there will be more changes to our trucks than in the last 120 years,' said Wolfgang Bernhard, head of Daimler's buses and lorries unit.

Mercedes-Benz's new battery-powered delivery van that has rooftop drones

5.2 Driverless technology

Grammar: Passive forms

6 Look at these passive forms. What tense are they? Do we know the person or thing responsible, i.e. who/what did the action, in these examples?

*The technology that **has been used** in lorries to improve predictive cruise control systems **will be deployed** in other areas ...*

→ page 122 See Grammar reference: Passive forms
→ page 116 See Pronunciation bank: Auxiliary verbs in passives

7A How many more examples of the passive form can you find in the article? What tense are they?

B In which example is the agent, or the person/thing responsible, known? Which preposition is used?

8 Extend the Present Perfect Simple passive sentences and questions with the adverbs in the box in the correct position. Which two actions are the most recent?

> already (x2)   just (x2)   yet (x4)

1 Has the order been delivered?
2 The order hasn't been delivered.
3 The order has been delivered.
4 The order has been delivered.
5 Have these invoices been paid?
6 These invoices haven't been paid.
7 These invoices have been paid.
8 These invoices have been paid.

9 Complete the passive sentences with the correct form of the verbs in brackets. There may be more than one possible answer.

1 In the last few years, self-driving systems for lorries and buses _____ (*develop*).
2 Logistics and new technologies _____ (*talk about*) at the commercial vehicles trade show earlier this year.
3 A self-driving lorry _____ (*already/design*) by ZF, the German car parts maker.
4 New technology that _____ (*develop*) for lorries in recent years _____ (*not/develop/yet*) in self-driving cars.
5 In a self-driving lorry, the driver can usually rest while goods _____ (*take off*) and then _____ (*put on*) the lorry.
6 In the future, logistical tasks such as processing shipping documents _____ (*do*) by truck drivers.
7 A new battery-powered delivery van _____ (*just/reveal*) by Daimler.
8 Mercedes-Benz have shown that a delivery van _____ (*can/make*) without pedals or a steering wheel.

Teacher's resources: extra activities

Speaking

10A What process is being described here?

> First, the machine is loaded with dirty items. Next, the washing detergent is poured into a compartment and the door is closed. After that, the controls have to be set at the right temperature. When the process is finished, the door can be opened. Finally, the washed items can be removed. If the items aren't clean, they haven't been washed properly at the correct temperature, or the appliance has been overloaded.

B You are going to describe a process that you know well. Your partner/group will have to guess what the process is. First, write some notes. Choose from these ideas.

> a process or procedure at home, at work or in your place of study
> your favourite recipe   how a particular product is/was made   how a sport is played

C Work in pairs or small groups. Explain your process to your partner/group. Can they guess what you are describing?

Self-assessment

- How successfully have you achieved the lesson outcome? Give yourself a score from 0 (I need more practice) to 5 (I know this well).
- Go to My Self-assessment in MyEnglishLab to reflect on what you have learnt.

5.3 COMMUNICATION SKILLS
Collaborating

Lesson outcome — Learners are aware of different ways to collaborate with other people and can use a range of phrases for agreeing and disagreeing.

Lead-in **1A** Imagine your colleague has said he/she can't meet a deadline. What would you do? Discuss.

Dear Matt,

I'm sorry to have to inform you that we have still not resolved the technical problems that we discussed at the last meeting. I know it was agreed that we would solve all the issues but the problems are highly complex and are taking much more time than expected to handle. I have put two new people into the team to help with this, but this will increase project costs. I have attached a new cost proposal for your attention.

In terms of deadline, I am concerned that we may not finish this before Phase 2 – the first customer pilot that is planned. Can we discuss the project timing and find a way to delay by one week, which will give us the time we need to get things back on track?

Many apologies, but these problems are very typical.

Raj

B Raj is based in India. He works for the IT company which is developing the e-learning platform for Matt's project. In pairs, read Raj's email and decide if these sentences are *true* (T) or *false* (F).
1 Raj has solved all the project's technical problems.
2 Raj informs Matt that project costs will rise.
3 Raj suggests that Matt should delay Phase 2.

C Work in pairs and discuss the questions.
1 How do you think Matt will feel when he reads the email? Why?
2 What should he say in his next face-to-face meeting with Raj?

VIDEO **2** ▶ 5.3.1 Watch as Matt discusses the situation with Stefanie.
1 Why does Matt think that culture is the problem?
2 What does Stefanie think about Matt's cultural explanation?
3 What is Stefanie's advice to Matt on how best to manage Raj and the situation?
4 Why is Matt unsure about following Stefanie's advice?

3A In small groups, discuss which collaboration style (option A or B) is best for Matt to use with Raj. As a class, decide which video to watch first.

Option A – Be demanding and focus on own goals: put pressure on Raj to correct the problems quickly. Threaten to talk to Raj's manager if the situation doesn't improve.

Option B – Be supportive and focus on common goals: emphasise the common challenges and objectives which they share in the project. Offer support to solve the problems.

B Watch the videos in the sequence the class has decided and answer the questions.

Option A ▶ 5.3.2
1 What does Matt say are 'significant problems'?
2 What risk, caused by project delays, does Matt discuss with Raj?
3 What is Matt's proposal to Raj on the cost of the extra work?
4 Overall, how successful is Matt's approach? Why?

Option B ▶ 5.3.3
1 What does Matt refer to as 'reasonable'?
2 How does Raj explain the cause of the project delay?
3 What is Matt's proposal to support Raj on the project?
4 Overall, how successful is Matt's approach? Why?

4 Discuss in pairs and agree what you can learn from Matt's experiences.
1 What did Matt do to manage Raj differently in the two videos?
2 What happened as a result?
3 Which approach – being demanding or supportive – is most effective? Why?

5 ▶ 5.3.4 Watch the Conclusions section of the video and compare what is said with your answers in Exercise 4. Note down three main learning points. How far do you agree with these points? Why?

Reflection **6** Think about the following questions. Then discuss your answers with a partner.
1 Which of the two collaboration styles do you prefer when working with others? Why?
2 What are one advantage and one possible disadvantage of your own personal style?

5.3 Communication skills: Collaborating

Functional language

Agreeing and disagreeing

7A Put these phrases from the video into the correct category in the table.
1. I know [they're right], but …
2. It *is* good yes, but …
3. That would be a [good] solution.
4. That makes sense.
5. Good thinking.
6. That's one way of looking at it, but …

Direct agreement	Expressing doubt	Direct disagreement
I completely agree [with you]. _____ _____ _____	That might [work / not work]. I'm not sure [that's the best solution]. _____ _____ _____	That's rubbish/nonsense! I don't agree at all. I'm afraid I disagree.

B In the video, the speakers communicated disagreement using expressions of doubt, not expressions of direct disagreement. Why do you think they did this? Does this happen in your own language?

8A Look at these exchanges between a manager (M) and an employee (E). Rewrite what the employee says so that it doesn't sound so direct.
1. **M:** We're very busy. We need to cancel all staff holidays in August.
   E: I don't agree at all.
2. **M:** I think we should outsource the IT department.
   E: I'm afraid I disagree.
3. **M:** Karine is the best person to negotiate with these clients.
   E: That's nonsense!

T Teacher's resources: extra activities

B Choose one situation in Exercise 8A and continue the dialogue until you reach an agreement. Use phrases from Exercise 7A.

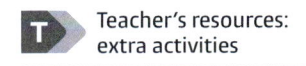

> **TASK**

9A Work in groups of four. Two of you are Pair A; two of you are Pair B. Look at the agenda for your department's meeting and prepare your arguments for the points you agree and disagree with.

Pair A: You agree with items 1 and 3 and disagree with items 2 and 4.
Pair B: You agree with items 2 and 4 and disagree with items 1 and 3.

Departmental meeting
1. Working hours: proposal to start work at 8.30 a.m. and finish half an hour earlier than now.
2. Lunch breaks: proposal to have two shifts for lunch: 12.00–13.00 and 13.00–14.00.
3. Dress code: proposal to ban trainers and T-shirts in the office.
4. Languages: proposal that all staff have an intermediate level in two foreign languages.

B Hold your meetings. Explain why you agree or disagree with each point and try to use phrases from Exercise 7A.

C Which pair presented the strongest arguments? Who disagreed directly most often during the meeting? Who expressed doubt most often?

Self-assessment
- How successfully have you achieved the lesson outcome? Give yourself a score from 0 (I need more practice) to 5 (I know this well).
- Go to My Self-assessment in MyEnglishLab to reflect on what you have learnt.

5.4 BUSINESS SKILLS
Negotiating

Lesson outcome | Learners are aware of the stages in a typical negotiation and can use a range of phrases for each stage of the negotiation process.

Lead-in

1A A negotiation can be defined as 'a discussion between two or more people to reach an agreement'. Work in pairs and discuss what kinds of negotiation you have in a typical week.

B Look at the list of qualities of an international negotiator. Which two qualities do you think are the most important? Why?

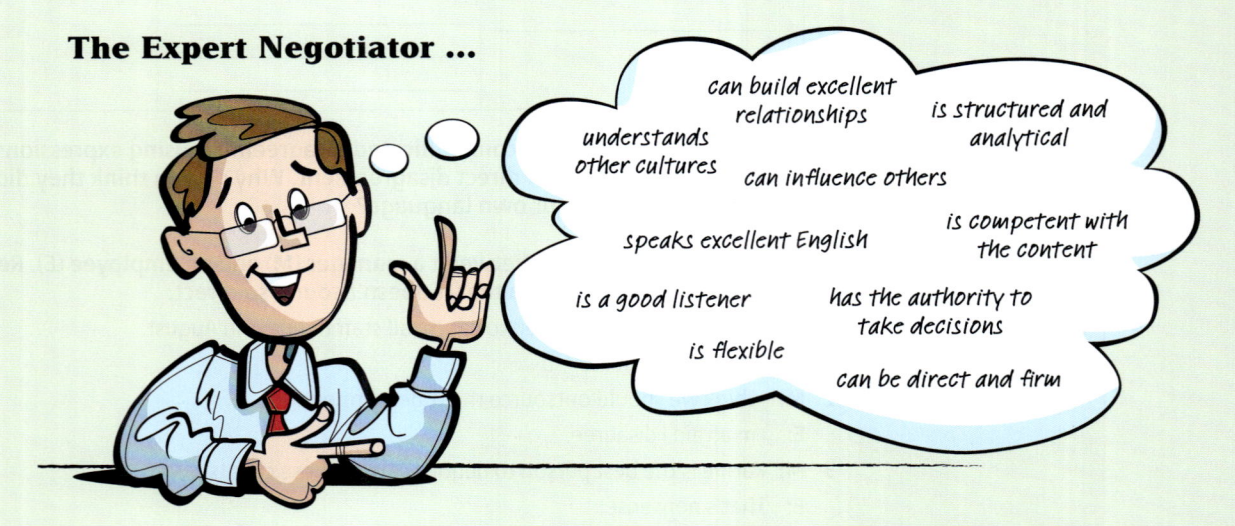

The Expert Negotiator …

- can build excellent relationships
- is structured and analytical
- understands other cultures
- can influence others
- speaks excellent English
- is competent with the content
- is a good listener
- has the authority to take decisions
- is flexible
- can be direct and firm

C How good are you at negotiating? What makes you a good (or bad) negotiator?

Listening

2 Read the background. Anne wants to negotiate new terms and conditions for TravelExec's services and has sent a four-step meeting agenda to Anders. In pairs, read the agenda and suggest what should happen in each step.

BACKGROUND

Anne Roberts is a purchasing manager for a sports clothing company, DesignPro, with its headquarters based in London. She is meeting Anders Rik, a salesperson from TravelExec, which organises all travel services (flights, taxi transfers, hotel accommodation) for DesignPro's staff who travel for business.

Meeting agenda
1. Welcome and opening
2. Proposals
3. Discussion to find agreement
4. Close

3A 🔊 5.01 Listen as Anne opens the negotiation with Anders, and answer the questions.
1. Why does Anne apologise to Anders at the beginning of the meeting?
2. What does Anne suggest are the main items to negotiate?
3. How does Anne suggest that they start the negotiation, and why?

B 🔊 5.02 Listen as Anne and Anders enter the second step of the negotiation. Note down the different proposals which they make for each of the three topics.

C 🔊 5.03 Listen as Anne and Anders discuss in more detail. What agreement is reached on each point?

D 🔊 5.04 Listen as Anne and Anders summarise and close the meeting.
1. Which topic do they make an additional agreement about? What is the agreement?
2. How does Anne close the meeting? How effective is it to close the meeting in this way?

4 In general, how effective do you think this negotiation was? Why?

5.4 Business skills: Negotiating

Functional language

Negotiating

5A Look at the expressions (1–12) from the recordings in Exercise 3. Match them with the correct points (a–l) in the four-step negotiation process.

1. To start, I'd like to hear from you first.
2. Just to clarify, you mean …
3. We agreed to …
4. Good to see you again. Are you well?
5. That seems reasonable.
6. How does that (all) sound to you?
7. Excellent. Well, that was [quick and efficient].
8. If you confirm that in an email to me, then I will …
9. I think we can do this, but we will need to …
10. What I'd like to discuss today is …
11. That's a little high; we were hoping for something lower.
12. My proposal would be that we …

THE FOUR STEPS OF NEGOTIATING

1 OPENING
- a Welcome ___
- b State agenda ___
- c Invite other party to present ___

2 PROPOSALS
- d Present own proposals ___
- e Request feedback on own ideas ___
- f Clarify other person's ideas ___

3 BARGAINING/DISCUSSION
- g Bargain to find an agreement ___
- h Give positive feedback on a proposal ___
- i Give negative feedback on a proposal ___

4 SUMMARY AND CLOSING
- j Summarise agreement reached ___
- k Confirm next steps ___
- l Close positively ___

B Look at some more examples of bargaining to find an agreement. Match the negotiation proposals (1–6) with the correct response (a–f).

1. How would you feel if we [reduced the price]?
2. Could you accept [a smaller volume]?
3. We can't agree to [lower prices] unless [you're flexible on payment].
4. What if we tried [a different approach to this]?
5. Can we look at [increasing the discount]?
6. Would you be prepared to [change to invoicing in dollars]?

a. What do you mean by [increasing]?
b. I'm happy to [link price and payment terms].
c. I think we'd find [price reduction] difficult.
d. I think that's quite reasonable for [the U.S. side of the business].
e. But [volume] is very important to us.
f. What did you have in mind?

T Teacher's resources: extra activities

> TASK

6A Work in pairs and read the professional context. You are going to prepare a negotiation between ATAX and LAURA.

Professional context
ATAX (the seller) and LAURA (the buyer) already have a contract in place. LAURA imports 2,000 coats per year, in three different colours and three different designs, for a unit price of €85 each. This includes a 15 percent discount on the standard unit price of €100. Payment terms are currently 45 days from date of invoice.

B In pairs, prepare the role of negotiator for either ATAX (see page 129) or LAURA (see page 131). Plan to negotiate five areas: the number of coats to buy/sell, the number of colours, the number of designs, the discount, and the number of days for payment. Prepare both the content (what you want to achieve in each of the five contract areas) and also the process – how you will manage each of the four negotiation steps.

C When you are ready, find two negotiating partners who have prepared the other role and negotiate a new deal.

D After your negotiation, discuss in your group what went well and what you found difficult during the negotiation. Then share your ideas with the class.

Self-assessment

- How successfully have you achieved the lesson outcome? Give yourself a score from 0 (I need more practice) to 5 (I know this well).
- Go to My Self-assessment in MyEnglishLab to reflect on what you have learnt.

5.5 WRITING: Letter of complaint

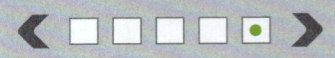

Lesson outcome: Learners can write a letter or email of complaint with supporting details.

Lead-in

1 Read the letter of complaint from one company to another. Choose the correct option in italics. Then compare in pairs.

Dear Sirs,

Re: Order # 4587 for 30 dishwashers

We ¹*arranged / ordered* 30 dishwashers for our hotel group last week on the understanding that they would be ²*delivered / carried* yesterday. Although you indicated that this might be difficult, you ³*assumed / assured* us that you could manage it.

However, only 10 machines arrived and, of those, two were ⁴*damaged / injured* and one did not work at all. Your driver was most unhelpful and told us to call you immediately, which we did. We tried to contact you several times but your customer service department did not answer our ⁵*chats / calls*. Despite sending you several emails asking you to contact us, so far we have had no response from you.

We are very surprised by this as we have been customers of your company for many years. However, if you do not ⁶*respond / answer* to this letter immediately, we shall be ⁷*made / forced* to withhold payment, find another supplier and request that you ⁸*distribute / collect* the ten machines already delivered.

We sincerely hope that this situation can be resolved to our mutual satisfaction.

We look forward to receiving your ⁹*punctual / prompt* response.

Jacob Besinger

Purchasing Manager

Functional language

2 Complete the table using words and phrases from the letter.

Problem (Para 1)
Last week, we ¹_____ 100 desks from you.
Unfortunately, some of the desks were ²_____ .
My ³_____ were not answered by your customer service department.

Extra details (Para 2)
You ⁴_____ the goods would arrive on time.
Ten of the desks were the wrong type.
We were unable to ⁵_____ your customer service department.

Demand (Para 3)
If you ⁶_____ to this letter immediately, we ⁷_____ to look for another supplier.
We ⁸_____ you collect the desks.
If you do not resolve this situation immediately, we shall have no alternative but to cancel our order.

Desired outcome (Para 4)
We ⁹_____ that this situation will be resolved to our ¹⁰_____ .
We look forward ¹¹_____ the correct goods as soon as possible.

T Teacher's resources: extra activities

L The letter of complaint contains examples of linking words. Go to MyEnglishLab for optional grammar work.

➔ page 122 See Grammar reference: Linking

TASK

3A Work in pairs. Make a list of as many business situations as you can which might require a letter of complaint. Then look at the list of problems on page 130 and complete the table with 'details' and 'demands'.

B Use a situation from the table in Exercise 3A and write a letter of complaint in around 180 words.

C Exchange letters with your partner. Did your partner organise the letter well? How many of the phrases in Exercise 2 did your partner use?

Self-assessment

- How successfully have you achieved the lesson outcome? Give yourself a score from 0 (I need more practice) to 5 (I know this well).
- Go to My Self-assessment in MyEnglishLab to reflect on what you have learnt.

Entrepreneurs

6

'It's not about ideas. It's about making ideas happen.'

Scott Belsky, co-founder of Behance

Unit overview

6.1 **Fairphone**
Lesson outcome: Learners can use vocabulary related to starting and financing a business.

Video: The world's first ethical smartphone
Vocabulary: Running a business
Project: Brainstorm and present new business ideas

6.2 **Young entrepreneurs**
Lesson outcome: Learners can use reported speech to report what other people have said and asked.

Reading: Leaving Harvard to start a business
Grammar: Reported speech
Speaking and writing: Talk to a journalist about your start-up

6.3 **Communication skills:** Influencing
Lesson outcome: Learners are aware of different ways to influence other people and can use a range of phrases for dealing with objections.

Video: Influencing styles: push and pull
Functional language: Dealing with objections
Task: Influencing others to overcome objections

6.4 **Business skills:** Presenting facts and figures
Lesson outcome: Learners can use a range of phrases to present facts and figures using visual information.

Listening: A presentation based on visual data
Functional language: Presenting visual information
Task: A presentation to an investor

6.5 **Writing:** Summarising
Lesson outcome: Learners can write a simple summary of factual work-related information.

Model text: Summary of a business talk
Functional language: Summarising
Grammar: Order of information in sentences
Task: Listen to a talk and write a summary

| **Business workshop 6:** p.98 | **Review 6:** p.109 | **Pronunciation:** 6.1 Consonant-vowel linking 6.3 Intonation and discourse marking in presentations   p.116 | **Grammar reference:** p.123 |

6.1 Fairphone

Lesson outcome — Learners can use vocabulary related to starting and financing a business.

Lead-in

1 Discuss these questions.
1 Why do people start their own businesses? How many reasons can you think of?
2 Under what circumstances would you start a business? What kind of business?
3 What are the three biggest attractions and disadvantages of running your own business?

BBC VIDEO

2 Bas van Abel, CEO of Fairphone, says he's created 'the world's first ethical smartphone'. What do you think he means by this?

3 ▶ 6.1.1 Watch the video and check your predictions. Discuss your ideas in pairs.

4 Watch the video again and complete the summary. Use one to three words in each gap.

> Fairphone is a company which started life as a(n) [1]_____ to give visibility to the wars in the Eastern Congo. Many conflicts are related to the mines where the [2]_____ for mobile phones come from. Then the campaigners decided to [3]_____ .
>
> The company grew very fast. Within the first two years the staff increased from two people to [4]_____ . Turnover* in the first eighteen months was sixteen million euros and in only three weeks more than [5]_____ people bought the phone before it was built.
>
> The Fairphone design is modular, which means that people can [6]_____ the components themselves. The company wants to help the economy in the Democratic Republic of Congo by getting minerals from conflict-free mines. They have also recycled [7]_____ old phones in order to reuse the minerals. Bas van Abel believes business is an important mechanism to actually [8]_____ . He did not start Fairphone to become [9]_____ phone company in the world but to show that there's [10]_____ for ethical business.

5 Work in pairs or small groups. Discuss these questions.
1 Who would buy Fairphone's mobile phone?
2 Would you consider buying a Fairphone? Why / Why not?
3 Based on what Bas said in the video interview, what do you think are the key points he wants to communicate to consumers?
4 How do you think he will measure the success of his company?
5 How would you describe his attitude to the business world?

T Teacher's resources: extra activities
T Teacher's resources: alternative video and activities

➡ page 116 See Pronunciation bank: Consonant–vowel linking

Vocabulary — **Running a business**

6 What do the words in the box mean? Complete the extracts from the video using the words and phrases.

> crowdfunding   set up   start-up

1 ... the fastest growing tech _____ of Europe ...

2 ... we made a turnover of sixteen million euros. [The] first actually was through _____ ...

3 ... you know that's why we _____ Fairphone ...

---

*turnover: the amount of business done in a particular period of time, measured by the amount of money obtained from customers for goods or services that have been sold

6.1 Fairphone

7 Complete the sentences using the words and phrases in the box.

> business angel   funding   go out of   pitch   profit   target market

1. When you _____ a business idea, you say things to persuade people to buy something, do something or accept the idea.
2. If you make a _____, you gain money by doing business, after your costs have been paid.
3. Half of all start-ups in the UK _____ business within five years.
4. A _____ is someone who gives new businesses money, often in exchange for a share of the company.
5. Money that is provided by an organisation for a particular purpose is _____ .
6. A company's _____ is the customers that the product or service is aimed at.

8A Complete the questions with the correct form of the words in brackets.

1. Where do you think is the best place to go to for _____ (advise) about starting a business?
2. Do you know the names of the _____ (found) of Apple, Facebook and Microsoft?
3. What are some of the difficulties of the fast _____ (grow) of a start-up like Fairphone?
4. Apart from crowdfunding, where else can entrepreneurs go to for _____ (finance) backing?
5. Do you think that Fairphone is a good _____ (invest) for the company's _____ (back)? Why? / Why not?
6. Do you think _____ (entrepreneur) talent is unique to some people?

B Work in pairs or small groups. Discuss the questions in Exercise 8A.

> Teacher's resources: extra activities

PROJECT: Setting up a business

9A Work in small groups. Imagine you want to start a business together. Follow these steps.
- Decide on your business. Use the ideas in the table if necessary.
- Think about what type(s) of consumers might be interested in buying your product(s) or service(s).
- How will you get financial backing for your project?

	Tech	Non-tech
Service	• App to arrange car sharing for long journeys • App to find restaurants offering gluten-free food	• Ironing service for busy people • Personal trainer who comes to your home or place of work
Product	• Smartwatch with lots of interesting features • Virtual reality video game	• High-quality handmade leather bags and shoes • Device to put over your mobile phone screen so it's easier to read it in the sunlight

B Present your business ideas to the class. Vote on the best idea.

Self-assessment

- How successfully have you achieved the lesson outcome? Give yourself a score from 0 (I need more practice) to 5 (I know this well).
- Go to My Self-assessment in MyEnglishLab to reflect on what you have learnt.

6.2 Young entrepreneurs

Lesson outcome — Learners can use reported speech to report what other people have said and asked.

Lead-in

1 Work in pairs. Do you think you need to go to university if you want to build a successful business?

2 Match the words in the box with the definitions.

| cool | fashionable | high flyer | prestigious | reliable | well-known |

1 admired as one of the best and most important
2 known by a lot of people
3 popular, especially for a short period of time
4 very attractive, interesting, etc. in a way that people admire
5 can be trusted or depended on
6 someone who is extremely successful in his/her job or in school

3 Work with your partner again. Think of one organisation, product, service or person which you could use the words in Exercise 2 to describe.
MIT is a prestigious university in Massachusetts.

Reading

4A Work in pairs and look at the article headline. Why do you think someone might decide to leave a prestigious university to start a business?

B Read the article quickly and check your predictions.

5 Read the article again and answer the questions.
1 What type of business is Traveloka?
2 How does it make money?
3 What evidence is there that the business is successful?
4 Which market(s) does Traveloka operate in?
5 How does Mr Unardi feel attitudes to his profession have changed in Indonesia?
6 Do you think he feels positive or negative about the future of the industry in Indonesia?

6 Work in pairs. To what extent do you think Ferry Unardi's success was due to luck, hard work or something else?

Teacher's resources: extra activities

FT

High flyer left Harvard to start his business

by Avantika Chilkoti

It may be difficult to get into Harvard Business School – but it is also difficult to leave after just one semester, which is exactly what Ferry Unardi did. Today he is running one of Indonesia's best-known start-ups, the online travel agent Traveloka.

'Everybody knows internet time works differently from normal time,' says Mr Unardi, 27. 'When I arrived at school, I underestimated the speed of change.' When Traveloka started out, he said few Indonesian websites were well designed or even reliable, and many consumers were uncomfortable making transactions online. However, Traveloka had 10 million visitors a month by the end of last year and today takes between 10 and 15 percent commission from flight and hotel bookings. He told me the company had partnerships with 33 airlines and hotels across Southeast Asia.

Mr Unardi met one of his partners while studying computer science at the prestigious Purdue University in the USA. He said his other partner had been a fellow intern at Microsoft. 'We always discussed the development of the internet industry in Indonesia and always thought about coming back,' Mr Unardi said.

When the three software engineers felt the time was right, with interested investors and a ready consumer base, they launched Traveloka as a search engine for the travel industry.

As with many start-ups up across Southeast Asia, the idea was not new. I asked him if any businesses had inspired them. 'We definitely had a lot of companies that we looked up to,' Mr Unardi says, and mentions Expedia and Priceline of the USA. 'Now, the rate of creativity and innovation is so high that it's inevitable somebody has done it previously.'

The CEO says that Indonesia's start-up scene is changing. 'That's the thing about programming and software – it's fashionable now,' he says. 'Now, you're cool if you do this, so it's interesting to see what type of people come in, and how they will take the industry forward.'

6.2 Young entrepreneurs

Grammar
Reported speech

> The company has partnerships with 33 airlines and hotels across Southeast Asia.

> My other partner was a fellow intern at Microsoft.

> Did any businesses inspire you?

7A Look at three comments Ferry Unardi made during the interview. How were these comments reported in the article?

B Answer the questions about reported speech.
1. What changes to verb tenses did the journalist make to report the interview?
2. What other changes are necessary to change direct speech into reported speech?
3. What changes are necessary to change a direct *yes/no* question into a reported question?

→ **page 123** See Grammar reference: Reported speech

8 Look at some more statements Ferry Unardi made and questions the journalist asked during the interview. Choose the correct option in italics to complete the reported speech.
1. 'My family don't understand what Traveloka does.'
   He said *his family didn't / my family don't* understand what Traveloka does.
2. 'I won programming competitions as a child.'
   He told *me he had won / that he had won* programming competitions as a child.
3. 'Do you miss anything about being a student?'
   I asked *he do you miss / him if he missed* anything about being a student.
4. 'E-commerce will grow quickly in Indonesia.'
   He *said e-commerce would grow / told e-commerce grow* quickly in Indonesia.
5. 'How did you get funding?'
   I asked *him how did you get / him how he had got* funding.

9A 🔊 6.01 Listen to some extracts from a job interview for an internship. Complete what the candidate told his friend afterwards using reported speech. Use a maximum of four words in each gap.
1. The interviewer asked _____ doing in my free time.
2. I told _____ hanging out with friends.
3. She asked _____ any previous work or voluntary experience.
4. I said _____ the dog for a walk every day.
5. She asked me what I _____ doing in five years' time.
6. I said _____ about that.

B Do you think he got the internship? Why? / Why not?

Teacher's resources: extra activities

Speaking and writing

10A Work in groups of four. Read the information and prepare for the roleplay.

Students A and B: You are new entrepreneurs. Think about the type of start-up you own and five key things you want to tell a business journalist about your company.

Students C and D: You are business journalists. You are going to interview a new entrepreneur about his/her start-up. Think of five questions you want to ask the businessperson.

B Regroup (Students A and C together and Students B and D together) and roleplay the interviews.

C Report back to your partner from Exercise 10A. Entrepreneurs: discuss what you want the journalist to put in the article. Journalists: decide what information will make an interesting article.

D Work individually. Entrepreneurs: write a short email to a friend reporting the interview. Journalists: write a short article based on your interview.

Self-assessment
- How successfully have you achieved the lesson outcome? Give yourself a score from 0 (I need more practice) to 5 (I know this well).
- Go to My Self-assessment in MyEnglishLab to reflect on what you have learnt.

6.3 COMMUNICATION SKILLS
Influencing

Lesson outcome: Learners are aware of different ways to influence other people and can use a range of phrases for dealing with objections.

Lead-in

1A Work in pairs. When is it helpful to be a good at influencing? What situations have you been in, or might you be in, when you need to influence someone?

B What would you say to influence people in each of these situations?
1 You want to get an extension on a work or study task, e.g. a report or an essay deadline.
2 You want to go to a specific restaurant or a film with a friend, and not a different one.

VIDEO

2A ▶ 6.3.1 Watch as Paula prepares to present PRO Manage's online courses to Pedro and Susan, potential customers from a chain of business schools in Mexico.
1 How does Paula describe herself?
2 How does Matt describe Pedro?
3 Do you think Paula's natural influencing style will be successful with Pedro? Why / Why not?

B Read the text and decide if the sentences (1–4) use a 'push' or a 'pull' style.

> **Influencing styles: push and pull**
> There are two influencing styles known as 'push' and 'pull'. With a **push** style, people try to influence through the strength of their ideas and opinions, their status, by listing benefits for the other person, and by getting the right people to support them. With a **pull** style, people show empathy and focus on finding out more about the other person's needs, interests and challenges. Together, they try to find a common direction.

1 Tell me more about why that would be difficult for you.
2 I think the best thing is to launch the product this month.
3 As project manager, I feel we should do it this way.
4 I can understand how you feel. Would this option work for you?

3A In small groups, discuss which influencing style (option A or B) is better for Paula to use in her pitch to Pedro and Susan. Give reasons for your answers. As a class, decide which video to watch first.
Option A – Paula tries to close the deal by highlighting the strengths of the offer (push).
Option B – Paula adapts her approach when she hears the reaction from Pedro (pull).

B Watch the videos in the sequence the class has decided. For Option A, decide if the sentences are *true* (T) or *false* (F). For Option B, answer the questions.

Option A ▶ 6.3.2
1 Paula reminds Susan and Pedro of the benefits of the online courses.
2 Susan sees the benefits of the online courses in their school, but Pedro is hesitant.
3 Paula designed the proposal especially for the Mexican business schools.
4 Paula varies her approach to persuade both Susan and Pedro.
5 Paula successfully persuades both of them.

Option B ▶ 6.3.3
1 What is the most important point Pedro is concerned about?
2 What else is he concerned about?
3 How does Paula adapt her style when she sees Pedro is hesitant?
4 Does Paula successfully persuade them?

4 Work in pairs. Discuss what lessons you have learnt about influencing people.

5 ▶ 6.3.4 Watch the Conclusions section of the video. What do we need to do when we are trying to persuade others? How far do you agree? Why?

Reflection

6 Think about the following questions. Then discuss your answers with a partner.
1 When trying to influence to others, do you mostly make statements or ask questions?
2 What is one advantage and one possible disadvantage of your influencing style?

6.3 Communication skills: Influencing

Functional language

Dealing with objections

7 The table below shows four steps for dealing with objections. Put these phrases from the video into the correct section of the table.

1 [I/We] totally understand your concern.
2 That's why [there's provision for us to support the platform].
3 Sorry, the most important thing for you is …?
4 Can I ask [why you don't think the finances will work out]?
5 That doesn't have to be a problem. [I/We/You] would/could/can …
6 How does that sound?

Acknowledge	Probe	Answer	Confirm
[I'm/We're] aware that … [I/We] appreciate that … That's a(n) [fair/good/ interesting] point. _____	What [is/are] your main concern[s]? _____	_____ _____	If I …, do we have a deal? Does that address your concern(s)? _____

8A Put the dialogue between a salesperson and a client into the correct order (1–9). Two lines have been done for you.

a I don't know. It's a lot of money. *1*
b It sounds good. Yes, we do!
c Is that interest-free?
d That doesn't have to be a problem. You could pay in instalments to spread the cost. Say 10 percent a month?
e I appreciate that this product is top of the range. When you say a lot of money, what sort of price did you have in mind?
f Yes, that's right. We can't afford to buy it right now.
g Yes, if I arrange that, do we have a deal?
h Sorry, the most important thing is your budget for equipment this financial year? *4*
i Well, you see, we've spent a lot on office equipment this year. And we can't afford to spend more on it this year.

B Work in pairs and practise the dialogue in Exercise 8A.

> **T** Teacher's resources: extra activities

TASK

9A Work in pairs. Look at the situations (1–4) and your partner's possible objections. Prepare your ideas and plan what you will say using phrases from Exercise 7. Then roleplay the conversations.

1 **Speaker A:** Persuade your colleague to come in to the office with you on Saturday.
 Speaker B: Your objection is that it's the weekend.
2 **Speaker B:** Persuade your friend to go bungee jumping with you.
 Speaker A: Your objection is that it's dangerous.
3 **Speaker A:** Persuade your boss to pay for your business school course this summer.
 Speaker B: Your objection is that it's expensive.
4 **Speaker A:** Persuade your boss to let you work from home one day a week.
 Speaker B: Your objection is that you need to have him/her in the office to talk to him/her.

B Work with another pair and discuss. Did you succeed in persuading your partner to do the things you wanted him/her to do? Did you follow the four steps from Exercise 7? Which phrases did you find useful?

Self-assessment

- How successfully have you achieved the lesson outcome? Give yourself a score from 0 (I need more practice) to 5 (I know this well).
- Go to My Self-assessment in MyEnglishLab to reflect on what you have learnt.

6.4 > BUSINESS SKILLS
Presenting facts and figures

Lesson outcome Learners can use a range of phrases to present facts and figures using visual information.

Lead-in **1** Think of a presentation you've given at work or during your studies. Work in pairs and discuss the questions.
1 Who was the audience? Did you adapt the content to this audience?
2 Was the presentation too long / too short / just right?
3 Which tools did you use, e.g. PowerPoint, a flipchart, etc.?
4 Was there visual data, e.g. images, tables, charts, videos? Were they useful or distracting?
5 What went well? What didn't go well?

2 In pairs, discuss what tips you can think of for preparing and delivering visual data in a presentation.

Listening **3A** Match the words and phrases (1–9) for presenting ideas or information about business sales with the correct definition (a–i).

1 market growth
2 target market
3 forecast
4 demographic
5 annual revenue
6 stock level
7 projected sales
8 loan
9 disposable income

a a financial calculation about a future trend
b the amount of money that a company brings in over a year
c the amount of spending money people have available after they have paid taxes
d an increase in demand for a product or service
e the expected future sales of a product
f the quantity of products kept in a shop or warehouse
g the customers that a company wants to sell to
h a particular section of the population, e.g. people aged 18 to 30
i an amount of money that is borrowed

B 🔊 6.02 Listen to two parts of the same presentation. Work in pairs and discuss the questions.
1 Which products does the company make?
2 What are the two biggest age demographics?
3 Is the mobile sector growing or slowing down?
4 Do they have enough stock?
5 Which products should they focus on in the next two years?

C 🔊 6.03 Listen to Part 2 again and look at the pairs of charts below. Which chart in each pair is the speaker talking about?

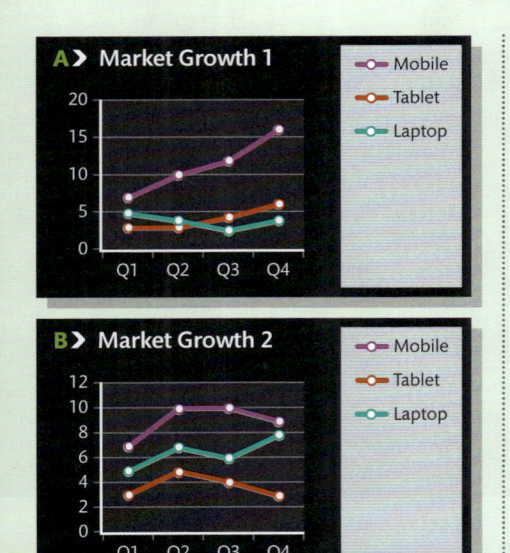

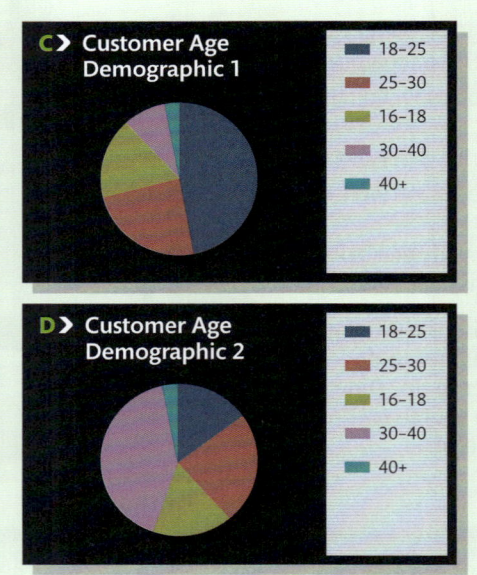

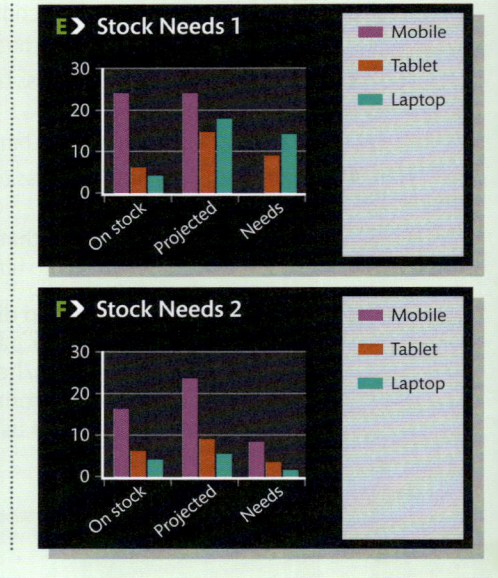

A > Market Growth 1

B > Market Growth 2

C > Customer Age Demographic 1

D > Customer Age Demographic 2

E > Stock Needs 1

F > Stock Needs 2

64

6.4 Business skills: Presenting facts and figures

Functional language

Presenting visual information

4 Complete the expressions from the recording in Exercise 3B with the words in each box below. If necessary, use the audioscript on page 149 to help you.

Part 1: the overview

> chart graph hand over
> next part notice pie
> right slide

1 In this _____ of my presentation, I'm going to tell you more about [the target market].
2 On this _____ you can see [three charts].
3 This _____ chart shows [us the age demographic of our target customers].
4 You can see [which ages the colours refer to] on the _____ .
5 You'll _____ that [the 18–25-year-old age group is our biggest target group].
6 Next, you can see [the growth of our market …] on this line _____ .
7 Finally, on this bar _____ , you can see [the stock levels we have].
8 I'd now like to _____ to [my colleague], who will give you more details.

Part 2: the details

> closely fact details
> interesting show you
> significant think

1 It is _____ that [the growth of the tablet product line has been slow].
2 These _____ confirm that [mobile devices, in general, are outselling tablets].
3 I'd also like to _____ [something on the customer age demographic pie chart].
4 It's _____ to see that [almost half of our customers are in the 18–25 age group].
5 This _____ proves that [our cases are highly desirable for this age group].
6 The last thing I want to you to _____ about is [our current stock levels].
7 Looking more _____ at the bar chart, you can see that [we have underestimated …].

5 Work in pairs. Choose one of the charts in Exercise 3C not described in the recording. Prepare a brief description of it to present to your partner using expressions from Exercise 4.

T Teacher's resources: extra activities

→ **page 116** See Pronunciation bank: Intonation and discourse marking in presentations

> **TASK**

6A Work in pairs. Read the information and plan your presentation together.

Professional context
You have recently set up a business from home, selling products online. You are growing and want to buy more stock to meet the demand.

The task
Prepare a short presentation to a bank or an investor, asking for a loan or investment. Your presentation should contain visuals (graphs/charts) and include the following key information:

- your context (e.g. the company name and product).
- information on your target market (age and type of customer).
- information about market growth (Is the market growing? If yes, how quickly?).
- stock levels (How much do you have at the moment? How much more do you need?).

Use this structure to organise your presentation and decide who will deliver each section:

- Introduction and overview
- Main topic
- Detail on two or three visuals (bar chart, pie chart, etc.)
- Conclusion and final message

B Give your presentation to the class. Ask for feedback about the structure and how you presented the facts and figures.

C When you are not presenting, listen to other presentations and make notes on the key information and other relevant points. Give the presenters feedback.

Self-assessment

- How successfully have you achieved the lesson outcome? Give yourself a score from 0 (I need more practice) to 5 (I know this well).
- Go to My Self-assessment in MyEnglishLab to reflect on what you have learnt.

6.5 WRITING
Summarising

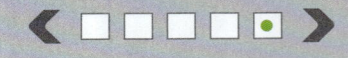

Lesson outcome — Learners can write a simple summary of factual work-related information.

Lead-in

1A 🔊 6.04 Listen to the first part of a talk by a successful entrepreneur. What is the main purpose of this part of his talk?
- a to give his audience advice
- b to explain the background to his business
- c to convince his audience to invest in a new project

B Listen again and complete the summary. Use one to three words in each gap. Ignore the underlined words.

George Johnson, founder of GJWoodToys, explains how he began his business

He mentions that he was working as a(n) ¹_____ when he started making ²_____ for his young children. However, these toys were so popular with other parents that he started selling them at ³_____, where they always sold out. His ⁴_____ was huge: parents and children who loved the toys. Originally he made them in his garage but, when two local stores became interested, he realised he had to expand even further and find ⁵_____. The initial funding came from ⁶_____ and remortgaging his house, but soon a big department store expressed interest in ⁷_____ for 50,000 units. As a result, he realised he had a potentially very successful business but, in order to fulfil the order, he would need a huge investment to expand. With the department store order, he started ⁸_____ to various backers: banks, crowdfunding schemes and ⁹_____. Finally, he was fortunate enough to find one who brought both the money and experience to the business.

C Listen again and read the audioscript on page 149. Check your answers to Exercise 1B.

Functional language

2 Match the tips (1–5) with the underlined examples in the summary in Exercise 1B. Some tips have more than one example.

1	Identify main topic/purpose	
2	Use synonyms where possible	
3	Paraphrase	
4	Use linking words to join sentences	
5	Use reporting verbs	

T Teacher's resources: extra activities

L The summary contains examples of how to order information in sentences. Go to MyEnglishLab for optional grammar work.

➡ **page 123** See Grammar reference: Order of information in sentences

TASK

3A Work in pairs. Turn to page 134 and read the summary of the final part of the talk. Discuss ways in which you could improve it and shorten it. Use the tips in Exercise 2 to help you.

B 🔊 6.05 Listen to the final part of the talk and read the audioscript on page 149. Write your own summary in around 250 words.

C Exchange summaries with your partner. How well did your partner use the five tips in Exercise 2? Did your partner include the same information as you?

Self-assessment
- How successfully have you achieved the lesson outcome? Give yourself a score from 0 (I need more practice) to 5 (I know this well).
- Go to My Self-assessment in MyEnglishLab to reflect on what you have learnt.

Working abroad 7

> 'Studying culture without experiencing culture shock is like practising swimming without experiencing water.'
>
> Geert Hofstede, Dutch social psychologist

Unit overview

7.1	**Global work cultures**	**Video:** Working abroad
	Lesson outcome: Learners can use vocabulary for talking about work cultures and adjectives for describing people's personality.	**Vocabulary:** Working abroad; Adjectives, prefixes, opposites **Project:** Research a different work or study culture
7.2	**Cultural anecdotes** **Lesson outcome:** Learners can use the Past Simple, Past Continuous and Past Perfect Simple to tell anecdotes.	**Listening:** Working in other cultures **Grammar:** Past Simple, Past Continuous and Past Perfect Simple **Speaking and writing:** Tell and write an anecdote
7.3	**Communication skills:** Decision-making **Lesson outcome:** Learners are aware of different ways to make decisions and can use phrases for expressing preferences.	**Video:** Decision-making styles **Functional language:** Expressing preferences **Task:** Discuss preferences and reach agreement
7.4	**Business skills:** Relationship-building **Lesson outcome:** Learners are aware of strategies for building relationships and can use phrases to keep a conversation going.	**Listening:** Conversations at a networking event **Functional language:** Keeping a conversation going **Task:** Meeting new people at an induction day
7.5	**Writing:** Making recommendations **Lesson outcome:** Learners can give advice, make suggestions and recommendations in a written report.	**Model text:** Report giving suggestions, advice and recommendations **Functional language:** Formal/neutral/informal language for recommendations **Grammar:** First and second conditional **Task:** Write a report giving suggestions, advice and recommendations

| **Business workshop 7:** p.100 | **Review 7:** p.110 | **Pronunciation:** 7.2 Phrasing and intonation in past sentences
7.3 Strong or weak? p.117 | **Grammar reference:** p.124 |

7.1 Global work cultures

Lesson outcome — Learners can use vocabulary for talking about work cultures and adjectives for describing people's personality.

Lead-in

1 Discuss these questions.

1 Have you ever worked or studied abroad, or do you know someone who has? Describe your/their experience. Did you/they experience 'culture shock'?
2 If you were going to relocate to work/study abroad, what would you do to prepare?
3 If people from another country come to work/study in your organisation, what are the most important cultural differences they need to be aware of?

VIDEO

2 ▶ 7.1.1 Watch the video. Write the first names of the speakers and match them with their countries. Some of the countries are not used.

> Argentina   Australia   Brazil   Denmark   Germany   New Zealand   Poland   Sweden   the Netherlands   Ukraine

1 _____ is from _____ .   3 _____ is from _____ .
2 _____ is from _____ .   4 _____ is from _____ .

3 Watch the video again and answer the questions.

1 What may employees need to do when working for international companies?
2 Why is working abroad not the same as travelling for pleasure?
3 What might happen after you break the ice and get to know a German person well?
4 What do Brazilians tend to be like?
5 What did Marcus find difficult but fun?
6 Why is it acceptable in Poland to say 'yes/no' and not say 'thank you' and 'please' so much?

4 Who said what? Match the speakers (E, R, M, H) with the sentences. Use two of the speakers twice. Then watch the video again and check your answers.

1 I thought I was very **fluent in** English when I, you know, when I lived at home.
2 But initially they are a bit more reserved, so don't **be put off** by that.
3 But then when you actually come to live here, you realise the **nuances** and phrases that you don't know at all.
4 The use of 'thank you' and 'please' – it's probably less **widely used**.
5 You always have lunch with someone – you never have your lunch **alone**.
6 You might be a little bit shocked that the Poles **tend to** be more abrupt, or that's how they will **come across**.

Teacher's resources: extra activities

Vocabulary   Working abroad

5 Look at the words and phrases in bold in Exercise 4. Discuss the meaning of the words with a partner and choose the best meaning or synonym, A, B or C.

1 A speak with a native accent
  B speak a language very well
  C speak fast
2 A make it difficult for someone to pay attention
  B arrange to do something later
  C get demotivated
3 A slight differences in manner
  B slight differences in colour
  C slight differences in meaning
4 A common or usual
  B popular or well-known
  C to be found everywhere
5 A feeling unhappy or lonely
  B without people you know
  C without help from anyone else
6 (*tend to*)
  A have a tendency to (*come across*)
  B be always annoying
  C move in a particular direction
  (*come across*)
  A easy for people to understand
  B meet or find by chance
  C seem to have particular qualities

7.1 Global work cultures

Adjectives, prefixes and opposites

6A What are the opposites of these words to describe people? Add a prefix such as *dis-*, *im-*, *in-* or *un-*, or write the antonym (opposite).

> direct   friendly   formal   honest   helpful   kind   polite   reserved
> sociable   respectful

B Complete these sentences with suitable adjectives. The first letters are given.

1 People in our culture come across as quite f_____ and communicative when you first meet them.
2 You should always be s_____ and generous with visitors. And we expect to be treated the same way when we go abroad.
3 It is common to say what you think with people in my country. If you're too i_____, people won't understand you, or might even think you are d_____ !
4 People here tend to be very understanding and h_____ if you have a language problem. But when I was working abroad, some people were rude to me because I didn't speak English fluently at first – that was mean and u_____ .
5 It is very important to be r_____ to managers and those in authority. You shouldn't be i_____ . Not respecting people is considered very i_____ in my country.

7 Work in pairs. Discuss these questions.

1 Why do people in your country go to work/study abroad? Which countries/regions are popular?
2 What are the advantages and disadvantages of working or studying abroad?
3 Would you like to work or study abroad? Why / Why not?
4 If you went to work/study abroad, which country would you choose? How long do you think it would take you to adapt?

T Teacher's resources: extra activities

PROJECT: Research a culture

8A Work in pairs or small groups. Do you know people who have come to work in your country? In what ways has their experience been positive or negative? Research ways of working or studying in a culture that's different to yours. Follow these steps.

- Interview a person you know who has a) worked/studied abroad or b) come to work/study in your country.
- Prepare 6–8 questions and record the interview on your mobile phones.
- Consider some of these points:

> being direct/indirect   customs and etiquette
> cultural misunderstandings   national character
> ways of working

- Use expressions like these for checking and confirming information:
  So, do you mean … ? Are you saying that … ? Can I just check, when you say, … ?

B Write ten dos and don'ts for people from abroad coming to work/study in your country. Use the expressions in Exercise 6 to help you.

Self-assessment

- How successfully have you achieved the lesson outcome? Give yourself a score from 0 (I need more practice) to 5 (I know this well).
- Go to My Self-assessment in MyEnglishLab to reflect on what you have learnt.

7.2 Cultural anecdotes

Lesson outcome Learners can use the Past Simple, Past Continuous and Past Perfect Simple to tell anecdotes.

Lead-in **1A** Work in pairs. These are some things people need to do to help them adapt when they are working/studying abroad. Which ones do you think are the most/least important? Why?

> finding somewhere to live   getting to know new friends and colleagues
> getting to know the region   joining a club   learning about the culture

B What else would you add to the list?

Listening **2** 🔊 7.01 Listen to three people with experience of working in other cultures and match the speakers with what they say (a–i). One of the items is <u>not</u> used.

Speaker 1 (Luis), talking about working in India: ____ , ____ , ____
Speaker 2 (Marcus), talking about working in Kenya: ____ , ____
Speaker 3 (Shivani), talking about working with a U.S. manager: ____ , ____ , ____

a The boss was too direct.
b Employees didn't want to say 'no'.
c The meeting started in a surprising way.
d The speaker was embarrassed and offended.
e The speaker saw the positive side of an unusual custom.
f The speaker had an argument with the boss.
g The speaker explains the meaning of 'loss of face'.
h The speaker left his/her job because it had been too stressful.
i The speaker was working with optimistic colleagues.

3 Listen again and decide if these sentences are *true* (T) or *false* (F). Correct the incorrect sentences.

Speaker 1
1 Luis once went to a meeting in Mumbai where there was a religious statue and the smell of food cooking.
2 The Indians wanted to create a positive atmosphere to help the meeting process.
3 'Loss of face' means embarrassing someone, or offending him/her.

Speaker 2
4 In Kenya, 'Hakuna matata' is an expression that means 'we shouldn't worry' but this optimism can lead to workers not finishing tasks by a given time.

Speaker 3
5 Shivani had become ill because she was working so hard, so she sent her boss an angry email, copying in all the team.
6 Shivani's boss was insisting on having the latest figures by the end of the month, so when Shivani didn't send them, she sent her boss an apologetic email.

4 Work in pairs. Discuss these questions. Give examples from your personal experience where possible.
1 How important is it in your culture to create a good atmosphere before a business meeting?
2 How important is it to work in an office with a positive, relaxed atmosphere?
3 Which of the speakers had the most negative experience? Why do you think that was?
4 How do you think this kind of communication problem could be avoided in the future?

T Teacher's resources: extra activities

7.2 Cultural anecdotes

Grammar
Past tenses: Past Simple, Past Continuous and Past Perfect Simple

5 Look at sentences 1–3 from the recording. Match the verb forms with uses a–c.
1 When I **went** into (the chairman's) office, I **was** surprised to see a shrine.
2 While I **was living** in Kenya, I **discovered** that optimism is highly valued in Kenyan society.
3 Later, they **admitted** that that they couldn't meet the deadline, even if they **had** previously **agreed** to it.

a Use the Past Perfect Simple to talk about a finished or completed past action or event that happened before another action or event in the past.
b Use the Past Simple to talk about finished or completed actions/situations, or past events that happen one after the other.
c Use the Past Continuous to talk about past actions or events that were in progress or happening at the same time.

➔ **page 124** See Grammar reference: Past tenses
➔ **page 117** See Pronunciation bank: Phrasing and intonation in past sentences

6 Match the sentence halves.
1 Just after the exam finished,
2 It was unfortunate because
3 The worst thing was they
4 Once, when we negotiated with a Chinese supplier, we thought
5 When we finally arrived at the meeting,
6 He decided that the best thing about his year abroad was

a he had forgotten to bring his presentation slides.
b that he'd learnt about a new language and culture.
c they had agreed to the deal, when in fact they hadn't.
d he suddenly realised he had made a mistake but it was too late.
e hadn't told us their CEO was coming to visit.
f they'd already had a break and eaten all the pastries!

7 Complete the sentences with the Past Simple or Past Continuous form of the verbs in brackets.
1 You _____ (not be) in the meeting yesterday, _____ (be) you?
2 While I _____ (travel) around India, complete strangers often _____ (ask) me personal questions about my marital status and how much money I _____ (earn).
3 I remember he _____ (still study) for his degree when he _____ (get) an opportunity to work abroad, but he _____ (not accept) it.
4 When I first _____ (join) this international company, I _____ (can not) adapt to the time differences for having online conferences but then it _____ (become) easier.
5 When you _____ (negotiate) with Americans, _____ (you/find) they usually said what they _____ (think) and were very direct?
6 When you _____ (do) business in Japan, _____ (be) you surprised at the way people _____ (hold) your business card and studied it carefully?

T Teacher's resources: extra activities

Speaking and writing

8A Work in pairs or small groups. Tell anecdotes about some of the situations in the box. Use past tenses from this lesson.

> an annoying boss/parent   a communication problem   an important meeting
> a special occasion with music   a stressful situation   a time you quit something
> the first time you were away from home   your first job

*Let me tell you about my experience of working/studying in/at …
At the time, I was -ing … ; Once, when/while I was … , I had to … ;
In countries such as … , it's very important to … . For example, when/while …*

B Write one of your anecdotes in 120–150 words. Use different past tenses. Look at the audioscript on pages 149–150 to help you.

Self-assessment
- How successfully have you achieved the lesson outcome? Give yourself a score from 0 (I need more practice) to 5 (I know this well).
- Go to My Self-assessment in MyEnglishLab to reflect on what you have learnt.

7.3 COMMUNICATION SKILLS
Decision-making

Lesson outcome — Learners are aware of different ways to make decisions and can use phrases for expressing preferences.

Lead-in **1A** People from different cultures make decisions in different ways. Work in pairs and answer the questions.
1. How do you make decisions with other people?
2. What is the most effective way for you to make decisions (for example, when organising an event like a party for a colleague or fellow student)?

B Read the information on how two different cultures approach decision-making.
1. Which culture, A or B, do you feel closer to?
2. What risks are there when someone from Culture A is working with someone from Culture B?

Culture A
It's important to have consensus. This means it's important to act as a group and have a discussion before decisions are made. The process of reaching a result is just as important as the result itself. Deadlines are useful to keep people focused, but they should be seen as flexible and can be moved around as circumstances or objectives change.

Culture B
It's important to be decisive. If the group can't reach a decision, then the person responsible should make one, based on the information available. Achieving results and reaching decisions are more important than the process of getting there. People who respect deadlines show both commitment and competence. Those who don't may be seen as unprofessional or disorganised.

VIDEO **2** ▶ 7.3.1 Watch as Stefanie and Paula prepare for a meeting with potential customers from a Mexican chain of business schools, Susan and Pedro.
1. What goal do they each have for the meeting?
2. Which approaches do they want to take? Why?
3. What problems do you foresee?

3A In small groups, discuss which is the best approach (Option A or B) for Paula and Stefanie to use to get commitment from their potential customers. As a class, decide which video to watch first.

Option A – Focus on your expertise and lead the discussion toward fixed dates and decisions you have in mind.

Option B – Focus on finding out more about their needs and priorities and make decisions together about dates and other steps.

Option A ▶ 7.3.2
Option B ▶ 7.3.3

B Watch the videos in the sequence the class has decided and answer the same questions for each video.
1. How do Susan and Pedro react to the approach taken?
2. What is the solution that is agreed? Who suggests it?
3. Overall, how successful was the decision-making process? Why?

4 In pairs, discuss how you think Paula and Stefanie felt at the end of each video. Think about the result and the decision-making process.

5 ▶ 7.3.4 Watch the Conclusions section of the video. Note down the three cultural differences mentioned and the recommendation for overcoming them. Have you experienced any of the differences? If so, how did you overcome them?

Reflection **6** Think about the following questions. Then discuss your answers with a partner.
1. Which communication style do you think is more effective when reaching decisions? Why?
2. Does your culture influence how you make decisions? How? What are one advantage and one possible disadvantage of your own personal style?
3. Following this lesson, decide one thing which you can do to handle working across cultures more effectively in the future.

→ **page 117** See Pronunciation bank: Strong or weak?

7.3 Communication skills: Decision-making

Functional language

Expressing preferences

happy to	keen
prefer [not] to	
sure	want

7 Complete these expressions of preference from the video with a word or phrase in the box.

1 I'm _____ to [keep the focus on our launch date].
2 I/I'd _____ [try to find consensus].
3 We're _____ [work around your needs].
4 I just _____ to [make sure that we're all being realistic].
5 I'm _____ that [we don't want to waste your time].

8A Match the beginnings of the phrases 1–7 with the endings a–g to complete more expressions of preference.

1 My preference is / would be (not)
2 I don't mind
3 I would rather (not)
4 I'm (not) keen
5 If it were up to me,
6 I would rather [we/you/they]
7 We'd prefer it if

a I'd [choose the red one].
b to [stick to our current supplier].
c [what we do / waiting for a bit longer].
d [had the meeting next week].
e [make the decision now].
f [you emailed us the details].
g on [the idea / changing our plan].

B Which phrase in Exercise 8A indicates that the speaker does not have a preference?

9A Complete the dialogue with the correct form of the verbs in brackets.

A: Where shall we hold next year's graduation ceremony? I'm not keen on ¹_____ (book) the same hotel again. The catering was terrible.
B: Yes, I'd rather we ²_____ (look) at other options, too.
A: If it ³_____ (be) up to me, I ⁴_____ (cancel) the whole event. It's such a headache to organise.
B: Don't worry! I'm happy ⁵_____ (do) some research. So, what are we looking for?
A: I'd prefer it if we ⁶_____ (choose) somewhere closer to the city centre.
B: Yes, but then it gets expensive. I'd prefer ⁷_____ (not increase) the cost. People don't mind ⁸_____ (go) to a hotel further away if it has good public transport links.
A: OK, I'll leave it with you.

T Teacher's resources: extra activities

B Work in pairs and practise the dialogue in Exercise 9A.

TASK

10A Work in pairs and look at the three situations. Discuss the points in the box and any ideas of your own. Talk about your preferences and try to come to an agreement.

1 You want to organise a team-building event for the staff in your department.

| accommodation | activities | duration | location | time of year | transport |

2 You want to redesign the room you are sitting in right now.

| colours | décor | equipment | furniture | lighting |

3 You want to open a new retail store in your town.

| advertising | location | pricing | product range | target market | type of store |

B Who had the strongest preferences in the group? Which phrases from Exercises 7 and 8A did you use? Which ones did you find difficult to use?

Self-assessment

- How successfully have you achieved the lesson outcome? Give yourself a score from 0 (I need more practice) to 5 (I know this well).
- Go to My Self-assessment in MyEnglishLab to reflect on what you have learnt.

7.4 BUSINESS SKILLS
Relationship-building

Lesson outcome — Learners are aware of strategies for building relationships and can use phrases to keep a conversation going.

Lead-in

1A Work in pairs and look at the topics in the box. Which do you talk about when you meet people for the first time? Which do you avoid talking about?

> family   hobbies/interests   professional experience and qualifications   politics
> relationships   religion   sport   travel   weather   work

B How do you build relationships with new people in a social situation, e.g. at a dinner?

Listening

2A Work in pairs. Look at the list of strategies for building relationships with new people and discuss which you think are the most important.

STRATEGIES FOR BUILDING RELATIONSHIPS

1. Be interested and ask questions.
2. Be careful your interest doesn't sound like interrogation.
3. Don't make assumptions about people from the first impressions you have of them.
4. Take time to get to know the other person.
5. Think about how they behave and the possible reasons why.
6. Find out and talk about things you have in common, e.g. interests, family, etc.
7. If possible, adapt your usual communication style to be closer to the other person's.
8. Try to talk about things the other person wants to talk about.

B 🔊 7.02 Listen to the beginning of an informal dinner at an international networking event.
1. Which topics does Peter try to talk about with Tadashi?
2. What topics do Peter and Pilar mention?
3. Which strategies from Exercise 2A does Peter use?
4. What first impression do you think Peter has of Tadashi and Pilar?
5. What impression do you think they have of Peter?

C 🔊 7.03 Listen to the next part of the conversation.
1. How does Peter adapt to make the conversation more comfortable for both Tadashi and Pilar?
2. Which topics do they talk about?
3. Which strategies from Exercise 2A does Peter use?

D 🔊 7.04 Listen to Peter later that evening, talking about what happened.
1. What conclusion does he reach about first impressions?
2. Which points from the list in Exercise 2A did he think about?

Functional language

Keeping a conversation going

3A Look at the example from Part 1 of the conversation. Then match the sentences 1–5 to responses a–e and follow-up questions or comments i–v to show how to make links in conversations. Check your answers in the audioscripts on page 150.

Initial question or comment	Response	Follow-up question or comment
1 What do you think of the elections?	a I went to Brazil.	i Yes, that's it.
2 What do you do?	b I'm working on one at the moment. We're making ads that will run in planes.	ii But you must have an idea. What do you think?
3 What sort of campaigns do you design?	c I don't know.	iii You're an accountant. Really? I'm a finance specialist. Who do you work for?
4 Where did you go on holiday?	d So you're in the middle, then?	iv Great!
5 You know, I also have two brothers, like you.	e I'm an accountant during the day and I play in a local band at weekends.	v That project sounds really interesting.

7.4 Business skills: Relationship-building

B Now match sentences from each column in the table below to make logical conversations.

Initial question or comment	Response	Follow-up question or comment
1 I've just come back from a trip to Tokyo. Have you ever been to Japan?	a Yes, that's right. I play for my local club most weekends. Do you play?	i Definitely! There are some fantastic theme parks and the food is amazing.
2 I understand you play a lot of tennis. Is that right?	b I'm working on a new project with the Milan team, but we're still trying to get funding.	ii Oh yes, I've heard about that. The funding process is really stressful, isn't it?
3 What are you working on at the moment?	c No, but actually I'm thinking about going next year with my family. Would you recommend it?	iii I do. Perhaps we should arrange a match sometime.

C Work in pairs and practise the three-part conversation structure. Use a conversation starter from Exercise 3B or your own idea. Use the phrases in Exercises 3A and B to help you.

- I've just come back from …
- I understand that/you …
- What are you working on at the moment?

T Teacher's resources: extra activities

> **TASK**

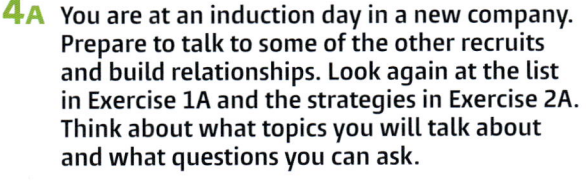

4A You are at an induction day in a new company. Prepare to talk to some of the other recruits and build relationships. Look again at the list in Exercise 1A and the strategies in Exercise 2A. Think about what topics you will talk about and what questions you can ask.

B Work in pairs. Introduce yourselves and spend a few minutes making small talk and building your relationship. Aim to talk about at least two to three topics. Try to reflect on the conversation while you are having it and adapt your approach if necessary.

C Think about what did/didn't go well.
- Which topics from Exercise 1A were discussed?
- Which strategies from Exercise 2A were used?
- Which phrases from Exercises 3A and B were used?
- Give each other feedback and make suggestions for how to improve next time you practise.

D Change partners and repeat the activity. Try to respond to the previous feedback and improve your approach.

Self-assessment
- How successfully have you achieved the lesson outcome? Give yourself a score from 0 (I need more practice) to 5 (I know this well).
- Go to My Self-assessment in MyEnglishLab to reflect on what you have learnt.

7.5 WRITING: Making recommendations

Lesson outcome | Learners can give advice, make suggestions and recommendations in a written report.

Lead-in

1 Read the extract from a formal report about a problem in project teams. Underline all the examples of suggestions, advice and recommendations. Then compare in pairs.

Report on cross-cultural project teams

Recently it has become obvious that staff need to be trained in cross-cultural working as we now have several project teams with members from different countries. For these projects to be most effective, it is advisable that everyone is aware of the cultural background of each team member. If people are not familiar with the differences, then cultural problems will become more complicated. Consequently, to avoid misunderstandings, it is essential that everyone in the team learns how each culture differs.

We therefore suggest that all staff in these teams do a suitable cross-cultural training course. You ought to do this quickly because, unless training is arranged with immediate effect, some projects will probably suffer. If this happened, it would be a disaster for the company.

Our recommendation would be to organise a course for the staff immediately. Another suggestion is to visit the other countries. If team members visited other members in their own countries, they would get to know each other better and develop better working relationships.

Functional language

2 Complete the table using the words in the box.

> advisable   obvious   ought   suggest   would

Formal
It is ^{1}_____ (that) everyone has training.
It is essential (that) you do it now.
I/We advise you to change supplier.
We strongly recommend (that) you add more designs.
Our recommendation ^{2}_____ be to merge with that company.
It is recommended (that) everyone attends the course.
It has become ^{3}_____ (that) our clients are not happy.

Neutral
You should increase prices.
My advice is to have a new marketing campaign.
One idea is to have drone deliveries.
One thing you could do is change the logo.
If I were you, I'd change your supplier.
I/We therefore ^{4}_____ (that) you recruit more staff.
You ^{5}_____ to have a sale.
We need to train staff better.

Informal
Have you tried speaking to her?
What/How about having a new logo?
Let's work together.
I think it's a good idea to work in teams.
Make sure (that) you change the order.
It's best to buy in bulk.
You'd better get some help.
Why don't we change the design?

T Teacher's resources: extra activities

L The report contains examples of first and second conditional sentences. Go to MyEnglishLab for optional grammar work

→ **page 124** See Grammar reference: First and second conditional

TASK

3A Work in pairs. Proofread the informal email on page 131 and find eight language mistakes. Think about grammar, missing words and unnecessary words.

B Look at the notes on a situation on page 129. Write a formal report of about 180 words giving suggestions, advice and recommendations about the best course of action.

C Exchange reports with your partner. How many functional language phrases did your partner use? Is there anything you think could be improved?

Self-assessment

- How successfully have you achieved the lesson outcome? Give yourself a score from 0 (I need more practice) to 5 (I know this well).
- Go to My Self-assessment in MyEnglishLab to reflect on what you have learnt.

Leadership

8

> 'If your actions create a legacy that inspires others to dream more, learn more, care more and become more, then, you are an excellent leader.'
>
> Dolly Parton, singer-songwriter

Unit overview

8.1 Learning to lead
Lesson outcome: Learners can use common verb and noun collocations related to work and leadership.

Video: Safari Vet School
Vocabulary: Leadership
Project: Research and write a short article about a great leader

8.2 Neuroleadership
Lesson outcome: Learners can use relative pronouns (*who*, *that*, *which*, *when*, *where*, *whose*) in defining and non-defining relative clauses when speaking and writing.

Reading: Business leaders need neuroscience
Grammar: Relative clauses
Speaking: Truth or lie game using relative clauses

8.3 Communication skills: Giving and receiving feedback
Lesson outcome: Learners are aware of different ways to give feedback and can use a range of phrases for giving and receiving feedback.

Video: Positive and developmental feedback
Functional language: Giving and responding to feedback
Task: Give and respond to developmental feedback

8.4 Business skills: Leading meetings
Lesson outcome: Learners are aware of techniques for dealing with interruptions and can use a range of phrases for leading and managing meetings.

Listening: Managing a team meeting
Functional language: Leading and managing meetings
Task: Lead a mini-meeting

8.5 Writing: Informing of a decision
Lesson outcome: Learners can write an email informing staff or colleagues about decisions taken.

Model text: Email about decisions made by Board of Directors
Functional language: Formal and semi-formal language for decisions
Grammar: Reduced relative clauses
Task: Write a formal email to inform staff of decisions made

| Business workshop 8: p.102 | Review 8: p.111 | Pronunciation: 8.1 Glottal stops 8.2 Phrasing and intonation in relative clauses p.117 | Grammar reference: p.125 |

8.1 Learning to lead

Lesson outcome | Learners can use common verb and noun collocations related to work and leadership.

Lead-in **1A** Discuss your views on these comments.
1 Great leaders are born not made.
2 Nobody really agrees about what the characteristics of a great leader are.
3 Being a leader is different from being a manager.

B Work in groups. Decide what the three most characteristic features of a leader are.

VIDEO **2** You are going to watch a video about a TV show called *Safari Vet School*. What do you expect to see?

3 ▶ 8.1.1 Watch the video and complete the notes.

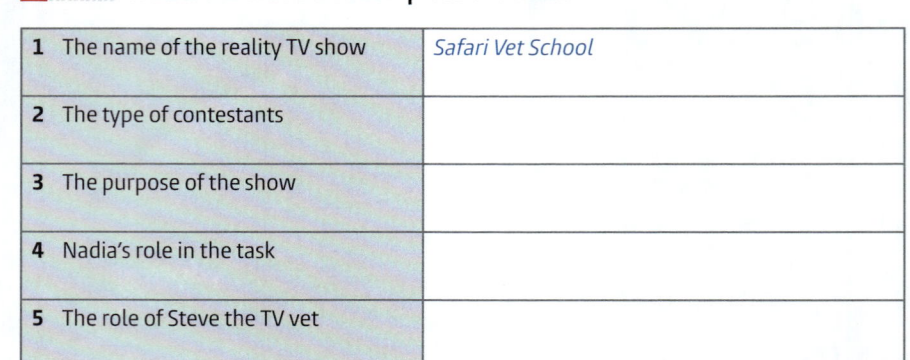

1	The name of the reality TV show	*Safari Vet School*
2	The type of contestants	
3	The purpose of the show	
4	Nadia's role in the task	
5	The role of Steve the TV vet	

4 Watch the video again and decide if these sentences are *true* (T) or *false* (F). Correct the incorrect sentences.
1 The contestants come from South Africa.
2 Nadia admits she feels intimidated by this challenge.
3 The animal must be treated quickly or it could die.
4 The Park Manager criticises them for not completing the task.
5 Nadia feels the team members were not happy with her.
6 Steve says Nadia asked her team too many questions.

5 Work in pairs or small groups. Discuss these questions.
1 In what ways do you think Nadia will be a good leader? How might she become a bad leader?
2 Do you agree with Steve that Nadia needed to consult her team more during the task? Why / Why not?
3 In what situations is it better for a leader to ask their team questions? In what situations should a leader take control?
4 Would you watch *Safari Vet School*? To what extent is it entertainment and to what extent is it educational? Which do you prefer?

Teacher's resources: extra activities

➔ **page 117** See Pronunciation bank: Glottal stops

Vocabulary **Leadership**

6 Match the two parts of the phrases you heard in the video. What are the verb and noun collocations?

1 ... knowing when to delegate
2 ... these are just as important in running
3 As team leader, Nadia has to make
4 ... you'd taken on too much

a key decisions ...
b responsibility?
c a team ...
d tasks.

78

8.1 Learning to lead

7 Replace the underlined phrase(s) in the sentences. Use one verb from the box in each sentence and put it in the correct position.

cope with   delegate   prioritise   run   set   trust (x2)   win

1. A good manager knows when to <u>give part of the work to a member of the team</u>.
2. Let's <u>put these tasks in order of importance</u> so we do the most important work first.
3. Staff must <u>feel sure that</u> their manager's judgement <u>is correct</u>.
4. She wants to <u>establish</u> short-term and long-term goals for her career.
5. You need a lot of skills to <u>be in charge of</u> a large department.
6. People <u>believe that</u> great leaders <u>are honest and will not do anything bad or wrong</u>.
7. I think it's very hard to <u>deal successfully with</u> failure.
8. The new manager is finding it hard to <u>gain</u> his staff's respect because he is younger than them.

8 Find the verb (1–6) which collocates with all the words in a group (a–f). Check new words in your dictionary.

1. cope with   a an effort, decisions, mistakes, people feel safe
2. give   b an example, high standards, priorities, the tone
3. make   c a crisis, constant change, stress, strong criticism
4. run   d a business, the country, a meeting, a team
5. set   e your instincts, the statistics, your team, each other
6. trust   f clear instructions, constructive feedback, praise, support

9 Work in pairs. Discuss these questions.

1. Do you find it easy to cope with stress? How do you cope with it?
2. How can managers best give support to their staff?
3. What should a manager do when staff make mistakes?
4. In what ways can a manager set an example for the team?
5. What can happen when managers and staff don't trust each other?

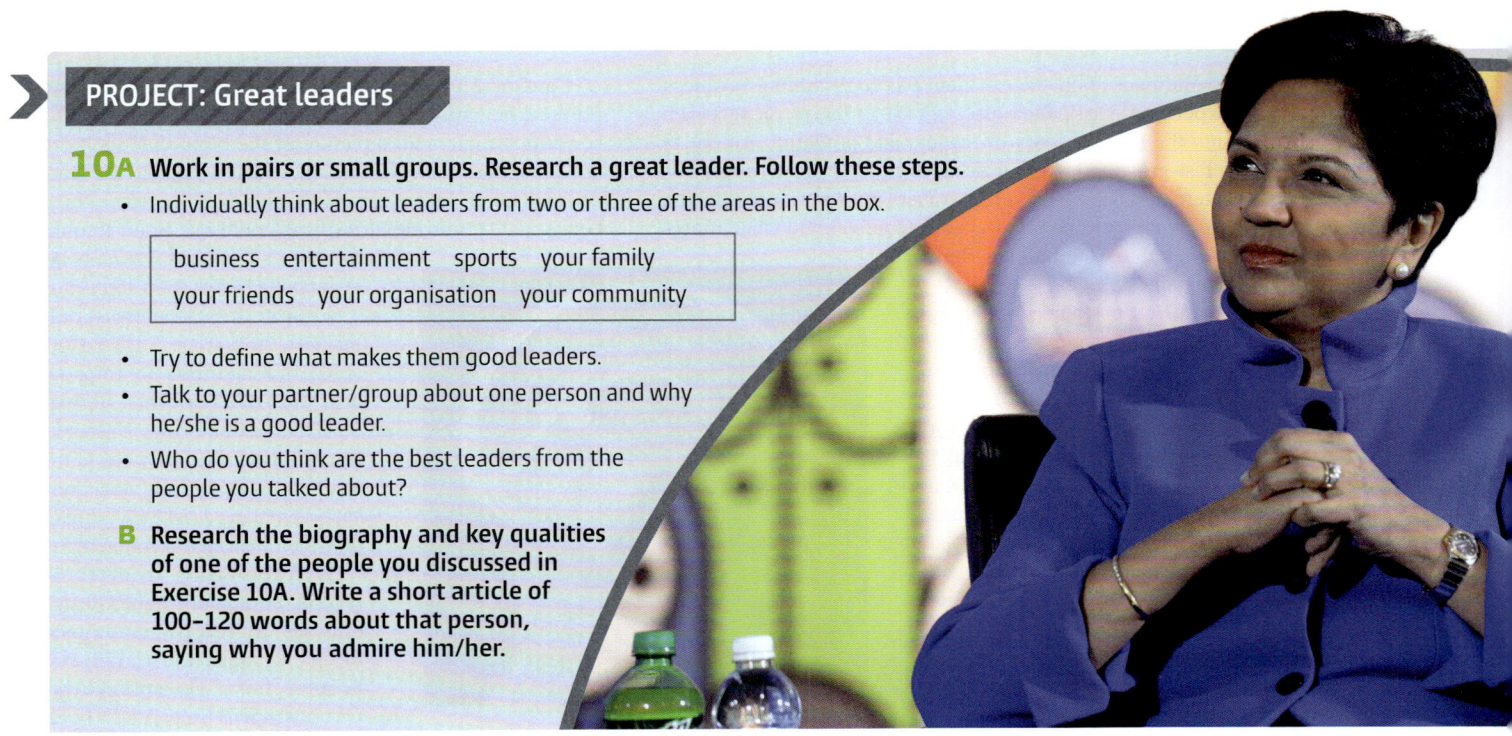

T Teacher's resources: extra activities

PROJECT: Great leaders

10A Work in pairs or small groups. Research a great leader. Follow these steps.

- Individually think about leaders from two or three of the areas in the box.

| business   entertainment   sports   your family |
your friends   your organisation   your community

- Try to define what makes them good leaders.
- Talk to your partner/group about one person and why he/she is a good leader.
- Who do you think are the best leaders from the people you talked about?

B Research the biography and key qualities of one of the people you discussed in Exercise 10A. Write a short article of 100–120 words about that person, saying why you admire him/her.

Indra Nooyi, Pepsi CEO

Self-assessment

- How successfully have you achieved the lesson outcome? Give yourself a score from 0 (I need more practice) to 5 (I know this well).
- Go to My Self-assessment in MyEnglishLab to reflect on what you have learnt.

8.2 Neuroleadership

Lesson outcome: Learners can use relative pronouns (*who, that, which, when, where, whose*) in defining and non-defining relative clauses when speaking and writing.

Lead-in

1 Look at the sentences. Can you work out the meaning of the bold words from the context? If you need further help, turn to page 129 and match the words with the definitions.

1 It is important to reward good **behaviour**.
2 There are opportunities for professional **development**.
3 She had great **empathy** with people.
4 The company seems to have a very old-fashioned **mindset**.
5 A moment's **reflection** will show the stupidity of this argument.
6 Children sometimes have strong **will**.

2 Work in pairs or small groups. Discuss these questions.

1 Does a good leader always need to have a strong will? Why / Why not?
2 Why is it important for leaders to have empathy?
3 Why is reflection important in leadership?

Reading

3A Look at the article headline. What do you think is the connection between neuroscience and business leadership?

B Read the article quickly. What is the writer's conclusion?
a In principle it is a good idea to train leaders' brains to improve their skills.
b Leadership brain-training techniques are generally unethical and high risk.
c It is relatively quick and easy to adapt a leader's mindset with brain training.

FT

Business leaders need neuroscience

'Do you want to sell it? Put a brain on it.' Molly Crockett, neuroscientist

Excitement about neuroscience is high among business experts. Neuroleadership, [1]which is based on research into the brain activity of leaders and potential leaders, is a fast-growing area. For decades experts saw managers as interchangeable. Then researchers started to identify the different types and mindsets of executives and what impact their behaviour had on their companies.

Now, 'I'm reading everything I can about neuroscience,' says Abbie Smith of Chicago Booth business school, [2]who has looked at the benefits for companies that appoint 'frugal'* executives. 'We take as a given that these behaviours indicate mindset. But the question is: what can change?'

Brains can. Dr Tania Singer recently presented [3]research which shows intensive exercises in empathy can break selfish habits and change 'the brain's hardware' so people become more altruistic. If we can work out how to change executives from one 'type' (selfish, say) to another (altruistic), it could open up whole new possibilities for training and development.

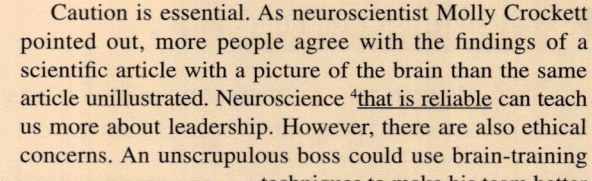

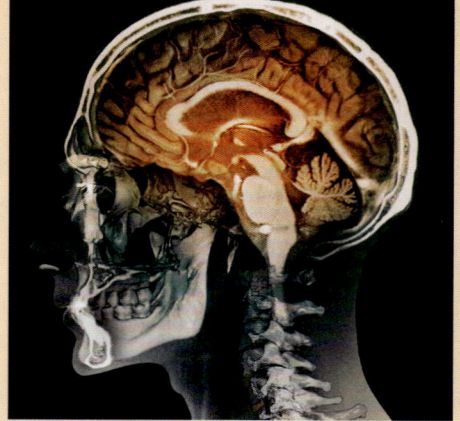

Caution is essential. As neuroscientist Molly Crockett pointed out, more people agree with the findings of a scientific article with a picture of the brain than the same article unillustrated. Neuroscience [4]that is reliable can teach us more about leadership. However, there are also ethical concerns. An unscrupulous boss could use brain-training techniques to make his team better at pursuing bad or short-term ends.

Despite this, leaders should pursue positive, thorough scientific methods to improve how the brain performs. Barbara Sahakian of Cambridge University found entrepreneurs were better adapted to taking 'hot' decisions, such as making a risky investment, than their managerial counterparts.

Extrapolating from those results, companies could design courses to retrain managers' brains to make the risk-averse become more entrepreneurial. One obstacle is time. A new book, *Neuroscience for Leadership* points out that to develop some of these skills still 'depends on tremendous motivation and will, and years of practice, reflection and feedback'. Most chief executives do not have years. But their successors do.

*frugal: careful to buy only what is necessary

8.2 Neuroleadership

4 Read the article again and answer the questions.
1 What does the writer say is the reaction of business experts to neuroscience?
2 What was the assumption about managers when studying organisations in the past?
3 How can neuroscience potentially help companies and managers?
4 What six 'types' of executives are mentioned in the article?
5 Why should companies be cautious about brain training?
6 What five key elements are required to develop neuroleadership skills?

Teacher's resources: extra activities

Grammar Relative clauses

A **defining relative clause** is part of a sentence that gives **essential information** about a person or thing.

5A Read the information about relative clauses. Then look at the underlined phrases (1–4) in the article. Which are defining and which are non-defining relative clauses?

B What are the relative pronouns that introduce the relative clauses? What are other common relative pronouns?

→ **page 125** See Grammar reference: Relative clauses
→ **page 117** See Pronunciation bank: Phrasing and intonation in relative clauses

A **non-defining relative clause** is part of a sentence that gives **extra information** about a person or thing.

6A Complete the sentences with suitable relative pronouns (*when, where, which, who, whose, that*). There may be more than one possible answer.
1 Business needs leaders _____ can adapt to complex and changing conditions.
2 Barack Obama, _____ father was a Kenyan economist, was born in Hawaii.
3 This is the brain-training app _____ I told you about.
4 Do you remember the day _____ you first started at the company?
5 A leadership style _____ is autocratic involves individual control over all decisions.
6 She is a manager _____ many people admire.
7 Oxford University, _____ twenty-seven British prime ministers were educated, has thirty-eight colleges.
8 Dr Tania Singer is the neuroscientist _____ we saw at the conference.

B In which sentences can we omit the relative pronoun? Why?

7A Combine the sentences using relative clauses.
0 Kyoto is in the central part of Honshu Island. It has a population of about 1.5 million.
Kyoto, which has a population of about 1.5 million, is in the central part of Honshu Island.
1 The workshop was cancelled at the last minute. She planned to attend it.
2 Leading a team must be very difficult. I wouldn't like to do it.
3 The university has a course on neuroleadership. I studied there.
4 Her book instantly became a bestseller. It was published last year.
5 The restaurant has a good selection of desserts. We often go there for lunch.
6 London is an expensive city. It is the capital of the UK.

Teacher's resources: extra activities

B When do you need to use commas with the relative clauses in Exercise 7A? When can you omit the relative pronoun?

Speaking

8A Prepare five sentences about your life using relative clauses. Make some true and some false.
I go to Frankfurt, where my mother's family live, every summer.
My sister, who works in Marketing, used to be a professional basketball player.

B Listen to each other's sentences and ask questions. Decide which sentences are true and which are false.
Oh really? Remind me, what's the name of Frankfurt airport?
That's interesting. Can you tell me which team she played for?

Self-assessment
- How successfully have you achieved the lesson outcome? Give yourself a score from 0 (I need more practice) to 5 (I know this well).
- Go to My Self-assessment in MyEnglishLab to reflect on what you have learnt.

8.3 COMMUNICATION SKILLS
Giving and receiving feedback

Lesson outcome — Learners are aware of different ways to give feedback and can use a range of phrases for giving and receiving feedback.

Lead-in **1** In pairs, read the definition of 'feedback' and discuss the questions.

> **feed·back** /ˈfiːdbæk/ ●●○ S3 W3 noun [uncountable]
> **1** advice, criticism, etc. about how successful or useful something is

1. Why is feedback important for you?
2. Why is feedback important in business?

VIDEO **2** ▶ 8.3.1 Watch as Matt prepares for the project-closing meeting, following the successful launch in Mexico and Japan. What sort of feedback is he looking for?

3A In small groups, discuss which is the best approach (option A or B) for giving feedback to your manager. As a class, decide which video to watch first.

Option A – Positive feedback
Feedback confirming what someone did well and their successes.

Option B – Developmental feedback
Feedback telling someone what they can improve on.

B Watch the two videos in the sequence which the class has decided on and answer the questions for each video.

Option A ▶ 8.3.2
1. What do they say Matt did well?
2. How does Matt respond?
3. Overall, how successful do you think the feedback meeting was? Why?

Option B ▶ 8.3.3
1. What do they say Matt could have done – or could do in the future – to improve?
2. How does Matt respond?
3. Overall, how successful do you think the feedback meeting was? Why?

C Work in pairs. Based on the two videos, what do you think are the benefits and the risks of each approach to feedback?

4 ▶ 8.3.4 Watch the Conclusions section of the video and make notes under the following headings. How far do you agree with the tips? Why?

Giving feedback	1 2
Receiving feedback	1 2
Overall conclusion	

Reflection **5** Think about the following questions. Then discuss your answers with a partner.
1. In general, which approach do you prefer when giving or receiving feedback?
2. Do you actively ask for feedback from others? Do you think it's a good idea? Why / Why not? Who do you ask for feedback from? What kind of feedback?
3. Following this lesson, decide one thing which you can do to give or receive feedback more effectively in the future.

8.3 Communication skills: Giving and receiving feedback

Functional language

Giving and responding to feedback

6 Put these examples of feedback from the video into the correct category in the table.
1. I think **you did a very good job of** [communicating with the team].
2. **It** [is/was] **your responsibility to** [make sure that we all knew each other], **but** …
3. **I think in future if** [you gave us all a timeline], **that might** [help].
4. **It** [is/was] **good that you** [asked Stefanie to help out].
5. [I'm always very busy, but] **I don't think** [you understood that].
6. **What** [Kenji's] **saying is that** [you often waited until things were urgent].
7. **You could have** [called each of us], **that would have been good**.

Positive feedback	Developmental feedback
I'm really impressed with/by [the work you did on …].	The [work wasn't completed on time], do you have any idea why?
	Not a big deal, but [for next time], remember to …

7 Now add these headings to the table for responding to feedback.

Explore
Respond and reflect
Thank

Responding to feedback		
1 _____	2 _____	3 _____
Great! Thanks Stefanie. I appreciate that feedback.	Can you be a bit more specific about …? Can you say more about what you mean by …? Can you give me an example of …?	I'm happy you feel that. Right, I'll [certainly] bear that in mind. I'll [certainly] take those comments into account.

8A Look at these situations. If you were the manager, what would you say?
1. A new member of staff seems very shy and never contributes ideas in meetings.
2. A fellow manager dominated a recent meeting with important clients and interrupted them all the time.
3. A member of staff has started arriving at work late. Other colleagues have noticed this.

B Compare your ideas in small groups. What were the best examples of developmental feedback?

Teacher's resources: extra activities

TASK

9A Work in pairs and roleplay the situations from exercise 8A. Take turns to give and respond to the feedback.

B Work with another pair. Choose your best roleplay from Exercise 9A and repeat it for the other pair. In your groups discuss how easy it was to give developmental feedback. Who responded best to feedback?

Self-assessment
- How successfully have you achieved the lesson outcome? Give yourself a score from 0 (I need more practice) to 5 (I know this well).
- Go to My Self-assessment in MyEnglishLab to reflect on what you have learnt.

8.4 BUSINESS SKILLS
Leading meetings

Lesson outcome: Learners are aware of techniques for dealing with interruptions and can use a range of phrases for leading and managing meetings.

Lead-in 1 Work in pairs and discuss which statement (a or b) in each pair you most agree with.
1. a Meetings are where decisions are made. People should argue strongly about their opinions and disagreement is not unusual.
   b Meetings are for having discussions and sharing opinions. The decisions should be made later by individuals.
2. a The leader is a just a facilitator. Everyone can speak freely when they want.
   b The leader controls the meeting. People must be invited to speak.
3. a Meetings must start and finish on time.
   b It's OK to start up to fifteen minutes late and finish late if necessary.
4. a There should be no external interruptions, e.g. mobile phone calls.
   b Important phone calls may be accepted during a meeting, but only for up to five minutes.

Listening 2 🔊 8.01 Listen to the beginning of a meeting and answer the questions.
1. Why has John arranged the meeting?
2. What is the goal of the meeting?
3. What are the five stages of the meeting? *focus on the goal, ...*

3 🔊 8.02 Read the *7 Golden Rules* and listen to the middle part of the meeting. Which strategies does John, the leader of the meeting, use to manage interruptions?

7 Golden Rules for managing interruptions in meetings
1. Allow the interruption, and then go back to the original speaker.
2. Acknowledge the importance of what the interrupter is saying.
3. Stop the interruption and let the first speaker finish.
4. Limit the length of speaking time.
5. Stop the interruption and check with the first speaker if the interrupter can continue.
6. Raise your voice and speak louder.
7. Move the focus back to the agenda and the process.

4A 🔊 8.03 Listen to the end of the meeting. What are the action points for each person?

B Listen again. Which of the following did John do?
1. Review the discussion
2. Review the decisions
3. Ask for confirmation of the decisions
4. Assign action points to different people
5. Ask for acceptance or understanding of the tasks
6. Set a day and time for the next meeting

Functional language Leading and managing meetings

5A Complete the phrases from the start of the meeting in Exercise 2 with the words in the box. If necessary, use the audioscript on page 150 to help you.

focusing   thinking   goal   called

Welcoming	Thanks, everyone, for coming to [this special meeting today].
Opening the meeting	I ¹_____ this meeting because [I need your help to prepare the presentation]. The ²_____ for this meeting is to [decide which information we want to present to senior management]. So, we have one hour. Let's start by ³_____ on [our goal, then we can collect and discuss some ideas and make some decisions]. OK, let's begin by ⁴_____ about [the management meeting].

8.4 Business skills: Leading meetings

B Now complete the phrases for dealing with interruptions with the words in the box.

agenda   back   concern   important   limit

Managing interruptions	I can understand what you're saying is [1]_____, but please let Angela finish. We can come to you next. Could you try to [2]_____ your [overview] to about [two minutes]? OK, [3]_____ to you [Philippe]. [Bettina], I understand your [4]_____ . [The market research results] aren't on today's [5]_____ .

C Put the words in the correct order to make sentences for the closing stages of a meeting.

Reviewing the discussion	1 has been / This / productive / a very / meeting 2 through / useful / both our successes and areas for concern / It was / to talk
Referring to action points	3 are / from this / action / meeting / points / The / … 4 of / Philippe / an overview / the media campaign / you'll prepare 5 tasks / OK / Is everyone / their / with / ? 6 have any / to do / they have / questions about / Does anyone / what / ?
Next steps	7 at 2 p.m. on / Let's meet / week / finalise everything / again to / Friday next 8 your completed tasks / of business / on Thursday / Please send me / before close

Teacher's resources: extra activities

> **TASK**

6A Work in groups of three. You are going to take turns to lead a mini-meeting on one of the topics below. Read the information, decide who will lead each meeting and prepare.

Meeting topics
1 Decide on an event for an **end-of-year party**. Discuss what needs to be planned, a timeline for planning and action points.
2 Decide on the **best time to do homework** from this course. Discuss your ideas and why you think your preference is best.
3 Share **a problem you're having in one area of your life**. Discuss the problem, identify possible solutions and decide the next steps.

Preparation
- Meeting leader: Use the categories and phrases in Exercise 5 to help you prepare. Think about the structure of the meeting.
- Meeting participants: Prepare the language and phrases you think you'll need to discuss the topic. During the meeting, you will try to interrupt another speaker once or twice.

B Hold your meetings on each of the topics.

C After each meeting, give feedback to the leader. Use the checklist to help you.

The leader:
1 started the meeting with a clear goal and process.
2 managed interruptions well.
3 reviewed the discussion and decisions.
4 assigned action points.
5 closed the meeting.

7 In your group, discuss how easy or difficult it was to lead each meeting. Give reasons for your answers.

Self-assessment
- How successfully have you achieved the lesson outcome? Give yourself a score from 0 (I need more practice) to 5 (I know this well).
- Go to My Self-assessment in MyEnglishLab to reflect on what you have learnt.

8.5 WRITING: Informing of a decision

Lesson outcome: Learners can write an email informing staff or colleagues about decisions taken.

Lead-in

1 Read the formal email informing managers of decisions made by the Board of Directors. Proofread the email and find eight spelling mistakes. Then compare in pairs.

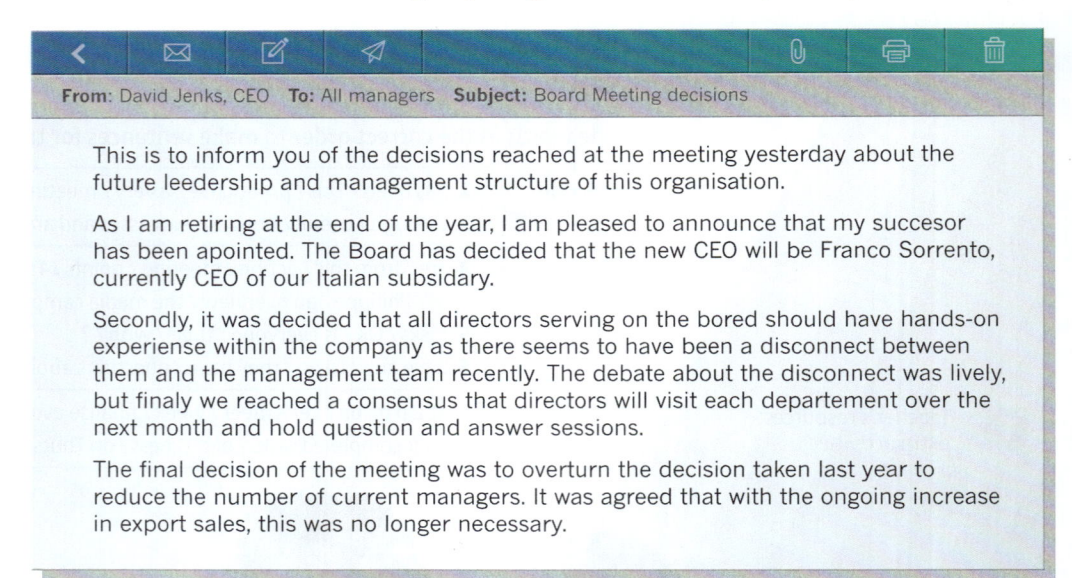

From: David Jenks, CEO **To:** All managers **Subject:** Board Meeting decisions

This is to inform you of the decisions reached at the meeting yesterday about the future leedership and management structure of this organisation.

As I am retiring at the end of the year, I am pleased to announce that my succesor has been apointed. The Board has decided that the new CEO will be Franco Sorrento, currently CEO of our Italian subsidary.

Secondly, it was decided that all directors serving on the bored should have hands-on experiense within the company as there seems to have been a disconnect between them and the management team recently. The debate about the disconnect was lively, but finaly we reached a consensus that directors will visit each departement over the next month and hold question and answer sessions.

The final decision of the meeting was to overturn the decision taken last year to reduce the number of current managers. It was agreed that with the ongoing increase in export sales, this was no longer necessary.

Functional language

2 Complete the table using the words in the box.

| agreed | announce | came | consensus | couldn't | inform | know | reach | tell |

Formal	Semi-formal
This is to ¹_____ you of our decision to …	I'm writing to ⁷_____ you about the decision to …
We are pleased/delighted to ²_____ that …	Just to let you ⁸_____ what was decided.
The Board has decided/agreed that …	Let me tell you what we decided.
We reached a ³_____ that/about …	We all agreed/decided that …
The final decision was to …	We've arranged to …
It was ⁴_____ that …	We thought that it was best to …
We failed to ⁵_____ an agreement about …	We ⁹_____ agree about …
We ⁶_____ to a decision that/about …	I'm happy to say that we've decided to …

→ page 125 See Grammar reference: Reduced relative clauses

Teacher's resources: extra activities

L The email contains examples of reduced relative clauses. Go to MyEnglishLab for optional grammar work.

TASK

3A Work in pairs. Read the informal email on page 131. Rewrite the email to make it more formal.

B Look at the meeting notes on page 135 and write a formal email of about 180 words to inform staff of the decisions made.

C Exchange emails with your partner. Which functional language phrases did your partner use? How many were different from the ones you used?

Self-assessment

- How successfully have you achieved the lesson outcome? Give yourself a score from 0 (I need more practice) to 5 (I know this well).
- Go to My Self-assessment in MyEnglishLab to reflect on what you have learnt.

Business Workshops

1 Office space p.88
Lesson outcome: Learners can exchange information about texts they have read and can contribute ideas in a discussion to design an office space.

Listening: Employee views on their workspace
Reading: Millennial-friendly workspaces
Task: Design a new office space

2 Kloze-Zone p.90
Lesson outcome: Learners can understand the challenges facing a retailer and can describe ideas for a promotional event and marketing campaign.

Listening: Customer and staff feedback on a clothing store
Task: Brainstorm a brand awareness campaign
Writing: An email summary of the campaign

3 Social media manager required p.92
Lesson outcome: Learners can compare CVs/résumés, talk about professional experience and ask and answer questions in job interviews.

Video and listening: Three video CVs
Listening: First interviews
Reading: Analysis of three CVs and covering letters
Task: Conduct a second interview

4 Supermarket wars p.94
Lesson outcome: Learners can use key information from a text to complete a chart and can make choices about company strategy, giving reasons.

Reading: Profiles of competing supermarket chains
Task: Select the best strategies for growth
Listening: Compare your strategies with a business news report

5 Robots wanted for a warehouse p.96
Lesson outcome: Learners can understand the details of supplier processes and can negotiate and summarise the key terms and conditions of a deal.

Listening: Criteria for choosing a supplier; Teleconferences with suppliers
Task: Negotiate and select a supplier
Writing: A formal email confirming the result of the negotiation

6 Doable crowdfunding p.98
Lesson outcome: Learners can understand the main points in crowdfunding pitches and can prepare and deliver a short crowdfunding pitch.

Video and listening: Three crowdfunding pitches
Speaking: Decide which crowdfunding project to back
Task: Prepare and deliver a crowdfunding pitch

7 Cross-cultural consultants p.100
Lesson outcome: Learners can exchange information about texts they have read and can give a brief presentation with recommendations for working across cultures.

Reading: Blog posts on cultural awareness
Listening: Interviews with staff about working internationally
Task: Recommendations for working in your culture
Writing: A formal email confirming the outcome of the presentations

8 Talent management p.102
Lesson outcome: Learners can understand details in conversations about training needs and can participate in a discussion to design a personal development plan.

Listening: Employees talking about their training needs
Reading: Profiles of training courses
Task: Design a development plan for an employee
Writing: An email to justify a training course

BUSINESS WORKSHOP 1 > Office space

Lesson outcome: Learners can exchange information about texts they have read and can contribute ideas in a discussion to design an office space.

Background

1 Read the background and discuss the questions with a partner.
1. What is 'arbejdsglæde'? Is there a similar concept in your country?
2. In what ways do you think the physical environment can make someone more or less productive or happy at work?
3. What physical features do you like most and least about the place where you work or study?

BACKGROUND

Ditigal is an internet media organisation offering music, news and entertainment to millions of subscribers. This dynamic, fast-growing enterprise, which is only seven years old, has over 300 employees. The company is planning to move into bigger headquarters soon.

Danish co-founder and CEO, Clara Jensen, is a strong believer in the concept of 'arbejdsglæde' – from 'arbejde', the Danish for *work*, and 'glæde', the word for *happiness* – literally meaning 'happiness at work'.

Jensen is aware that employees who enjoy their work environment will be more engaged, productive, innovative and happy. This in turn will lead to greater customer satisfaction and success for the organisation.

Giving everyone a voice is a core value of the company and Jensen wants her employees' input on design of the new offices.

Finding out what employees think

2A As part of the consultation process, employees at Ditigal were asked what they would change about the current workspace. Look at the survey results and complete the sentences.
1. The most popular request was for _____ .
2. This was followed by the need for _____ and _____ .
3. More than _____ the staff commented on problems with noise.
4. One in two people wanted _____ .
5. Three in ten people wanted the option to _____ .

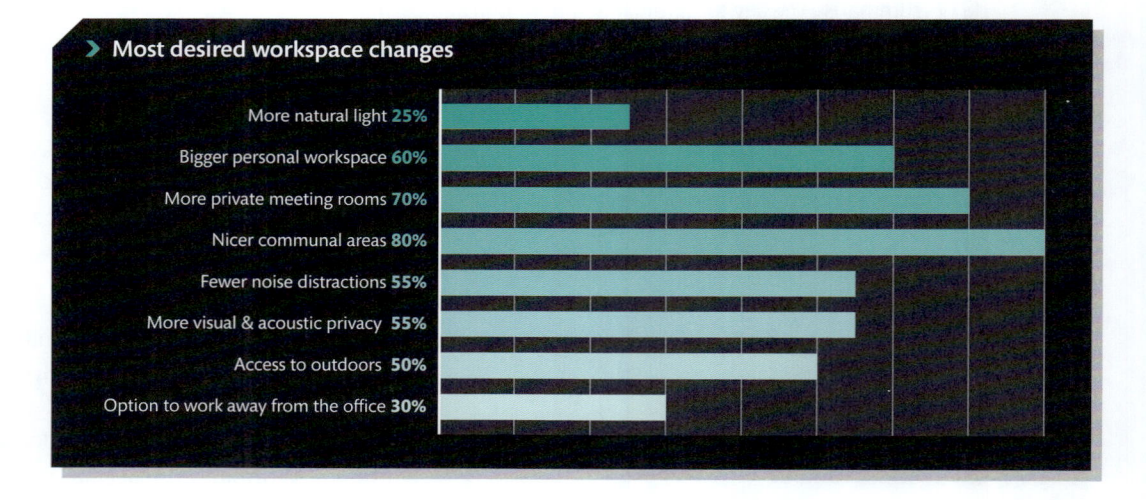

> **Most desired workspace changes**

More natural light	25%
Bigger personal workspace	60%
More private meeting rooms	70%
Nicer communal areas	80%
Fewer noise distractions	55%
More visual & acoustic privacy	55%
Access to outdoors	50%
Option to work away from the office	30%

B Work in pairs. What other conclusions would you draw from the graph?

3 🔊 BW 1.01 Listen to some employees giving their views. Which speaker talks about a) the communal areas, b) the office layout and c) the general impression?

4 Listen again and summarise the main suggestion(s) each person has for changes to the workspace.

Teacher's resources: extra activities

Business workshop 1

The office as somewhere to enjoy

Teacher's resources: extra activities

5A Work in pairs. Find out about what some companies are doing to make their offices happy places to work.

Student A: Read the article on this page.
Student B: Read the article on page 132.

B Tell your partner in your own words about the article you read. Which of the office features mentioned in the articles would be most attractive to you?

FT

Picnic tables and Xbox

Digital start-up GoCardless is typical of a millennial-friendly workplace. Its open-plan office in a warehouse in East London centres on a hub of picnic tables and an Xbox. Its 50-strong team is frequently treated to lunch and monthly company evenings.

For 28-year-old co-founder Hiroki Takeuchi, these perks are not just gloss and gimmicks. 'The way we built the environment is just the way we wanted to work ourselves,' he says. Mr Takeuchi is one of a new generation of chief executives creating a workplace that blends the office and the home while forking out on a healthy 'social budget' to promote team interaction.

'In a way, it's rooted in work and play not being necessarily completely separate things. We want this office to be somewhere you enjoy your time. Not somewhere you come for a set number of hours and then go home as quickly as you can,' he says.

At a time when technology allows individuals to work almost anywhere, companies need to give a younger digitally literate generation a good reason to come into the office. This is where stylish physical environments play a role.

The trend has been led by U.S. tech firms, such as Google and Facebook, that focused on the innovative use of office space when they could no longer compete for young talent on salary and on the previous generation's sweetener of the company car. What they are competing on now is really attractive community-based workplaces.

But employers should think carefully before opting for a fully open-plan office. People think young people want the office to be a constant brainstorm. But even for highly collaborative, creative work, you still need space to focus.

Contrary to expectations, technology has not led to the death of the office but has raised the need for better designed workplaces.

6A Work in small groups. Discuss your ideas for the new Ditigal headquarters. Clara Jensen, the CEO, says you can use your imagination. For now at least, there is no budget restriction.

> **Remember to think about:**
> - what will be most attractive to young staff.
> - how many zones you want to create and the purpose of each.
> - what messages you want to transmit to visitors.
> - how you want your staff to feel when they're at work.
> - what will attract workers into communal spaces.
> - what decor and artwork you would like.

▶ TASK
Design a new office space

B Work in pairs with someone from another group. Present your ideas. Are there any new ideas you would like to incorporate into your office design?

7 Turn to page 130 and read the email to find out what happened after the first year in the new headquarters. Decide what action the company should take now.

Self-assessment

- How successfully have you achieved the lesson outcome? Give yourself a score from 0 (I need more practice) to 5 (I know this well).
- Go to My Self-assessment in MyEnglishLab to reflect on what you have learnt.

BUSINESS WORKSHOP 2

Kloze-Zone

Lesson outcome: Learners can understand the challenges facing a retailer and can describe ideas for a promotional event and marketing campaign.

Background

1 Read the background and answer the questions with a partner.
1. What kind of company is Kloze-Zone?
2. What kind of brand is it?
3. What are the responsibilities of an assistant store manager?
4. What kinds of problems is the newly opened Berlin store having?
5. What will be the possible benefits of solving these problems?

BACKGROUND

Kloze-Zone is a successful Japanese fast-fashion retailer that has expanded globally. It now has over 1,500 stores in 60 countries and a reputation for quality clothing for young people at affordable prices.

The retailer has taken on assistant managers in its newly opened stores in international locations. Their duties consist of helping the store manager, supervising staff, dealing with deliveries, helping customers, etc.

However, some stores that have recently opened are not doing well. Kloze-Zone has problems with brand awareness in Europe as well as poor sales, for example, in Berlin. In addition, customers complain about long queues and demotivated staff, while shop assistants say they are under-staffed and work long hours.

Depending on their performance, assistant managers will be promoted to store managers in new locations in the near future.

Customer and staff satisfaction

2A Work in pairs. You are assistant store managers in the newly opened store in Berlin. You are in a staff meeting discussing ways to boost sales in the new store. What questions can you ask <u>customers</u> to check their satisfaction with the in-store experience? Consider these points:

- window displays
- promotional offers
- in-store customer service
- fitting rooms
- waiting time for payment

B What questions can you ask <u>staff</u> to check their satisfaction with working in the store? Consider these points:

- training / opportunities for promotion
- working hours, breaks and holidays
- staff discounts
- staff turnover
- work atmosphere

Feedback from customers and staff

3A 🔊 BW 2.01 Listen to some comments from customers and staff about Kloze-Zone. Match the speakers (1–6) with the problems (a–h). You need to match some speakers with more than one problem.

a. Window displays do not always engage customers. ____
b. Fast fashion is mostly marketed at women. ____
c. Staff work long hours: from 9 a.m. to 7 p.m., including Saturdays and Sundays. ____
d. The store should have more promotions and offers for customers. ____
e. They should have more interesting marketing campaigns. ____
f. Shop assistants don't help customers in the fitting rooms. ____
g. Staff turnover is fairly high in some locations. ____
h. Brand awareness is low. ____

B Which of the issues mentioned relate to customers and which ones to staff? Which ones relate to both?

Teacher's resources: extra activities

Consumer ratings

4 Look at the consumer ratings for Kloze-Zone and its main competitor, the Spanish retailer Fun & Sun. What are the main problems for Kloze-Zone? Discuss your answers in pairs.

A: The bar chart shows that consumers think Fun & Sun clothes are better quality than those of Kloze-Zone.

B: Yes, but they also think both retailers offer good value for money.

A: That's true. However, as we can see from the chart, the Kloze-Zone brand is not nearly as recognisable as Fun & Sun.

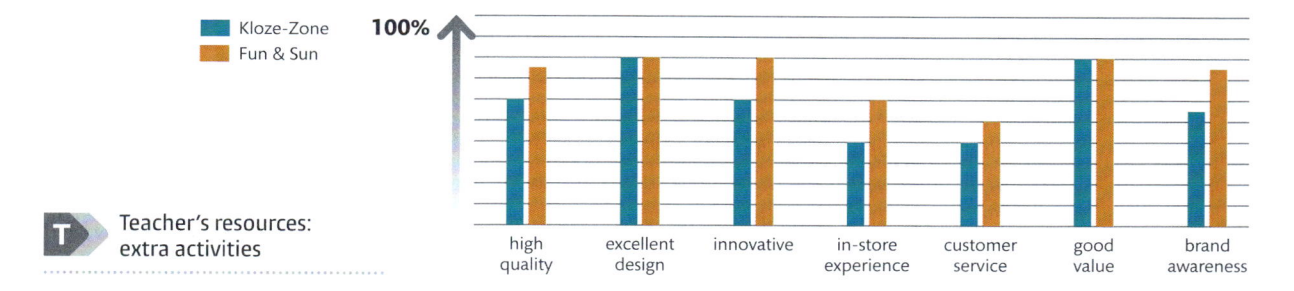

■ Kloze-Zone
■ Fun & Sun

Categories: high quality, excellent design, innovative, in-store experience, customer service, good value, brand awareness

T Teacher's resources: extra activities

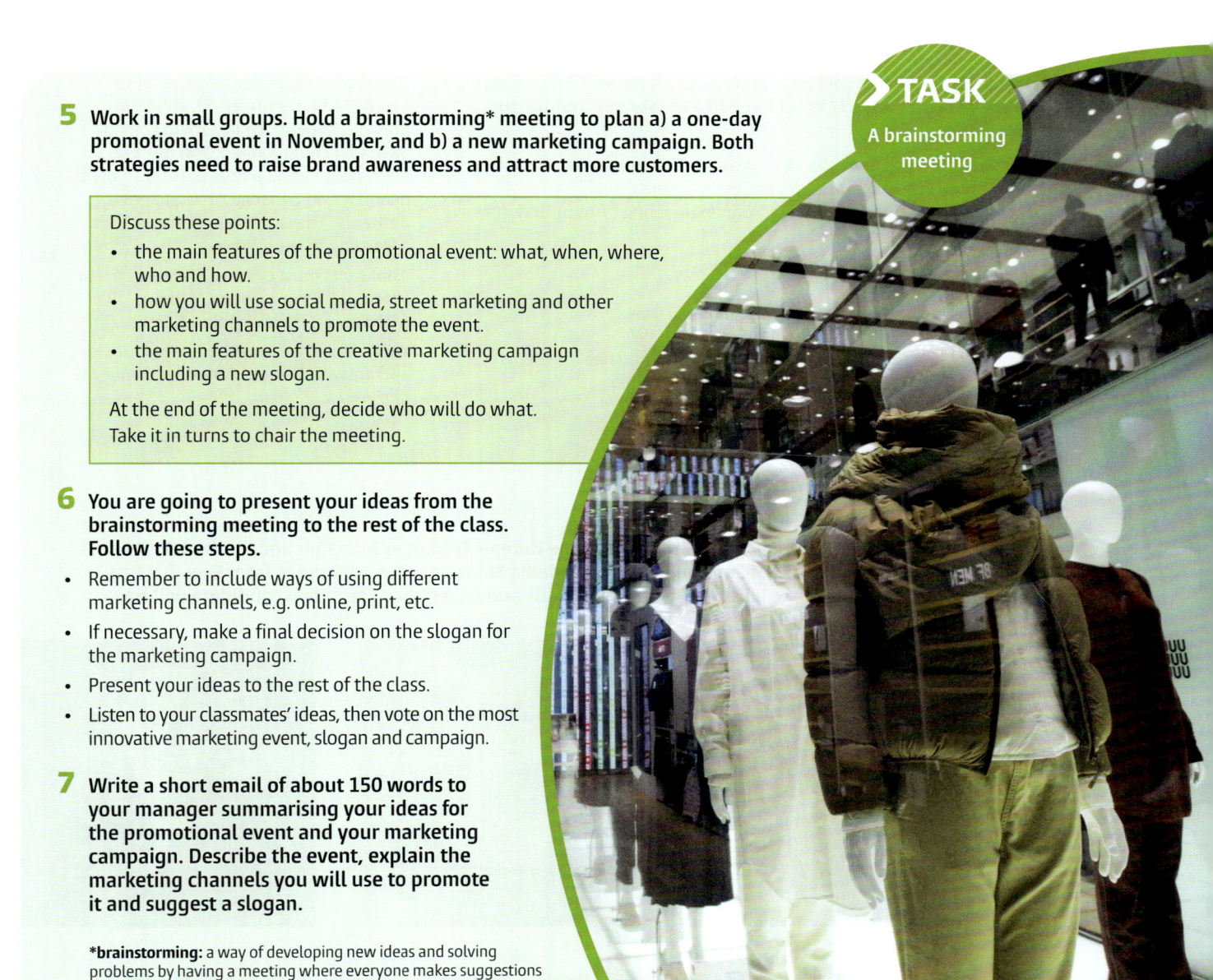

> **TASK**
> A brainstorming meeting

5 Work in small groups. Hold a brainstorming* meeting to plan a) a one-day promotional event in November, and b) a new marketing campaign. Both strategies need to raise brand awareness and attract more customers.

Discuss these points:
- the main features of the promotional event: what, when, where, who and how.
- how you will use social media, street marketing and other marketing channels to promote the event.
- the main features of the creative marketing campaign including a new slogan.

At the end of the meeting, decide who will do what. Take it in turns to chair the meeting.

6 You are going to present your ideas from the brainstorming meeting to the rest of the class. Follow these steps.
- Remember to include ways of using different marketing channels, e.g. online, print, etc.
- If necessary, make a final decision on the slogan for the marketing campaign.
- Present your ideas to the rest of the class.
- Listen to your classmates' ideas, then vote on the most innovative marketing event, slogan and campaign.

7 Write a short email of about 150 words to your manager summarising your ideas for the promotional event and your marketing campaign. Describe the event, explain the marketing channels you will use to promote it and suggest a slogan.

*****brainstorming:** a way of developing new ideas and solving problems by having a meeting where everyone makes suggestions and these are discussed

Self-assessment

- How successfully have you achieved the lesson outcome? Give yourself a score from 0 (I need more practice) to 5 (I know this well).
- Go to My Self-assessment in MyEnglishLab to reflect on what you have learnt.

BUSINESS WORKSHOP 3 > Social media manager required

Lesson outcome Learners can compare CVs/résumés, talk about professional experience and ask and answer questions in job interviews.

Background

1 Read the job advert and answer the questions with a partner.
1 What kind of job is being advertised?
2 Who is the employer?
3 Is experience necessary for the job? What kind of work experience would be useful?
4 What kind of candidate are they looking for? What kinds of qualities and skills are required?
5 Would you apply for this job? Why? / Why not?
6 What would you say about yourself in a one-minute video CV?
7 Why do you think some companies like to ask for video CVs?

SOCIAL MEDIA MANAGER REQUIRED

Do you have a proven track record in communications and marketing? Are you a social media addict? Would you like to join our multilingual, creative team?

Media Solutions is a prestigious media company specialising in media and PR* solutions for clients worldwide. We are based in the city of Copenhagen, although our clients range from engineering firms in Germany to High Street chains in Singapore.

Job responsibilities include:
- Managing and contributing to our social media sites
- Improving the profiles of key clients in social media
- Delivering easy-to-read social media reports and updates for clients
- Liaising with both the marketing team and key clients
- Reporting to the Head of Communications

Candidates with relevant experience in social media are preferred, although previous experience in a management position is not required. You must be a team player and be able to work to tight deadlines. Knowledge of languages is desirable. The salary is negotiable according to experience.

Applicants must send a CV with a covering letter and a short video CV to our HR Manager at: jobs@mediasolutions.com.

Your video CV should be one minute long and answer the question, *Why should we hire you?*

*PR: Public Relations

Video CVs

2 Work in pairs. Student A is the Human Resources Manager and Student B is the Head of Communications at Media Solutions. Use your notes from Exercise 1 to make a list of the qualities, skills and experience your ideal candidate will have.

3A ▶ BW 3.01 🔊 BW 3.01 Watch or listen to each applicant, Amalia, Birte and Cindy. Take notes about their qualities, skills and experience. What are your first impressions of each candidate?

B Work with your partner again. Compare your notes and first impressions. Who is the best at selling herself? Why?

4A Read the CVs of <u>two</u> of the candidates. The headings are missing from Birte's CV. Which headings could you use? Use the CV of the other candidate to help you.

Student A, the Human Resources Manager: Go to page 132 to read Amalia's CV. Then go to page 137 to read Birte's CV.
Student B, the Head of Communications: Go to page 134 to read Cindy's CV. Then go to page 137 to read Birte's CV.

B Who would you hire at this stage? Make notes about the two CVs you read and then compare your ideas with your partner.

The candidate needs to be someone who ...
I'd prefer someone who has ...
I'd hire/employ Amalia/Birte/Cindy because she has good ... skills ...
I think we should hire/employ Amalia/Birte/Cindy because of her experience in ...

	Strengths	Weaknesses
Amalia:		
Birte:		
Cindy:		

T Teacher's resources: extra activities

Analysis of covering letters

5 Look at the covering letters / emails from the applicants on page 133. Which of the candidates write effectively? Give reasons for your answers. Who would you hire at this stage?

First interviews

6 🔊 BW 3.02 Listen to extracts from the interviews in which the candidates answer the question, *What is your proudest achievement?* Make notes and then decide which one of the three candidates you are going to call for a second interview: Amalia, Birte or Cindy. Compare your ideas with a partner.

T Teacher's resources: extra activities

7 Work in new pairs and agree on which candidate you have decided to call for a second interview. Student A is the Human Resources Manager and Student B is your chosen candidate. Follow these steps.

Student A: Human Resources Manager
- Prepare some questions for the interview. You will ask the candidate some general questions about his/her education and work experience. Include three or more difficult questions, for example why you should hire him/her, and ask for examples of his/her proudest achievement and his/her communication skills.
- Make sure you describe the job position and the responsibilities involved.
- Be prepared to answer the candidate's questions at the end.

Student B: Candidate
- Think about what questions you expect to be asked in the interview and prepare your answers. Think about why they should hire you, and be ready to give examples of your proudest achievement and your communication skills.
- Deal with difficult questions using different strategies and expressions.
- Be prepared to ask the interviewer questions at the end about the job position and the responsibilities involved.

> **TASK**
> Second interviews

Social media profiles

8A The company checked the candidates' social media profiles after the interviews before making a final decision. Read the information on page 136 then discuss the company's decisions with your partner.

B Do you agree with the company's final choice? What other factors could influence their final decision?

Self-assessment

- How successfully have you achieved the lesson outcome? Give yourself a score from 0 (I need more practice) to 5 (I know this well).
- Go to My Self-assessment in MyEnglishLab to reflect on what you have learnt.

BUSINESS WORKSHOP 4 > Supermarket wars

Lesson outcome | Learners can use key information from a text to complete a chart and can make choices about company strategy, giving reasons.

Background

1 Compare the two photos. How often do you go shopping in places like these? What are the advantages and disadvantages of shopping in each place?

2 Read the background. To what extent does this represent the situation in your country? Discuss with a partner and give examples.

BACKGROUND

The supermarket sector is highly competitive throughout the world. In many countries a small number of retailers control a large proportion of the grocery market. In Australia the industry is dominated by just two main competitors, while the USA has four major players and South Africa has five. Market research group Kantar reports that four supermarket chains have two-thirds of the market in the UK.

In many European markets the competition has become even more intense in recent years. This is because discount supermarket chains selling similar products for much lower prices have gained a considerable market share.

However, the supermarket industry has not been able to expand across international borders well. Major chains from the USA, France and the UK have not had much success in the largest retail markets in Asia, such as Japan and China.

Consumer habits

3A Read the newspaper article about changing consumer habits. What are the four ways it mentions that people can do their shopping? What reasons does the article give for changing shopping habits? Can you think of any other possible reasons?

Recent studies show that hypermarkets in many countries are becoming less popular. Today's busy consumers don't want to waste time driving to 'big box' stores and walking down long aisles with loaded shopping trolleys. More and more people want the convenience of shopping closer to home or near where they work. They also want to reduce waste by shopping more often and for smaller quantities.

This shift in consumer habits means that smaller neighbourhood shops are becoming popular again and big supermarket chains have reintroduced smaller convenience stores in towns and cities.

Online shopping and home delivery services are also growing in popularity. Many big retail chains have started to offer a Click & Collect service allowing customers to shop online and pick up their shopping at a time and store that is convenient for them.

B How might these changing consumer habits affect the business strategies of the big supermarket chains?

Business workshop 4

Three supermarket chains

4A Work in groups of three. Each of you read <u>one</u> of the profiles of the three supermarket chains on pages 128, 133 and 137. What type of supermarket is it? Do you have any supermarkets similar to this in your country?

B Read the profile again and answer the questions.
1. What is the supermarket chain's approach to pricing and/or costs?
2. What impression do you get of the in-store experience?
3. How would you describe its product range?
4. What are the main challenges the chain faces?

5A Share the information you have about each supermarket chain and complete the pie chart and bar chart together. What conclusions can you draw from the charts?

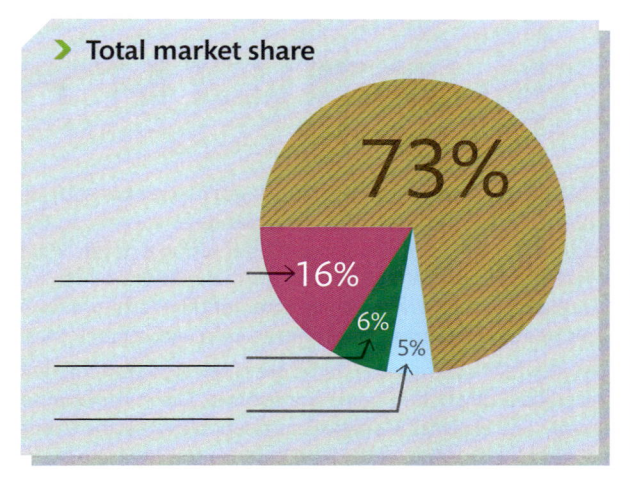

> **Total market share**

73%
16%
6%
5%

> **Product range on sale in stores**

30,000
20,000
10,000
0

T Teacher's resources: extra activities

B Which supermarket do you think faces most challenges? Why?

6A Work in small groups. Choose one of the supermarket chains in Exercise 4A. Look at the list of possible strategies. Which strategies would be best for your chosen supermarket? You can use more than one and suggest ideas of your own. Give reasons for your decisions.

> **TASK**
> Growth strategy

- Build bigger and better stores
- Sell off non-core businesses
- Invest in remodelling existing stores
- Rent out store space in hypermarkets to other companies
- Produce own-brand high-end products
- Use more locally sourced suppliers and products
- Reduce the number of product lines to cut costs
- Enter large overseas markets such as Asia
- Introduce more product lines and luxury goods
- Buy or rent more small stores in town centres
- Introduce a loyalty card and personalised discount vouchers
- Offer a Click & Collect service in urban areas

Remember to think about:

- [ ] Competition in the market
- [ ] Changing consumer habits and preferences
- [ ] The options offered by smartphones and digital technologies
- [ ] The risks of doing nothing

B Work in new groups with students who thought about the other supermarket chains. Tell each other about the chain you chose and the strategies you think best for it.

7 🔊 BW 4.01 Listen to a recent business news report about the supermarket industry. Which strategies is each company pursuing? How do they compare to your ideas?

Self-assessment
- How successfully have you achieved the lesson outcome? Give yourself a score from 0 (I need more practice) to 5 (I know this well).
- Go to My Self-assessment in MyEnglishLab to reflect on what you have learnt.

BUSINESS WORKSHOP 5 > Robots wanted for warehouse

Lesson outcome: Learners can understand the details of supplier processes and can negotiate and summarise the key terms and conditions of a deal.

Background

1 Read the background and answer the questions with a partner.
1. What kind of company is Meble BDB?
2. What does the Polish Minister of Development hope for the furniture market?
3. Why do Meble BDB want to use new technology in their warehouse?

BACKGROUND

Meble BDB is a furniture company based in Poznań, Poland, that manufactures quality furniture. The furniture industry in Poland is a success, so the company has increasingly been processing more international orders. Poland is now the third largest exporter in Europe, after Italy and Germany, and the sixth in the world. The Minister of Development recently visited an international furniture fair and said, 'We want Polish furniture to be exported all over the world with a label "Made in Poland".'

At Meble BDB's warehouse, furniture is selected from high shelves and items are packed carefully before being transported. Given the number of increased orders recently, the Logistics Manager has been talking to the Company Director. They have decided to introduce robotics technology to automate the process of selecting and lifting goods from shelves. Their aim is to minimise human error, avoid damage and deal more efficiently with the goods being prepared for shipment.

Criteria for choosing suppliers

2A Work in pairs. Student A is the Company Director of Meble BDB and Student B is the Logistics Manager. What are your criteria for choosing a supplier of robotics technology? Individually, number the factors in order of importance (1 = the most important).

after-sales service and maintenance   delivery terms   guarantees   price   quality

X is far more / much more / a lot more important than Y.
X is just as / not nearly as important as Y.

B Compare and discuss your answers with your partner. Can you think of any other factors?

3 🔊 BW 5.01 Listen to Tadeusz (Ted), the Company Director of Meble BDB, and Anna, the Logistics Manager, discussing their criteria. Answer the questions.
1. Which factors do they mention?
2. What other concerns do they have?
3. Who is more in favour of automation?
4. What are the next steps for Tadeusz and Anna?

Teacher's resources: extra activities

Business workshop 5

Analysis of proposal

4A 🔊 BW 5.02 Listen to two teleconferences between Meble BDB and the suppliers. Complete the notes.

SUPPLIER A: NOVAROBOT, SINGAPORE	SUPPLIER B: BOT-AUTOMATION, JAPAN
Strengths:	Strengths:
Installation:	Installation:
Guarantee:	Guarantee:
Training:	Training:
Maintenance:	Maintenance:
Discounts offered:	Discounts offered:
Payment terms: to be discussed	Payment terms: to be discussed

T Teacher's resources: extra activities

B Compare your notes with your partner. Which supplier would you prefer to work with at this stage?

> **TASK**
> Negotiating with suppliers

5A You are going to roleplay further discussions between Meble BDB and the two suppliers. In groups of four, assign the roles of:
Tadeusz Walentowicz, Company Director of Meble BDB
Anna Woźniak, Logistics Manager of Meble BDB
Tony King, representative of Novarobot, the Singaporean supplier
Kin Izumi, representative of Bot-automation, the Japanese supplier

B Look at your information and prepare your questions and answers for the discussion.
Tadeusz, look at page 130.   Tony, look at page 135.
Anna, look at page 136.   Kin, look at page 128.

C Work as a group in two pairs, Tadeusz and Kin together, and Anna and Tony together. Roleplay your initial negotiation and take notes of key information and points of agreement.

6 Regroup with Tadeusz and Anna together, and Tony and Kin together. Compare and evaluate your negotiations and discuss the questions.
1 How satisfied were you with the outcome/result of the negotiation?
2 What do you still need to discuss or confirm in the next stage of the negotiation?
3 Tadeusz and Anna, which supplier will you continue negotiating with? Why?

7 Work in groups of four. Two students represent Meble BDB and two students represent the chosen supplier. Hold the second stage of the negotiation to confirm the final terms and conditions. Try to focus on the key points.
- Refer to the points in the criteria for choosing a supplier in Exercise 2A and the information from Exercise 5.
- Remember to take notes.
- At the end of your negotiation, make sure you summarise the terms you have agreed with the other party.

Writing

8A Regroup in pairs, the two students from Meble BDB together, and the two students representing the chosen supplier together. Write a formal email of between 160 and 180 words to the other party, confirming the main points agreed.

B Read the other party's email and check that you all understood the same terms and conditions.

Self-assessment
- How successfully have you achieved the lesson outcome? Give yourself a score from 0 (I need more practice) to 5 (I know this well).
- Go to My Self-assessment in MyEnglishLab to reflect on what you have learnt.

BUSINESS WORKSHOP 6

Doable crowdfunding

Lesson outcome: Learners can understand the main points in crowdfunding pitches and can prepare and deliver a short crowdfunding pitch.

Background

1 Read the background and discuss the questions with a partner.
1. Have you ever visited a crowdfunding site like Doable?
2. Have you or has anyone you know ever backed a crowdfunding project?
3. What types of project would you consider backing? e.g. a filmmaker, a musician, a new app, a new video game, etc.
4. What types of rewards would most interest you? e.g. free products, discounts, etc.

BACKGROUND

Crowdfunding websites allow businesses which want to raise funds for their projects to gain access to lots of potential backers. People generally contribute to a project because they feel a connection to it, or want the rewards offered, or simply like the presentation of the project.

Doable is a crowdfunding platform that raises finance for creative, personal and business projects. Entrepreneurs can upload their presentations pitching their idea. The site is open to entrepreneurs and backers from all over the world. Contributions can be as little as €10 and as much as €3,000. The average is €25.

The site takes 5 percent of each contribution, is free to the user and easily syncs with social media. If a project doesn't receive the target amount by the deadline, potential investors get their money back. The site provides users with advice on how to present a crowdfunding pitch.

Getting a backer

2 ▶ BW 6.01 🔊 BW 6.01 Watch or listen to three extracts from crowdfunding pitches on Doable's website. What does each speaker want backing for?

Teacher's resources: extra activities

3 Watch again and complete the notes about each project on Doable's website. Use one to three words.

Ben Fischer Theatre Company

This award-winning theatre company performs at ¹_____ all over the world. Our latest production of Brecht's *The Good Person of Szechwan* has just been ²_____ . A fire destroyed all our ³_____ . Before the ⁴_____ pays the compensation to rebuild and replace everything, we need to raise €10,000 to complete our ⁵_____ . All donations to our cause will be repaid.

Alison's Tees

I'm Alison Chadwick, the founder of this company which allows you to ⁶_____ T-shirt.
It's simple, fun and creative. You can choose the colour and style and you can have any design or logo you like, including photos. All our T-shirts are 100 percent ⁷_____ and ethically sourced. We need your support to help us develop ⁸_____ so our users can design and ⁹_____ their own tees on their ¹⁰_____ .

Holidapp

Our new tour guide mobile app is like ¹¹_____ on your mobile phone. The app is ¹²_____ and quick and easy to use. For ¹³_____ you will get an expert guide to many destinations in Europe and the USA. Our guide contributors receive ¹⁴_____ of the revenues generated by their guides. We need your backing to ¹⁵_____ of production, audio recording, programming and photography.

98

Business workshop 6

Making a successful pitch

4 Here is some advice Doable suggests for crowdfunding pitches. Match the advice (1–5) with the extracts from the pitches (a–e).

1 Compare your project to something backers already understand
2 Attack the problem
3 Suggest a sense of solidarity and community
4 Use coolness
5 Offer an incentive or reward

a We're helping independent cotton farmers.
b … you will receive discounts on tickets …
c It's like an audio guide but on your smartphone.
d … your very own unique T-shirt. Friends will be amazed.
e No more shopping for hours looking for something you actually like.

5A Discuss in pairs. Which project would you back and how much would you contribute? Why?

B Many successful crowdfunded projects use the same method of finance again and again. How could the three businesses in Exercise 2 return for crowdfunding in future? What other rewards could they offer backers?

T Teacher's resources: extra activities

> **TASK**
> Prepare and give a crowdfunding pitch

6 Work in small groups. Write a crowdfunding pitch of your own. You can:
- choose from the new projects below for one of the three companies in Exercise 2, or
- think of an idea of your own for one of the three companies, or
- use your own ideas for a completely new company.

Remember to:
- Create a short video script (maximum two minutes long).
- Sum up your project in as few words as possible.
- Include some of the advice from the Doable website that you saw in Exercise 4.
- Decide your scheme of rewards for potential backers. Think about what will most attract them. Structure the rewards according to the amount they contribute.

Ben Fischer's Theatre Company
Following our sell-out world tour the actors and crew are now back in our Berlin studios preparing for next year's season. We plan to produce a contemporary version of the musical The Threepenny Opera, first performed in 1928. This is your chance to back our latest venture. We also welcome your feedback on the development of the play.

Alison's Tees
Exciting news! We wanted you, our backers, to be the first to know that we're expanding into a brand new range of bags for work and leisure. Our design team have come up with some beautiful concepts and you still get to choose your own style, colour and design. To find out more listen to founder Alison Chadwick on Doable.

Holidapp
By popular demand, we're adding high-quality videos to our travel guide app. Now you will be able to see our expert guides as they share their knowledge of their towns and cities with you. You also view the locations they take you to and have close-up images of major buildings and artwork if you want. Help Holidapp to become even better!

7 Use your smartphone to video your presentation.

8 Watch the other presentations. Which project would you back? Why?

Self-assessment
- How successfully have you achieved the lesson outcome? Give yourself a score from 0 (I need more practice) to 5 (I know this well).
- Go to My Self-assessment in MyEnglishLab to reflect on what you have learnt.

BUSINESS WORKSHOP 7

Cross-cultural consultants

Lesson outcome: Learners can exchange information about texts they have read and can give a brief presentation with recommendations for working across cultures.

Background

1 Read the background and answer the questions with a partner.
1. What services does Connecting Cultures offer?
2. Why does Betker Finance need intercultural training?
3. What kind of feedback has Betker Finance received from international employees?
4. What will happen if this course is effective with the managers?

BACKGROUND

Connecting Cultures is a consultancy based in Amsterdam that specialises in cross-cultural training for businesses. Betker Finance, a Dutch multinational dealing in financial services, has asked the consultancy for courses in business communication. Dutch managers from Betker Finance often go on business trips and have meetings with colleagues and sales staff from around the world, including Europe, Japan, India and Brazil.

Following an internal employee satisfaction survey, international employees say some managers are not familiar with working practices in different cultures and often come across as very direct, even impolite. As a result, the Dutch managers have requested training to improve communication with international colleagues and clients to help their understanding of international markets. If the course is successful, Betker Finance will offer similar cultural training to all its employees.

Company blog

2A Look at the introduction to a blog post on cultural awareness and answer the questions.
1. Can culture be defined as the behaviour of one nationality?
2. How can people's behaviour differ in different cultures?
3. Does an individual have the same personality characteristics as the people from his/her country?
4. What do you think the five areas to consider when doing business internationally will be?

CONNECTING CULTURES BLOG

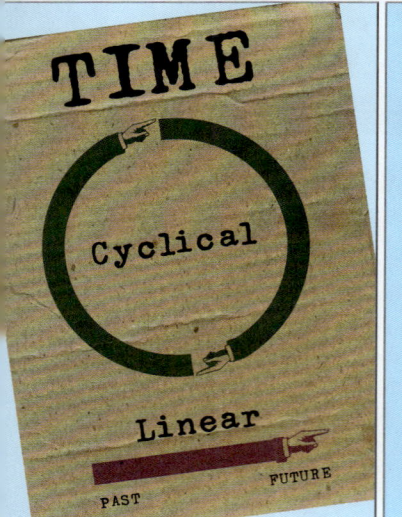

The way we do things around here

The best definition of culture I ever heard was from an expert who told me culture is about 'the way we do things around here'. This is true for a region, a community, a business sector or any organisation. What does this mean? Well, it means that accountants from one country will probably have similar ways of thinking and working to accountants in another culture. On the other hand, behaviour may differ enormously when it comes to areas such as being direct, or attitudes to time.

Here are five areas we should consider when doing business internationally. Of course, there are many more, but we hope these tips help you survive your next meeting or interview with an international client or supplier. These are just general guidelines, and although you may find information on websites about a particular culture, remember that an individual may not share the same characteristics as the 'national' character. We should NEVER fall into the trap of stereotyping people, e.g. 'all Americans and Germans are very direct.' Instead, we could say, 'Americans and Germans tend to be more direct than people from Asia or the UK.'

If you'd like more information on these issues and our training courses, please contact us at Connecting Cultures, and we'll help you connect with your partners and clients!

By Sofie Vroom

B Work in groups of three. You are going to read different parts of the blog post. Make notes and then exchange information about the topics and key points with the rest of your group. Which five topics are mentioned?

Student A: Look at the extract on page 136.
Student B: Look at the extract on page 131.
Student C: Look at the extract on page 135.

T Teacher's resources: extra activities

C How is your culture different from other cultures in terms of the topics mentioned?

What international colleagues say

3 A 🔊 **BW 7.01** You are consultants for Connecting Cultures. You are interviewing international staff from Betker Finance about working with their colleagues in the Netherlands. Match the ideas (a–g) with the speakers (1 and 2).

a business relationships are based on trust
b face-to-face meetings are preferred
c family members often work together
d it is rude to say 'no'
e they're not very punctual
f they are multi-active
g they believe in first impressions

B 🔊 **BW 7.02** Listen to interviews with speakers 3 and 4 and correct the summary notes about their experiences. There are six errors in each.

> SPEAKER 3 says the manager seemed very indirect. She thinks it's good to have an agenda to a meeting, but in their culture, they always make coffee before getting down to business. It's important to get the number of the other person to establish a conflictive atmosphere and they like to do business with people they don't like.
>
> SPEAKER 4 thinks the Dutch sales representative didn't talk a lot and didn't understand Japanese. The visitor thought they had finished the meal, when they had only started! The sales rep seemed a little emotional when he said he would check with his boss. He was surprised that she quickly confirmed points that they had agreed on. Hopefully, the next meeting will be more musical.

T Teacher's resources: extra activities

C Work in pairs. How could Betker Finance avoid these misunderstandings in the future?

> **TASK**
> Present a recommendation

4 A Work in pairs or small groups. Betker Finance have asked for your initial recommendations for doing business in your culture. Use all sections of the blog and the interviews to help you. Follow these steps.

1 Discuss these questions:
- What are the characteristics of your culture?
- What national stereotypes are there? Is there any truth in these stereotypes?
- Are there any considerations in your culture that could make or break a deal when working internationally? Give examples.

2 Prepare recommendations for Betker Finance on how to avoid misunderstandings when they do business in your culture. Consider these points:
- attitudes to time and how this affects ways of working.
- how being linear-active, multi-active or reactive might affect a business trip.
- how being direct vs. indirect affects business meetings and conference calls.
- attitudes to authority; how visitors should behave towards authority figures in your culture.
- attitudes to the collective vs. the individual in your culture and how this affects business communication.

B Take turns to present your recommendations. Listen to each other and ask questions at the end of each presentation.

C Which group do you think Betker Finance should contract? Why?

5 Write a formal email of between 180 and 200 words to the director at Betker Finance, confirming the group you have chosen. Give reasons for your choice based on your discussions in Exercise 4C.

Self-assessment

- How successfully have you achieved the lesson outcome? Give yourself a score from 0 (I need more practice) to 5 (I know this well).
- Go to My Self-assessment in MyEnglishLab to reflect on what you have learnt.

BUSINESS WORKSHOP 8

Talent management

Lesson outcome: Learners can understand details in conversations about training needs and can participate in a discussion to design a personal development plan.

Background

1 Read the background and discuss the questions with a partner.
1. What types of products do you think Grupo Tula distributes to retailers?
2. Why do you think a growing number of multinational companies are adopting English as an official or second language for business?
3. What type of training might a recent graduate in his/her first job need?
4. Why might managers need different types of training throughout their careers?
5. What are some of the pros and cons of companies recruiting managers externally or appointing internal staff to more senior positions?

BACKGROUND

Grupo Tula is a Mexican distributor* of consumer electronics. It has recently merged with a South Korean multinational and is expanding rapidly across the world. The CEO recently introduced English as the company's official language. Managers at the company's headquarters are encouraged to conduct all business in English.

Grupo Tula wants well-trained managers able to respond to the complexities of global markets, changing technologies and business competition. As part of its training programme the company develops high-performing employees for leadership roles in the organisation.

Employees set objectives based on feedback from their managers, and have personal development plans. They receive training to improve the technical and business skills they need for their current and future management roles. Continuous personal development is an essential element of the company's strategy. All management training is conducted in English and tailored to individual needs.

*__distributor:__ intermediary between a manufacturer and a retailer

Training needs

2 ◆ BW 8.01 Listen to three employees talking about their training needs. Which job do you think each person does? Complete the job titles in the notes below.

> Operations Manager   Senior Finance Manager   Trainee Sales Manager

3 Listen again and complete the notes. Use one to three words in each gap.

CRIS MARTINEZ
JOB: _____

He has done a lot of [1] _____ courses over the years.

He wants to build up a [2] _____ with [3] _____ in Grupo Tula to share ideas and solutions.

He says [4] _____ should be part of a senior manager's job.

ALEX CORTÉS
JOB: _____

She wants to learn to get [5] _____ from her staff.

She has to negotiate with [6] _____ within and outside Mexico.

She doesn't feel confident [7] _____ and wants to improve her [8] _____.

DANNI LEE
JOB: _____

He's doesn't know if he is focusing on [9] _____ and feels [10] _____.

He wants some software training, especially [11] _____.

He also wants to know how to [12] _____ one day.

Teacher's resources: extra activities

4 Who do you think seems most resistant to leadership training? Why do you think that is?

Business workshop 8

Training options

5 Match the programme descriptions 1–5 with the course titles in the box.

> coaching   executive decision-making   presentations   team-building
> time management

1 _____
Improve your productivity with this series of ten weekly online videos. Learn about setting priorities, getting things done, dealing with interruptions, reducing procrastination and much more. These practical tips will help you to get more out of your day, focus on the most important tasks and become more productive.

2 _____
A leader's success depends on the staff's contribution to business goals. This course gives you the tools and techniques you need to become a great mentor to your staff. In twelve days over a period of five months you will learn how to give effective feedback, inspire your team and improve their performance.

3 _____
Excellent public speaking skills are essential to many managers in today's business world. This three-day intensive course is aimed at non-native English speakers. You will learn how to hone your skills to make a greater impact and sound more persuasive in this fun, highly practical course.

4 _____
As a strategic leader, it is your responsibility to ensure that your organisation is moving in the right direction. This two-day course studies the latest neuroscience research into how effective decisions are made. Through theory and practice, executives will be able to apply these ideas to their own real-world projects.

5 _____
Learn strategies and techniques for creating successful group dynamics and getting people working effectively together on this six-week blended course. Develop skills that enhance communication and trust. Make sure your team members share goals so they can plan, communicate and work effectively.

6 Read the course descriptions again. Which type(s) of training:
a   is the shortest course? __
b   is on the internet? __
c   is run over the longest period? __
d   develop communication skills? __ , __ and __
e   are most useful for managers with staff? __ and __

Teacher's resources: extra activities

7 Which type of course(s) would most interest you at the moment? Why?

> **TASK**
> Design a leadership development plan

8A Work in small groups. Choose one of the employees from Grupo Tula and design a development plan. Use your own ideas as well as the training options on this page. Think about:

- the person's position in the company and training preferences.
- short- and long-term training needs.
- how he/she can be encouraged to do continuous professional development.
- ways to train and develop leaders, such as on-the-job activities, online courses, coaching.
- possible new training techniques like computer games, m-learning and blended learning.

B Take turns to present your development plans. After listening to the other groups, would you like to make any changes to your plan?

9 The Training Manager has asked all course applicants to write a short justification of why they need the course. Imagine you are applying to do one of the courses from your development plan in Exercise 8A. Write a short email of between 100 and 120 words to the training manager, formally requesting the course.

Self-assessment

- How successfully have you achieved the lesson outcome? Give yourself a score from 0 (I need more practice) to 5 (I know this well).
- Go to My Self-assessment in MyEnglishLab to reflect on what you have learnt.

1 REVIEW

1.1 Roles and responsibilities

1 Complete the text using the words in the box.

| after   care   charge   for   head   involves   leads |
| makes   reports   with |

Grigor's new job ¹_____ meeting new clients and he ²_____ to the Sales Manager. He is responsible ³_____ presenting the products and winning orders. His boss, who ⁴_____ the sales team, motivates his staff well. As ⁵_____ of Sales he sets them targets every month. He looks ⁶_____ them very well and it is a happy team. Grigor works closely ⁷_____ the distribution team and ⁸_____ sure that orders are delivered on time. He also has to take ⁹_____ of the paperwork. Grigor hopes to be in ¹⁰_____ of his own company one day.

1.2 Future forms

2 Choose the correct option in italics.

1 I was late this morning. I'm sure I *'m going to get / 'm getting* a warning from the boss.
2 The office *opens / is opening* at 10 o'clock on Fridays.
3 What do you think? *Are we going to sell / Do we sell* more this month?
4 He's decided he *asks / 's going to ask* his boss for a pay rise today.
5 What time *are you meeting / do you meet* him at the station later?
6 What? The course finishes at 6 p.m.? *I'm going to / I miss* my train.
7 They've closed the airport because it *snows / 's going to snow* more this afternoon.
8 I *'m seeing / see* the new clients later today.

Functional language

1.3 Greetings, introductions and goodbyes

3 Complete the dialogue using the phrases in the box.

| a bit of a delay   first time   for coming   have you met |
| in person   in such a rush   let's go and say hello |
| not bad, not bad   see you again |

A: Hi! How's it going?
B: ¹_____ . What about you?
A: Fine thanks.
B: Good trip?
A: We landed only 30 minutes late. ²_____ at Frankfurt Airport.
B: ³_____ Julia Knopf before? She runs the marketing office.
A: Yes, I have. Nice to ⁴_____ .
C: You too.
B: Excuse me. Sorry to be ⁵_____ like this, but I've got a meeting in five minutes. Before I leave, ⁶_____ to Miranda Scales. She works in head office.
A: Hi Miranda, I'm Jack Levine from the New York office. Nice to finally meet you ⁷_____ .
D: You too. So, ⁸_____ in London?
A: Yes, it is.
D: Well thank you ⁹_____ to this meeting.
A: You're welcome.

1.4 Asking and answering questions in first meetings

4 Choose the correct option in italics to complete the dialogue.

A: Can I ¹*offer / take* you a drink?
B: That ²*could / would* be great, thanks.
A: Where are you ³*positioned / based* at the moment?
B: In Geneva, but I was in Rome for two years before that.
A: Do you ⁴*work / report* to Roger Kleitz?
B: Yes, I do. Do you know him?
A: I ⁵*worked / joined* with him last year.
B: When did you ⁶*join / attend* the company?
A: Five years ago.
B: Are you ⁷*open / free* for lunch today?
A: Sorry, I'm meeting Matt Miller.

1.5 Ordering information

5 Put the sentences in the correct order.

Dear Mr Umbala

a I've therefore arranged, after a coffee break, for the Quality Control Manager to take you through the procedures.
b Please do not hesitate to contact me if you have any questions before the visit.
c We look forward to seeing you on October 7th at our factory premises.
d The Production Manager will meet you at the entrance at 9.30 to show you and your colleagues around.
e After that you will understand how we manage to maintain the highest quality control.
f Yours sincerely
g I will join you and the other managers for lunch at 1 p.m. in our staff restaurant.
h In the afternoon we can meet in my office to discuss the details of your order.
i I am writing to confirm that we have organised your visit to our factory on October 7th.
j I understand that you are particularly interested in the quality control we do.

Brian Watkins

2 REVIEW

2.1 Marketing and brands

1 Complete the text using the words in the box.

| approach   base   core   devalued   growth |
| history   loyalty   marketing   stretching   venture |

We have decided to take a cautious ¹_____ to expansion, because we know there is a lot of bad ²_____ with many companies whose brand-³_____ strategies have led to the brand being ⁴_____. This in turn can cause the brand ⁵_____, which had built up over years, to disappear. Thanks to our interactive ⁶_____, which has broadened our client ⁷_____, sales of our beauty products have seen very fast ⁸_____ over the last two years. We've now decided to move away from our ⁹_____ business and to ¹⁰_____ into the ultra-luxury spa hotel business.

2.2 Connectors

2 Choose the correct option in italics to complete the text.

¹*Recently / Previously / As well as* we decided that the brand needed refreshing so we discussed what to do. We got together with focus groups ²*such as / also / and* elicited customer feedback to determine how our brand is currently perceived. ³*Then / Previously / While* our branding consultants got to work on the new logo. ⁴*As well as / In addition / For instance*, we asked staff to come up with some ideas for a new logo, too. ⁵*However / Although / But* the consultants produced some great ideas, a design from a member of staff was finally chosen. ⁶*Now / Recently / When* we still have a lot of work to do before the product range can be launched with the new branding and the ad campaign finalised, but we are confident we are making changes for the better.

Functional language
2.3 Giving and responding to advice

3 Complete the advice given by a manager using the phrases in the box.

| why don't we   we need   you shouldn't |
| have you tried   this would be   it's important |

A: I never seem to have enough time to do my work.
B: ¹_____ planning your work for each day and week? That can help. ²_____ to sort this problem out now. ³_____ for each team member to meet the deadlines. ⁴_____ be missing them so often. ⁵_____ have a look at your tasks for this week together now? I think ⁶_____ an opportunity for you to improve your organisational skills.

2.4 Signposting in presentations

4 Complete the missing words. The first letters are given.

Let's ¹b_____ with the most important part – the new line of products.
²F_____, I'd like you to ³t_____ a look at this slide. It shows the new packaging and logo, which I think look really great. Secondly, the products themselves have been redesigned and now look much fresher and more up-to-date. ⁴F_____, this last slide outlines plans for our digital marketing campaign.
As I said ⁵e_____, we aim to attract younger customers. This is very ⁶i_____ if we want to remain competitive.
I'd like to thank everyone for their input on this project. The Marketing Manager will say ⁷m_____ about that later. Well, thank you very much for ⁸l_____. I'll hand over to Fran now.

2.5 Accepting and declining an invitation

5 Match the sentence halves.

1 I'm afraid
2 We very much
3 I'd like to
4 I'm writing
5 It would be great if
6 I'm sorry
7 Unfortunately, I
8 I'd love to come

a can't make the open day as I am away.
b to your open day but I'm away.
c but I can't come to the open day.
d to invite you to our open day next Friday.
e look forward to seeing you at our open day.
f invite you to our open day.
g you could come to the open day.
h that I will be unable to come to the open day.

105

3 REVIEW

3.1 Getting a job

1 Complete the text using the words in the box. Some words are not used.

> applied   character   clichés   come   competition
> competitive   employee   employer   gained
> intern   internship   jobseeker   motivated
> motivation   responsibility   sort   stand

As a(n) [1]_____, Jim has not been very successful so far. He has [2]_____ for over a hundred jobs, but not one potential [3]_____ has invited him for an interview. Why is this? Maybe he doesn't [4]_____ across well in his CV in a very [5]_____ job market. While he was at university, he [6]_____ some experience during a(n) [7]_____ with a big company. His manager found him very [8]_____ and hard-working. Unfortunately, Jim's job applications don't [9]_____ out from the crowd so now he has paid an expert to [10]_____ the problem out. The expert says Jim uses too many [11]_____ in his CV and he needs to add something which shows his [12]_____.

3.2 Indirect questions

2 Rewrite the direct questions as indirect questions.

1 What degree did you do?
   We'd like to know _____.
2 Why do you want to work for us?
   Could you tell me _____?
3 Where do you expect to be in five years' time?
   Can you tell me _____?
4 What will my responsibilities be?
   I'd like to know _____.
5 Why do you think you're the right person for the job?
   Could tell us _____?
6 How long were you working in China?
   We'd like to know _____.

Functional language
3.3 Active listening

3 Complete the dialogue using the phrases in the box.

> don't understand what   exactly do you mean
> tell me a bit more   you are frustrated   what I meant

A: Hi, Sam. I'm afraid we're not going to meet the project deadline.
B: OK, why don't you [1]_____ about it?
A: We're going to be at least a week late. There are some issues which are out of our control.
B: What [2]_____ by 'out of our control'?
A: Well, the construction workers have gone on strike because of a few small incidents.
B: I [3]_____ you said about going on strike.
A: Well, three people had small accidents and now they want more money because they say the work is dangerous, but I disagree.
B: So you don't think they should get more money?
A: That's not [4]_____. I don't believe the work is more dangerous than any other project but I do think they've got a point about the pay.
B: I can see that [5]_____ with the situation. If we offer them a small bonus if they can get the work done on time, do you think they'd accept?
A: I don't know, but we can try.

3.4 Useful phrases for candidates

4 Complete the text. Use only one word in each gap.

Thank you for your [1]_____ today. I'm really interested in this job. Could you tell me more [2]_____ it, please? For example, could you tell me what a normal day is [3]_____ and can I speak to some of the people I would be working [4]_____? And, finally, when can I expect to [5]_____ from you if I've been successful or not?

3.5 Useful phrases for covering letters

5 Choose the correct option in italics to complete the covering letter.

Dear Sir or Madam

Please find my CV [1]*advertised / attached*. I have just [2]*studied / completed* my management degree and would like to be [3]*considered / thought* for the [4]*post / placement* of Trainee Manager. I worked for a multinational company last summer and [5]*proved / appeared* that I could work under pressure.

I would very much [6]*regard / appreciate* the opportunity of an interview.

4 REVIEW

4.1 Business strategy collocations

1 Complete the text using the words in the box.

| cut   developed   emerging   lines   major |
| margin   missed   risks   tackle   takeover |

One of our rivals has just made a(n) ¹_____ bid for our company. In the last year, sales have suffered greatly due to cheaper product ²_____ coming from new ³_____ markets and we are no longer one of the ⁴_____ players in this industry. We have tried various strategies to ⁵_____ the problem, but we are not making enough money to survive. We have ⁶_____ opportunities to move into different markets and have not ⁷_____ a suitable strategy to ⁸_____ costs and maintain a healthy profit ⁹_____. We are not in a position to take any more ¹⁰_____ and I feel that accepting the bid is now our only option.

4.1 Word building – verbs, nouns and adjectives

2 Complete the sentences with the correct form of the word in capitals.

1 His ideas were totally _____ and changed the way the company worked. INNOVATE
2 The _____ of our business is due to the success of our new product. EXPAND
3 We are not doing well due to our _____ to appeal to a younger market. FAIL
4 A press release announced the _____ before staff were told about it. ACQUIRE
5 When we _____ the company, we kept all the staff. TAKEOVER
6 If this new strategy _____, we will be making a profit again. SUCCESS

4.2 Modal verbs

3 Choose the correct option in italics to complete the sentences.

1 We *shouldn't / don't have to* miss the project deadline.
2 You *don't have to / mustn't* work late tonight if you don't want to.
3 New regulations state everyone *will have to / must* wear hard hats at all times.
4 It's a good idea to do a training course. You *have to / should* book it now.
5 We recommend you clean the machine regularly. Ideally, you *should / must* clean it every two weeks.
6 You *shouldn't / mustn't* eat or drink at your desk. It's not allowed.

Functional language
4.3 Offering and asking for help

4 Complete the dialogue with the phrases in the box.

| I'd really like   is there anything else   I can manage |
| need a hand   thanks for   would be |
| would you like me   would you mind |

A: I haven't got the sales figures and this report has to be finished by the end of the day.
B: ¹_____ to find them for you?
A: ²_____ offering but I think ³_____ to find them.
B: ⁴_____ I can do? ⁵_____ to help if I can.
A: ⁶_____ collating those market reports? That ⁷_____ helpful.
B: Of course. No problem. ⁸_____ with anything else?
A: No, thanks. I think that's everything.

4.4 Leading and participating in problem-solving meetings

5 Complete the dialogue using one word in each gap.

A: Can you ¹_____ what the issue is exactly?
B: We're losing customers because of our pricing strategy.
A: Would it be ²_____ to reduce our prices?
B: If we ³_____ that, we'll reduce our profit margin.
C: To ⁴_____ up on what Adam just said, could we the reduce price for a short while?
D: I think that ⁵_____ a lot of sense.
A: And we'll need to look for new suppliers for the future.
D: I'm happy to ⁶_____ that on.

4.5 Reporting problems, reasons and results

6 Write sentences using the words in brackets.

0 Product recalled. Safety issues. (because)
The product was recalled because of safety issues.

1 Sales fell. Poor product quality. (due to)
_____

2 Poor product quality. Unhappy customers. (led)
_____

3 High costs. Customers bought cheaper rival products. (result of)
_____

4 Product was redesigned. Attract new customers. (order)
_____

5 The new strategy. Production problems. (resulted)
_____

5 REVIEW

5.1 Logistics

1 Choose the correct option in italics to complete the text.

Many companies use ¹*courier / robot* companies instead of the ²*posting / postal* service. However, this has made traffic ³*crowding / congestion* in cities worse in the past few years. Instead of delivering to customers' homes, some companies now use collection ⁴*lockers / couriers*. One main customer concern about online shopping is the safe delivery of their goods, so suppliers must make sure that they are ⁵*properly / rightly* packed.

5.1 Word building – verbs, things and people

2 Complete the text with the correct form of the words in brackets.

The rise of online shopping means that fast ¹_____ (deliver) of goods is key to a company's success or failure. Consequently, ²_____ (manufacture) or retailers must ensure that the ³_____ (distribute) of orders is carefully planned and this is the job of a ⁴_____ (logistics). Furthermore, the ⁵_____ (pack) needs to be sufficient to keep goods safe. Some companies ⁶_____ (operator) their own vehicles for transporting ⁷_____ (pack) to customers, but others use specialist companies.

5.2 Passive forms

3 Complete the passive sentences.
1. We must buy new software.
   New software _____.
2. They have already found a new factory.
   A new factory _____.
3. The company will launch a new product.
   A new product _____.
4. We have just changed the design.
   The design _____.
5. They didn't finish the project on time.
   The project _____.
6. They couldn't return the goods.
   The goods _____.

Functional language
5.3 Agreeing and disagreeing

4 Complete the dialogue using the phrases in the box.

agree at all   I'm afraid   I'm not sure   that's might work   rubbish   that makes

A: We need to recruit more staff urgently.
B: I don't ¹_____. We only need to reorganise the shifts and then we can manage with the existing staff.
A: ²_____ the best solution.
B: Why not?
A: The staff are already overworked. Many are doing overtime and they're making more mistakes.
B: That's ³_____. They're not overworked.
A: ⁴_____ I disagree with you. Look, why don't we recruit five temporary staff until we've caught up?
B: It ⁵_____ I suppose.
A: Then we can review the situation and decide what to do.
B: ⁶_____ sense. OK.

5.4 Negotiating

5A Choose the correct option in italics to complete the sentences.
1. How does that *develop / sound / go* to everyone?
2. My *proposal / offer / purpose* would be that we look at increasing our orders.
3. *Look forward / Good / Welcome* to see you again.
4. That seems *good idea / sensitive / reasonable*.
5. To *discuss / end / start*, I'd like to ask Mike to outline the key points for discussion.

B Match sentences 1–5 in Exercise 5A with negotiating steps a–e.

a Welcome   d Request feedback
b Invite others to present   e Give feedback
c Present suggestion

5.5 Useful phrases for letters of complaint

6 Choose the correct option in italics to complete the text.

Two days ago, we ¹*took / received / delivered* our order from you. ²*Unfortunately / Unluckily / Unfavourably*, the order was incorrect. We ordered 2,000 units but only 1,800 arrived.

If you do not ³*react / answer / respond* to this letter immediately, we will be ⁴*forced / required / bound* to look for another supplier and ⁵*appeal / request / require* that you collect the 1,800 units from our warehouse.

We hope that this situation will be ⁶*committed / resolved / determined* to our mutual ⁷*satisfaction / approval / fulfilment*.

6 REVIEW

6.1 Running a business

1 Complete the text using the words in the box.

| advice   angel   crowdfunding   financial |
| founders   funding   go out of   investment   profit |
| set up   start-ups   target market |

Look online and you'll find experts happy to give ¹_____ to those who want to ²_____ a new business. If you have a great idea that you think will sell, you need to get to know your ³_____ because, sadly, the majority of ⁴_____ will ⁵_____ business in the first year. You might make a small ⁶_____ in the first year, but can you sustain it? Many ⁷_____ of new companies look for a business ⁸_____ who believes the business is a good ⁹_____ in order to get the ¹⁰_____ needed to expand. Finding an investor who can offer not only ¹¹_____ help but also experience is often the ideal solution, although recently ¹²_____ , where lots of people provide small amounts of money, has become very popular as an alternative.

6.2 Reported speech

2 Complete the reported speech.

1. 'We finished by lunchtime today.'
   The manager said they _____ day.
2. 'What's your plan for the new business?'
   He asked me _____ .
3. 'They won't be working here in a year's time.'
   I said _____ in a year's time.
4. 'Have you been working in hospitality for long?'
   They asked him _____ for long.
5. 'The Sales Manager will visit tomorrow.'
   I told her _____ day.
6. 'I can finish the report now.'
   He said he _____ .
7. 'Where do you work?'
   They asked me _____ .

Functional language

6.3 Dealing with objections

3 Chose the correct option in italics to complete the sentences.

1. Does that solution *address / challenge* your concerns?
2. That *makes / sounds* like a very good idea.
3. What sort of price did you have in *idea / mind*?
4. I'm *aware / know* that the price is an issue for you.
5. You could *spend / spread* the cost by paying in instalments.
6. Is the instalment payment plan interest- *rate / free*?
7. We *appreciate / support* that you have budget restrictions.

6.4 Presenting visual information

4 Choose the correct option in italics to complete the text.

In this ¹*slice / part* of my presentation, I'm going to talk about sales. On this ²*graph / slide* there are two visuals. The ³*pie / round* chart shows our share of the overall market and you'll ⁴*notice / understand* that we now have a 5 percent share. The ⁵*line / straight* graph shows our monthly sales totals and it's ⁶*significant / considerable* that growth has been very steady this year. Looking more ⁷*nearly / closely* at it, it's ⁸*interesting / correct* to see that sales did not decrease in the traditionally slow summer months.

6.5 Summarising

5 Match the sentences 1–5 with the summary tips a–e. Focus on the parts in bold.

1. Xavier, the winner of the New Business Award, **talks about** how he started his company. ____
2. There were many **problems** at the beginning. Some **issues** were out of his control. ____
3. He **explains** how he managed to maintain customer loyalty. ____
4. As costs kept going up, he made a decision not to put his prices up. **Costs rose but he kept prices the same.** ____
5. **However**, **as a result** of this he managed to keep his loyal customers and attract new ones, **so** sales increased greatly. ____

a identifying main purpose/topic
b paraphrasing
c using synonyms
d using linking words
e using reporting verbs

7 Review

7.1 Working abroad

1 Complete the text using the words and phrases in the box. Some are not used.

> be put off   come across   common   fluent
> alone   nuances   rude   tend to

Working abroad can present difficulties, especially if you are not ¹_____ in the language of the country and you may ²_____ by a lack of understanding of cultural differences. Your colleagues might ³_____ as rather impolite, but it may simply be that their culture is just more reserved. People from a culture which is more indirect ⁴_____ appear less friendly than those from a culture where it is ⁵_____ practice to be more direct. Remember that it can take a few weeks or months to get used to living and working in different cultures. Be patient and make an effort to get to know your colleagues socially so that you don't spend too much time ⁶_____ .

7.1 Adjectives, prefixes and opposites

2 Add the correct prefix to make the opposite of the words in brackets.

When I first started working in Venezuela, people thought I was ¹_____ (sociable) when I refused to join them for lunch and dinner. They thought I was being ²_____ (friendly), but it was because I was shy; not because I was being ³_____ (respectful). I hadn't been ⁴_____ (honest) when I said that I spoke good Spanish on my CV, but I did have problems following ⁵_____ (formal) conversations. My studies had been rather ⁶_____ (helpful) in that area.

7.2 Past tenses: Past Simple, Past Continuous and Past Perfect Simple

3 Complete the text with the most suitable past tense form of the verbs in brackets.

Many years ago, while I ¹_____ (work) as the HR Manager for a multinational, I ²_____ (make) a big mistake. My job ³_____ (involve) recruiting engineers for our overseas branches. After I ⁴_____ (recruit) someone, I ⁵_____ (prepare) them for the cultural differences. One engineer ⁶_____ (insist) on taking his young family with him immediately to East Africa and the Engineering Director agreed. But, after three weeks, he ⁷_____ (resign) and ⁸_____ (return) to the UK. I ⁹_____ (warn) him before leaving that life would be very different there, but he ¹⁰_____ (not listen). He came home because his family ¹¹_____ (not be able) to get tomato ketchup so they ¹²_____ (can not) eat their food. Crazy but true!

Functional language
7.3 Expressing preferences

4 Complete the sentences using the phrases in the box.

> I'd cancel the meeting   I'd prefer it if
> not pay in advance   the boss isn't keen
> to change the design   we don't mind

1 If it were up to me, _____ .
2 _____ waiting a few days.
3 _____ you'd organise the trip for everyone.
4 They would rather _____ .
5 _____ on the new plans.
6 My preference would be _____ .

7.4 Keeping a conversation going

5 Put the dialogue into the correct order. The first line is done for you.

a What do you do? 1
b Did you go there for business or a holiday?
c I'm sure you'll enjoy it. It's a very interesting country.
d I'm designing an ad campaign for a large car producer.
e Yes, I'm looking forward to it.
f So you can't tell me? That's OK, I shouldn't have asked. I'm sorry I'm a bit tired today. I've just come back from Korea.
g What are you working on at the moment?
h No, but I'm going there next month for business.
i Business. Have you ever been there?
j I'm a graphic designer.
k I'm afraid not. It's all secret at the moment.
l Oh right, can you tell me which company it's for?

7.5 Making recommendations

6 Choose the correct option in italics to complete the text.

It has become ¹*suitable / obvious / probable* that many staff have problems working across cultures. Therefore, we strongly ²*recommend / mention / note* that all staff have cross-cultural training, and it is ³*optional / advisable / advisory* that you organise this immediately. My ⁴*instruction / approval / advice* is to find a good outside company which specialises in this. In fact, if I ⁵*shall be / am / were* you, I'd contact Jack Higgins from BVC. They used a good company last year. We ⁶*ought / should / must* to contact all staff as soon as possible and draw up a schedule for them to attend.

8 REVIEW

8.1 Leadership

1 Complete the text using the words in the box.

> cope   delegate   gives   make   praise   prioritise
> sets   takes   trust   won

Why is it that some people just seem to be hopeless at being a manager, unable to ¹_____ key decisions or ²_____ with crises? One manager I know just refuses to ³_____ any important tasks to his team and only ever ⁴_____ critical feedback because he does not allow his staff to do the work they are employed to do. He is always stressed because he ⁵_____ on too much responsibility. For some reason, the senior management team ⁶_____ his judgement and opinions and see nothing wrong. On the other hand a friend of mine works for someone with excellent leadership skills. He has ⁷_____ the respect of his staff and helps them to ⁸_____ tasks. He ⁹_____ goals with them, and always motivates them to do their best and he never forgets to give them ¹⁰_____ when they have done well.

8.2 Relative clauses

2A Complete the sentences with *when, where, which, who, whose*.

1 The conference, _____ was held in the Bahamas, was really useful.
2 The hotel _____ we had the training session was amazing.
3 This factory, _____ was built 100 years ago, will be replaced next year.
4 Our Chief Financial Officer, _____ has been with us for ten years, is retiring next month.
5 The business guru, _____ new book came out this week, is giving a talk here next week.
6 He's the person _____ has applied for the manager's position.
7 She's the Chief Executive Officer _____ company has won many awards.
8 2017 was the year _____ we first made a reasonable profit.

B In which sentence can we also use *that*? And in which sentence can we omit the relative pronoun?

Functional language

8.3 Giving and responding to feedback

3 Choose the correct option in italics to complete the mini dialogues.

A: I think you did a really good ¹*work / job / task* of planning the office relocation.
B: I'm happy you ²*are / mean / feel* that way. It was quite difficult to get everything done so quickly.

C: I think in future you should ask a colleague to help you.
D: Thanks, that's interesting. I'll ³*bear / put / have* that in mind.

E: I'm very ⁴*impressed / aware / good* with the quality of your work.
F: I really ⁵*understand / appreciate / realise* that feedback. Thanks.

G: It was your responsibility to get the task done on time but your team was late.
H: Oh! I'll certainly take those comments into ⁶*mind / feedback / account*.

8.4 Leading and managing meetings

4 Choose the correct option in italics to complete the dialogue.

A: Thanks for ¹*coming / attending / being* to the meeting, which I know I ²*held / made / called* at very short notice. The ³*agenda / goal / thinking* for this meeting is to find ways to cut costs. We have one hour for this meeting so let's start by ⁴*talking / focusing / thinking* on possible new suppliers.
B: What about my request for more staff?
A: I understand your ⁵*difficulty / concern / business* but that isn't on today's ⁶*diary / paper / agenda*.

8.5 Informing of a decision

5 Match the sentences halves.

1 This is to inform you
2 Just to let you know that we
3 The final decision
4 In today's meeting, we came
5 We thought that
6 We reached
7 I'm writing

a to a decision about packaging design.
b an agreement about the new pay structure.
c to inform you of the policy changes.
d of our decision to introduce new contracts.
e are having a meeting tomorrow morning.
f it was best to change the date of the interviews.
g was to ask people to suggest ideas for a logo.

Pronunciation bank

Introduction

Pronunciation is important because even if you use the right words and the right grammar, you won't be able to communicate effectively if listeners can't understand your pronunciation easily. Awareness of the key elements of pronunciation will also help you to understand spoken English better.

Syllables, stress and intonation

Different words have different numbers of syllables:
- 1 syllable   grow, growth
- 2 syllables   prod·uct, re·port
- 3 syllables   in·ter·view, pro·duc·tion
- 4 syllables   in·ter·view·er, co·or·di·nate
- 5 syllables   char·ac·ter·is·tic
- 6 syllables   re·spon·si·bil·i·ty

In words with more than one syllable, one of the syllables is stressed, i.e. clearer, louder and longer than the other syllables, and it carries the main intonation, i.e. the movement of the voice up or down:

| PRODuct | INterview | INterviewer |
| rePORT | proDUCtion | coORdinate |

In longer words and compound nouns there is often a secondary stress, i.e. a less strong stress earlier in the word:

characteRIStic   responsiBILity   mobile PHONE

Stress is important in making words recognisable, and stress and intonation are used to highlight important information:

A: Are you still using that same old comPUter?   **B:** No, I've got a NEW one.
A: Did you get it as a PREsent?   **B:** No, I BOUGHT it.

The sounds of English

These are the sounds of standard British English and American English pronunciation. See also the section 'Varieties of English' on the following page.

Consonants	
Symbol	Keyword
p	pen
b	back
t	tea
t̬ (AmE)	city
d	day
k	key
g	get
tʃ	church
dʒ	judge
f	fact
v	view
θ	thing
ð	this
s	soon
z	zero
ʃ	ship
ʒ	pleasure
h	hot
m	more
n	nice
ŋ	ring
l	light
r	right
j	yet
w	wet

Vowels		
Symbol BrE	Symbol AmE	Keyword
ɪ	ɪ	kit
e	e	dress
æ	æ	bad
ʌ	ʌ	but
ʊ	ʊ	foot
ɒ		odd
ə	ə	about
i	i	happy
u	u	situation
iː	i	feel
ɑː	ɑ	father
ɔː	ɔ	north
uː	u	goose
ɜː	ɚ	stir
eɪ	eɪ	face
aɪ	aɪ	price
ɔɪ	ɔɪ	boy
əʊ	oʊ	no
aʊ	aʊ	mouth
ɪə	ɪr	near
eə	er	fair
ʊə	ʊr	jury

/t̬/ means that many American speakers use a voiced sound like a quick /d/ for the /t/ in words like *city, party, little*.
ː shows a long vowel

Sounds and spelling

In English, the relationship between spoken and written language is particularly complicated.

The same sound can be spelt in different ways, e.g.:
- /əʊ/   sl**ow**   g**o**   l**oa**n   t**oe**   alth**ough**   kn**ow**
- /s/   **s**ell   **sc**ien**ce**   **c**ent

The same letter can be pronounced in different ways, e.g.:
- the letter *u* can be pronounced /ʌ/ as in c**u**t, /ʊ/ as in f**u**ll, /ɔː/ as in s**u**re in British English or /ɪ/ as in b**u**sy;
- the letter *s* can be pronounced /s/ as in **s**ell, /z/ as in ea**s**y, /ʃ/ as in ten**s**ion or /ʒ/ as in deci**s**ion.

Using a dictionary

Once you are familiar with the phonetic symbols in the table in The sounds of English section, you will be able to use a dictionary to find the pronunciation of any word you are unsure about. As well as the sounds in a word, dictionaries also show word stress. Look at this dictionary entry for *controversial*:

> **con·tro·ver·sial** /ˌkɒntrəˈvɜːʃəl/ *adj* causing a lot of disagreement, because many people have strong opinions about the subject being discussed

- The ' sign shows you that the syllable immediately after it is stressed.
- The ˌ sign shows you that the syllable immediately after it has secondary stress.
- The ː sign shows you that the vowel is long.

Simplifications

In normal everyday speech, however, words often do not have the same pronunciation as shown in dictionaries. This is important for listening. Vowels in stressed syllables are usually pronounced clearly, but otherwise speakers make various simplifications:
- Some sounds are missed out, e.g. *facts* can sound like 'facs', *compete* can sound like 'cmpete', *characteristic* can sound like 'charrtristic'.
- Some sounds are merged together, e.g. *on Monday* can sound like 'om Monday', *ten groups* can sound like 'teng groups', *this show* can sound like 'thishow'.

Varieties of English

English is of course spoken by some people as a first language, but it is spoken by much larger numbers of people who learn it as an additional language and use it as a lingua franca for international communication.

There is a large amount of variation in how English is pronounced:
- Variation among traditional 'native' accents such as British, American and Australian. There are even considerable differences between the accents of different regions of the United Kingdom.
- Variation among accents of English as a lingua franca, with many of the differences caused by the influence of speakers' first languages, e.g. Japanese speakers often do not distinguish between /l/ and /r/, and Spanish speakers often add an /e/ at the front of words beginning with /sp/, /sk/ and /st/.

Consonant sounds are generally similar in different varieties, but there is much more variation in vowel sounds – both the number of vowel sounds used and the exact quality of the sounds.

In the audio and video recordings which accompany this course – and in your everyday life and work – you will hear speakers from various English-speaking and non-English-speaking backgrounds communicating successfully with each other despite such differences in pronunciation. For example, many speakers do not use the /θ/ sound of '**th**ink' and the /ð/ sound of '**th**en', but this does not generally affect their ability to make themselves understood. Particularly important things to concentrate on include:
- word stress,
- stress and intonation in phrases and sentences, for highlighting important information,
- consonant sounds,
- groups of consonants at the beginning of words – e.g. **str**ong,
- the difference between long and short vowels.

Good pronunciation does not necessarily mean speaking like a 'native' speaker; it means being understood by others when communicating in English. Awareness of pronunciation principles and regular pronunciation practice will help you improve your speaking, but also your listening comprehension.

Pronunciation bank

Lesson 1.1
Word stress

> We can record the stress pattern of a word by using large and small circles. For example, *photographer* has four syllables and the second syllable is stressed:
>
> pho·tog·ra·pher   oOoo

1 Work in pairs. Write the words in the correct place in the table according to their stress pattern.

> advertising   coordinate   director   involves
> manager   marketing   operator   programme
> report   resources   responsible   website

1	Oo	
2	Ooo	
3	Oooo	
4	oO	
5	oOo	
6	oOoo	

2 🔊 P1.01 Listen and check. Then listen again and repeat.

3 Work in pairs. Use one large coin and (up to) three small coins to show one of the stress patterns in Exercise 1. Your partner says one of the words that has this stress pattern, and uses it in a phrase or sentence.

Lesson 1.3
Intonation and politeness

> In order to sound polite and interested, we use a varied intonation when we ask questions.

1 🔊 P1.02 Listen to two versions of three questions. Which version sounds polite and interested, the first or the second?
1. Are you very busy at the moment?
2. Where are you based?
3. Do you travel a lot for work?

2 🔊 P1.03 Listen to the polite and interested versions again. Mark the word with the main stress in each. Then listen again and repeat.

3 Work in pairs. Take turns to ask one of the questions, sounding either polite and interested or impolite and uninterested. Answer in the same style.

Lesson 2.1
Stress in compound nouns and noun phrases

> In compound nouns and noun phrases, the main stress may fall on either word. For example:
> JEWELLERY brand   soft DRINK

1 Work in pairs. Underline the word with the main stress in each pair of words.

> advertising campaign   brand image
> client base   company logo   core business
> luxury brand   mobile phone   online advertisement
> product placement   TV programme

2 🔊 P2.01 Listen and check. Then listen again and repeat.

3 Work in pairs. Take turns to make sentences including two of the compound nouns and noun phrases in Exercise 1.

Lesson 2.2
Connectors: intonation and pausing

> Some connectors used at the beginning of sentences have a fall–rise intonation and a slight pause between the connector and the rest of the sentence. For example:
>
> *Recently, Asian brands have started to appear in U.S. shops.*

1 🔊 P2.02 Listen to the sentences and repeat the underlined connectors. Copy the intonation.
1. <u>Previously</u>, there were very few Asian brands in European shops.
2. <u>In recent years</u>, France has become a popular destination for Chinese customers.
3. <u>For example</u>, luxury handbags and watches are popular in Asia.
4. <u>In addition</u>, Asian shoppers are keen on scarves and jewellery.

2 Work in pairs and practise saying the sentences in Exercise 1.

Pronunciation bank

Lesson 3.1
Stress in derived words

> When we add endings to words, the stress sometimes stays on the same syllable and sometimes moves. For example:
> reCRUIT → reCRUITment
> FLEXible → flexiBILity

1 Work in pairs. Look at the words. In which pairs does the stress stay on the same syllable? In which does it move?

> character → characteristic
> communicate → communication
> effect → effective
> interview → interviewer
> responsible → responsibility

2 🔊 P3.01 Listen and check. Then listen again and repeat.

3 Work in pairs. Ask and answer the questions using words from Exercise 1.
1 What do you think is the most positive aspect of your c_____?
2 How important is body language for e_____ c_____?
3 Is it the r_____ of an i_____ to help the candidate make a good impression?

Lesson 3.2
Voice range and intonation in indirect questions

> In indirect questions, it helps to create an impression of politeness and friendliness if the voice starts at a high level and falls quickly on the main stress.

1 🔊 P3.02 Listen and repeat the indirect questions. Try to imitate the voice range and intonation.
1 Can you tell me what your greatest weakness is?
2 Could you tell me about your work experience?
3 I'd like to know if you've ever done any voluntary work.

2A Prepare six indirect questions to ask your partner.

B Work in pairs. Ask and answer the questions you wrote in Exercise 2A.

Lesson 4.3
/iː/, /ɪ/, /eɪ/ and /aɪ/

> These vowel sounds can be spelled in various ways. For example:
> /iː/ m**ee**t, k**ey**   /ɪ/ dec**i**sion, man**a**ge
> /eɪ/ gr**ey**, **ei**ght   /aɪ/ s**i**de, tr**y**

1 Work in pairs. Put the words below in the correct column, according to the pronunciation of the letters in bold.

> adv**i**ce   br**ie**fed   b**u**siness   ch**a**nge   coll**ea**gue
> d**ay**   **i**dea   l**i**mited   op**i**nion   p**eo**ple   r**ai**se   st**y**le

/iː/	/ɪ/	/eɪ/	/aɪ/

2 🔊 P4.01 Listen and check. Then listen again and repeat.

3 Work in pairs. Take turns to point to words in Exercise 1, and say sentences containing the words.

Lesson 4.4
Intonation in 'OK'

> The intonation of 'OK' is never completely predictable, but there are typical patterns.

1 🔊 P4.02 Listen to four extracts from a meeting and match them with the uses below.
a Getting people's attention: ____
b Asking someone to agree with you: ____
c Showing you understand and agree: ____
d Showing you understand but don't necessarily agree: ___

2 Work with a partner and practise the extracts and intonation patterns.
1 OK, let's get started. Good morning, everyone.
2 A: … we contract a call centre to handle first contacts, and then they contact our sales staff.
   B: OK, but I'm not sure how that would work.
3 A: You may be right.
   B: OK, then I think we need to look at recruitment as the quick solution.
4 I'll send Stefanie over to Tokyo for a couple of weeks, OK?

Pronunciation bank

Lesson 5.1
Pausing and stress in presentations

> In presentations, pay special attention to words that are stressed and the places where speakers pause for effect.

1 🔊 **P5.01** Listen to two versions of the beginning of a presentation. Which is more effective and why?

> Online shopping is now a major part of the retail sector. It is convenient and often cheaper than buying in traditional stores. E-commerce operators have invested heavily in their logistics systems so that consumers receive a quick and efficient service.

2 🔊 **P5.02** Listen to the more effective version again. Mark the pauses and underline the words the speaker stresses.

<u>Online</u> <u>shopping</u> is now a <u>major</u> <u>part</u> of the <u>retail</u> <u>sector</u>. | It is …

3 Work in pairs. Take turns to give the presentation.

Lesson 5.2
Auxiliary verbs in passives

> **Auxiliary verbs in passives are usually weak forms or contractions.**
> If the items aren't clean, they haven't <u>been</u> /bin/ washed at the right temperature or the appliance <u>has</u> /həz/ been overloaded.
>
> **If we use strong forms, it is usually to emphasize contrast.**
> **A:** Why hasn't the order been delivered?
> **B:** It <u>has</u> /hæz/ been delivered. It was delivered this morning. (B stresses *has* to contrast with A's idea that the order hasn't been delivered.)

1 Is each of the words in *italics* in these exchanges weak or strong?

1 **A:** *Has* the order *been* sent?
  B: Sent? It's already *been* delivered!
3 **A:** When *were* these invoices paid?
  B: I think they *were* paid last week. Let me check – yes, they *were*, on Wednesday.
4 **A:** I don't think driverless vehicles *can* be tested safely.
  B: They *can* be – they *can* be tested in closed areas.

2 🔊 **P5.03** Compare with a partner, then listen and check.

3 Work in pairs and practise the exchanges in Exercise 1.

Lesson 6.1
Consonant–vowel linking

> In spoken English, a consonant at the end of a word is often linked to a vowel at the beginning of the next word.

1 🔊 **P6.01** Listen and repeat these phrases.
millions‿of people
make‿a phone
but‿on the other hand
the situation‿in‿Eastern Congo

2 Work with a partner. Mark where there will be consonant-vowel links in this extract.

… that's why we started a company instead of, you know, doing art projects, for example.

3 🔊 **P6.02** Listen and check. Then listen again and repeat.

4 Take turns to say the phrases in Exercises 1 and 2.

Lesson 6.4
Intonation and discourse marking in presentations

> When you present information, use a fall-rise intonation for an introductory phrase, then pause, and then use a falling intonation for the information itself.
>
> On this graph | you can see how demand has grown recently.

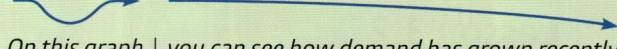

1 🔊 **P6.03** Listen to these presentation extracts. Mark where the speaker pauses.

1 Today, I'd like to tell you about our latest product.
2 I'll begin by giving you some background.
3 In the next part of the presentation I'd like to present some more technical details.
4 As you can see from the chart, Poland is one of our biggest markets.
5 I'm going to finish by telling you a little story.

2 Work in pairs and practise saying the sentences in Exercise 1.

Pronunciation bank

Lesson 7.2
Phrasing and intonation in past sentences

> In sentences with various past tenses, we often use a fall-rise intonation for the background information at the beginning of the sentence and then a falling intonation for the main information.

1 🔊 **P7.01** Listen and mark the main information.
1 While Luis was working in India, he was surprised to see a shrine on the table in the chairman's office.
2 Even if they'd previously agreed to a deadline, they later admitted they couldn't meet it.
3 Because her boss had copied in all the members of the team, Shivani was so embarrassed that she quit her job.

2 Work in pairs and practise saying the sentences in Exercise 1.

Lesson 7.3
Strong or weak?

> Some very common words such as *a, an, and, are, as, have, the, to*, etc. are usually spoken in their weak forms, unless they are stressed, for example for contrast.
> A: Are /ə/ these your glasses?
> B: Yes, they are /ɑː/ – thanks!

1 🔊 **P7.02** Listen and repeat this extract.
I don't agree *that* /ðət/ deadlines *can* /kən/ never *be* /bɪ/ moved around – I think they *can* /kæn/ *be* /bɪ/ sometimes.

2 Work in pairs. Do you think the words in *italics* will be strong or weak?
1 *The* process is *as* important *as the* result.
2 Deadlines *are* useful *to* keep people focused – *that's* their main purpose.
3 I think consensus is important – what *do you* think?
4 If we can't all reach *an* agreement, what *do you* think we should *do*?

3 🔊 **P7.03** Listen and check. Then work in pairs and practise saying the sentences.

Lesson 8.1
Glottal stops

> The sound /t/ is sometimes replaced by a glottal stop, in which the air is stopped in the throat. Some regional accents of English, and some individual speakers, use glottal stops more than others.

1 🔊 **P8.01** Listen to the exchange, first with /t/ and then with a glottal stop.
A: When are we going to star**t**?
B: Straightaway.

2 🔊 **P8.02** Listen and underline where /t/ is replaced by a glottal stop.
1 Great leaders are born not made.
2 Nobody really agrees about what the characteristics of a great leader are.
3 We forgot the whole point was just to start the truck.

3 Work in pairs. Take turns to say the sentences using either /t/ or a glottal stop. Tell your partner which of the sounds you heard.

Lesson 8.2
Phrasing and intonation in relative clauses

> In speech, non-defining relative clauses are usually separated from the rest of the sentence by pauses which correspond to commas in writing. Non-defining relative clauses are also often spoken on a lower pitch than the rest of the sentence. Defining relative clauses are not separated from the rest of the sentence in these ways.

1 🔊 **P8.03** Listen to two sentences. Which is defining and which is non-defining?

2 🔊 **P8.04** Listen and repeat the sentences.
1 A My sister, who works in marketing, used to be a singer.
  B I've got two sisters. The one who works in marketing used to be a singer.
2 A This is the new app I was telling you about the other day.
  B The new app, which I was telling you about the other day, is selling well.

3 Work in pairs. Practise saying the sentences.

117

Grammar reference

1.2 Future forms

We can talk about the future using a variety of forms depending on the function:

- We use the **Present Simple** for **events scheduled to happen** (something that is timetabled).

  I **have** a job interview tomorrow.

  Our train **doesn't leave** until 8.30 this evening.

  Does the departmental meeting **start** at 9 o'clock on Monday as usual?

- We use the **Present Continuous** for **plans/arrangements** (something you have confirmed for the future). This often involves other people.

  I'**m visiting** the suppliers tomorrow.

  He's on holiday so he **isn't coming** to the meeting on Friday.

  Are you **having** a leaving party next week?

- We can use **be + going to + infinitive** in two different ways:

  i to talk about **personal intentions** (something you want to do).

  I'**m going to get** to the office early tomorrow.

  We **aren't going to change** the software.

  Is she **going to come** to the meeting?

  Note: We use the Present Continuous more for plans/arrangements with other people and *be + going to +* infinitive for personal intentions. However, often we could use either form because many events can be seen as either plans/arrangements or intentions.

  I'**m visiting** the suppliers tomorrow. (This is a plan/arrangement between the supplier and myself.)

  I'**m going to visit** the suppliers tomorrow. (This is my intention.)

  I'**m going to get** to the office early tomorrow. (This is my intention.)

  I'm getting to the office early tomorrow. (This is **not** correct because it is not a plan/arrangement.)

  ii to talk about **predictions when something is probable** (something you expect to happen).

  He's very good. I think he'**s going to get** promoted soon.

  Look at this office! It'**s not going to be** big enough for four people.

  She does a great job. I'm sure they'**re going to make** her Chief Executive.

1.5 Present Simple and Continuous

We can use the **Present Simple** to talk about:

- **permanent situations**.

  He **supervises** the production line.

  He **works** in the finance department.

- **general facts**.

  Water **freezes** at 0 degrees.

  It'**s** one of the biggest companies in the world.

- **repeated/regular actions**.

  They **work** in an office.

  She **deals** with customers.

We can use the **Present Continuous** to talk about:

- **things happening at the same time as we are speaking or writing**.

  We'**re waiting** for a delivery.

  He'**s showing** Mr Jones around the factory.

- **temporary situations**.

  I'**m staying** with a friend while I'm in London this week.

  He'**s acting** as Head of Finance while his boss is on maternity leave.

- **future plans/arrangements**.

  We'**re meeting** the clients tomorrow morning.

  She **is visiting** our offices next week.

There are some **verbs which are rarely used in the continuous**. These include:

be, believe, contain, dislike, hate, hear, know, like, love, need, own, possess, smell, sound, understand.

There are also some common **verbs which change their meaning** in the Present Simple and Present Continuous. These include:

- think

  I **think** you're going to find it very interesting. (This is my opinion.)

  I'**m thinking** about the induction day. (This is the topic.)

- have

  I **have** a good car. (= have got / own / possess)

  He'**s having** breakfast. (= eating)

- see

  I **see** your point. (= understand)

  I'**m seeing** him tomorrow. (= meeting)

2.2 Connectors

Connectors are words or phrases that signal to the reader or listener how things relate to one another in a text or speech, and help to support understanding. They can also be used to manage and direct the focus of the reader or listener.

There are different categories of connectors depending on the role they perform in the sentence. For example:

- **adding ideas**, e.g. *and, also, as well as, in addition.*

  As well as *discussing the in-store customer experience, we* **also** *need to look at brand awareness if we want to improve sales figures.*

  In addition, *we feel that our stores should use new technologies to attract customers.*

- **contrasting ideas**, e.g. *although, but, however, while.*

  Initial response to our new product range has been positive. **However**, *there is still a lot of work to do to reach our target.* (*Note:* we use a comma <u>after</u> *However*.)

  I think she's a great brand ambassador, **although** *I don't like her music very much.* (*Note:* we use a comma <u>before</u> *although*.)

  Certain luxury brands are popular in some countries, **while** *different brands are popular in other markets.*

- **referring to time**, e.g. *earlier (this year), in recent years, now, previously, recently, when.*

  In recent years, *Chinese customers have started to combine holidays abroad with shopping expeditions.*

- **giving examples**, e.g. *for example, for instance, such as.*

  There are many successful global luxury brands, **such as** *Bulgari, Chanel and Hermès.*

  Our stores use new technologies, **for instance**, *we have created an app that lets the assistant know when a loyal customer enters the store.*

- **sequencing**, e.g. *first of all, then, to start with.*

  If you'd like to go into marketing, **first of all**, *you should feel passionately about brands.*

  The success of our brand is due to two factors. **To start with**, *we have a well-designed, great product.* **Then** *we have the support of many, many loyal customers.*

2.5 Verbs + *-ing* vs. infinitive

When a verb is followed by another verb, the first verb dictates the form the second verb takes. There are various possibilities:

- **verbs which take *to* + infinitive**

  afford, agree, arrange, attempt, claim, decide, demand, deserve, expect, fail, guarantee, hesitate, hope, learn, manage, offer, plan, prepare, promise, refuse, seem, tend, would like

  They have **decided to sponsor** *the exhibition.*

  We'**d like to invite** *you to our offices in Delhi to meet the team.*

- **verbs which take *-ing***

  avoid, consider, delay, deny, dislike, enjoy, finish, involve, justify, miss, postpone, practise, risk, suggest

  He **denied writing** *the email to the boss.*

  They **postponed launching** *the new product for six months.*

- **verbs + preposition which take *-ing***

  apologise for, insist on, look forward to, put off, succeed in

  He **apologised for arriving** *at the meeting late.*

  We **look forward to seeing** *you soon.*

- **verbs which take *to* + infinitive or *-ing* with a change in meaning**

  forget, go on, remember, stop, try

  I **remember discussing** *modern art with you last month.* (Here *remember* refers to a past action, something the person knows happened.)

  Please **remember to bring** *this invitation with you.* (Here *remember* refers to a future action, something the person needs to do.)

  She **tried to write** *an email to apologise, but she couldn't find the words.* (Here *tried* refers to something the person wanted to do, but wasn't able to.)

  She **tried writing** *an email to apologise, but he still isn't talking to her.* (Here *tried* refers to something the person did, but which didn't work as planned.)

- **verbs which take *to* + infinitive or *-ing* with little or no change in meaning**

  begin, continue, hate, intend, like, love, prefer, start

  They **began arguing / to argue** *the moment the meeting started.*

Grammar reference

3.2 Direct questions

The usual word order in question forms is:

(Question word(s)) + auxiliary verb + subject + main verb + object/time/place/manner, etc.

Have you worked in sales before? (no question word(s))

Why did you decide to travel for a year? (*why* = question word)

Direct questions can be open or closed. Closed questions have a *yes/no* answer, while open questions start with a question word or words, for example, *what, who, when, where, why, how*, etc.

Do you have any experience for this position? (CLOSED)

Are you prepared to travel? (CLOSED; invert the verb *be*)

Why would you like to work for us? (OPEN)

Indirect questions

We often use **indirect questions** to be more polite with people we don't know very well, e.g. in an interview, or when a question is more difficult or challenging.

There are different ways of starting an indirect question. For example:

- **Can/Could you tell me/us …**

  Can you tell me how many people work in the department?

  Could you tell us what your greatest strengths are?

- **I'd/We'd like to know if/wh- question word(s) …**

  I'd like to know what the starting salary will be.

  We'd like to know if you have experience in this sector.

  Note: *I'd/We'd like to know …* does not need a question mark (?).

In closed questions, *I'd/We'd like to know …* and *Can/Could you tell me/us …* are followed by *if/whether*, while in open questions they are followed by a question word or words.

I'd like to know if you provide any training. (= *Do you provide any training?* (CLOSED))

I'd like to know what kind of training you provide. (= *What kind of training do you provide?* (OPEN))

Can/Could you tell me whether I will need to travel? (= *Will I need to travel?* (CLOSED))

Can/Could you tell me how often I will need to travel? (= *How often will I need to travel?* (OPEN))

Note: Always check the word order in indirect questions as there is no inversion of the subject and the (auxiliary) verb.

I'd like to know who I will report to. (not … *who will I report to.*)

3.5 Past Simple and Present Perfect

We can use the **Past Simple** to talk about:

- **events that took place at a definite time in the past**.

  In this case, we often use the Past Simple with time expressions such as *yesterday, last week, at 8 o'clock, three years ago*, etc.

  I organised a surfing team at my university.

  Last year we won the national inter-university surfing competition.

- **finished time in the past**.

  I lived there for ten years. (This means that I don't live there anymore.)

- **details of something that happened in the past**.

  I've been there several times. In fact, I went there last week.

We can use the **Present Perfect** to talk about:

- **indefinite time in the past**.

  In this case, we either don't know when something happened or we don't consider when it happened important.

  I have spent the last three summer holidays working for a local surfing company. (In this case, we don't know exactly when, but it was sometime before now.)

- **past actions or states which are relevant now.**

  In this case, we often use the Present Perfect with expressions such as *already, before, ever, never, recently, always, still* and *yet*.

  I've just completed a sports education degree.

  I have always kept up-to-date with current trends.

  Have you ever worked for Microsoft?

4.2 Modal verbs

We can use a range of modal verbs to talk about obligation, necessity, prohibition and recommendation. For example:

- We use **have to** + infinitive when we talk about actions that are necessary and obligations. These obligations can include laws, rules and regulations.

  *Companies **have to pay** 20 percent corporate tax in the UK.*

  In British English it's also common to use **have got to** when speaking.

  *I**'ve got to go** to the dentist's tomorrow.*

  - We can also use the modal verb **must** + infinitive when we talk about actions that are necessary or obligations. We can generally use either **have to** or **must** in most cases.

  *Companies **have to pay** 20 percent corporate tax in the UK.*
  *Companies **must pay** 20 percent corporate tax in the UK.*

  However, we use **have to** more frequently for external rules and **must** more frequently for obligations we make for ourselves.

  *I **have to get** to work early tomorrow. There's a meeting at 9 o'clock.*
  *I **must get** to work early every day. It's when I get my best work done.*

  We use **have to** when we need to use a past, future, present perfect, gerund or infinitive form.

  *Did you **have to do** a test as part of the interview process?*
  *We **will have to cut** prices in order to compete.*
  *The European Bank **has had to lower** interest rates again.*
  ***Having to work** shifts at the hospital is not easy.*

  We can use both **have to** and **must** for strong recommendations.

  *You **have to visit** the National Portrait Gallery. It's brilliant!*
  *You **must tell** the hotel you want a room with a sea view.*

- We use **should/shouldn't** + infinitive to make recommendations and suggestions and to give advice and opinions.

  *If you ask me, we **should catch** the earlier train.*
  ***Should** I **call** the supplier if they haven't replied to my email?*
  *We **shouldn't leave** the air-con on when we leave the office. It's a waste of energy.*

- We use **mustn't** + infinitive to say that it is important or necessary not to do something or that it is not allowed.

  *We **mustn't lose** market share to our competitors.*
  *Staff **mustn't talk** about company strategy in public.*
  *Passengers **mustn't use** mobile phones during take-off.*

- We use **don't have to** + infinitive to say that it is not necessary or compulsory to do something, but that you can do it if you want.

  *You **don't have to wear** smart clothes but clean clothes are essential.*
  *I **don't have to work** tomorrow. It's a public holiday.*

Be careful because **mustn't** and **don't have to** have very different meanings.

*You **mustn't** smoke anywhere in the building. (This is not permitted.)*
*You **don't have to** go outside to smoke here. (This is not necessary.)*

4.5 Comparison

We can use a variety of structures to make comparisons. These include:

Comparative adjectives

- **short adjectives**

  For adjectives with one syllable (and some two-syllable adjectives, e.g. *clever, quiet, narrow*), add **-er**:

  *They prefer to visit **bigger** supermarkets.*

  Note: There are some common exceptions. For example:
  good – better; bad – worse

- **adjectives ending in -y**

  For adjectives ending in *-y*, drop the **-y** and add **-ier**:

  *The company boss is **wealthier** than we thought.*

- **long adjectives**

  For some adjectives with two syllables and for most adjectives with three syllables, use **more** or **less**:

  *Local stores are offering a **more limited** range of products.*

- **not as … as**

  To say that two things are not the same, use **not as … as**:

  *The HR department is **not as** noisy **as** Sales.* (This means that Sales is noisier than the HR department (though the HR department may be noisy, too).)
  *The training session was**n't as** interesting **as** I had expected.* (This means that I expected the training session to be more interesting than it was.)

Emphasising comparisons

- We can use words such as *much, far, considerably, slightly* and *a bit* before a comparative adjective to make the comparison stronger.

  *We wouldn't go, even if prices were **much lower**.*
  *The launch was **far more difficult** than we expected.*

- We can also **repeat the comparative adjective** to indicate that something is changing over time.

  *Customers have to wait **longer and longer**.* (This means that the average time customers are waiting is becoming progressively longer.)

Comparing nouns

- We can use words and expressions such as *more, less, fewer* and *not as much/many … as* to compare nouns. For example:

  *There are **not as many** staff members **as** before to help them.*
  *The company wanted **fewer** out-of-town **stores**.*
  *This year customers spent **less money** than last year.*

Grammar reference

5.2 Passive forms

Past, present and future

We make past, present and future **passive forms** using the appropriate form of the auxiliary verb **be + past participle** of the main verb. We use the passive form when we don't know who or what is responsible for an action (the agent), or the agent isn't important, or when we simply want to emphasise the importance of an action rather than the person/thing responsible for doing it. We often use the passive instead of the active form to describe systems and processes and in formal writing (technical manuals, reports, scientific writing, etc.). When we include the agent we use the preposition *by*. For example:

- **Agent not known**

  *First the goods **are packed** and then the lorry **is loaded**.*
  *The goods **were** badly **damaged** in transit.*
  *The shipment **will be delivered** on Friday.*

- **Agent known**

  *The paperwork is done **by our shipping agent**.*
  *The invoice was paid **by the client** last month.*
  *The parcel will be sent **by courier**.*

  Be careful with word order in questions.

  ***Was the bill paid** last week?* (no question word(s))
  *What time **will the shipment be delivered**?* (*what time* = question words)
  *How many people **were involved** in the process?* (*how many* = question words)

  If you want to be more direct, or simply use fewer words, it's best to use the active form.

  Who packed this? (rather than *Who was this packed by?*)

Present Perfect Simple passive

We form the passive of the **Present Perfect Simple** using the auxiliary verb **have + been + past participle** of the main verb.

*This robot **has been designed** to deliver packages.*
*It **hasn't been done** properly.*
***Have** these invoices **been paid**?*

Remember, we often use the adverbs *already*, *just* and *yet* with the Present Perfect Simple. We use **already** to **confirm that something has been done** (often earlier than expected), and we use *just* to **show that something has been done recently**. We usually use **yet** in **negatives** and **questions**. Be careful with the word order with all three adverbs.

*These goods have **already** been sent.*
*Your order has **just** been sent by courier.*
*I'm afraid the order hasn't been fulfilled **yet**.*
*Have the goods been delivered **yet**?*

Passive form of modal verbs

We form the passive with **modal verbs** using *have to / can / could*, etc. + *be* + past participle of the main verb. Remember, we use *have to*, *should* and *must* to talk about obligations and *can*, *could* and *might* to talk about possibilities.

*The orders are processed and then they **have to be packed**.*
*Packages **must be left** in collection lockers.*
*Parcels **can be delivered** by robot or drone.*
*Goods **could be damaged** in transit if they are not well packed.*

5.5 Linking

We can use a range of linking words to introduce differences, but the language structures following them vary. For example:

- **But** connects two statements or phrases when the second one adds something different or seems surprising after the first one. **Though** is like *but* and adds a fact or opinion that makes what you have just said seem less definite or less important.

  *We visited the offices **but/though** the manager wasn't there.*

- **Although** contrasts one clause with another in the same sentence.

  ***Although** we visited the offices, the manager wasn't there.*

- **Even though** is used to introduce a statement that makes the main statement coming after it seem surprising.

  ***Even though** we visited the offices, the manager wasn't there.*

- **Nevertheless** and **However** are often used to begin a sentence. They can also be used in the middle of a sentence to join two different ideas.

  ***However/Nevertheless**, he said he would meet us the following day.*

- **Despite** and **In spite of** are used to say that something happens or is true even though something else might have prevented it. *Note:* You cannot use *of* with *despite*.

  ***Despite** sending the order in early, delivery was still late.*
  ***Despite the fact that** we sent the order in early, delivery was still late.*

- **In spite of** means the same as *despite* but is used differently unless you add *the fact that*. It is usually followed by a noun phrase.

  ***In spite of** all the problems, we still managed to complete the project.*
  ***In spite of the fact that we sent** the order in early, delivery was still late.*

- **Whereas** makes comparisons and says that something is true of one person, thing or situation but is different for another.

  *This supplier offers better quality **whereas** the other one offers better design.*

6.2 Reported speech

When we tell someone what another person said, we usually change the verb tenses from direct speech:

- **Present Simple → Past Simple**

  '*I **want** to go to Harvard Business School.*'

  *She said (that) she **wanted** to go to Harvard Business School.*

- **Present Continuous → Past Continuous**

  '*I'**m studying** to be a software engineer.*'

  *She said (that) she **was studying** to be a software engineer.*

- **Present Perfect → Past Perfect**

  '*I'**ve worked** in the company for three years.*'

  *She said (that) she **had worked** in the company for three years.*

- **Past Simple → Past Perfect**

  '*I **went** to Paris on business.*'

  *She said (that) she **had been** to Paris on business.*

Modal verbs also change: *can* changes to *could*; *will* changes to *would*; *may* changes to *might*, *must* changes to *had to*, etc.

'*I'**ll** phone the client.*'

*She said (that) she **would** phone the client.*

'*We **must** finish the project on time.*'

*She said (that) they **had to** finish the project on time.*

We often use the verbs **say** and **tell** when reporting what someone said. Both verbs can be followed by a clause with or without *that*.

Note: The verb *tell* needs an indirect object or an object pronoun before the clause.

'*We must finish the project on time.*'

*She **said (that)** they had to finish the project on time.*

*She **told me (that)** they had to finish the project on time.*

Changes to personal pronouns and adverbs of time and place

We often need to **change the pronoun** and **the adverbs of time and place** when we change from direct speech to reported speech.

'***We** spoke earlier **today**.*'

*He said (that) **they** had spoken earlier **that day**.*

'*I'll phone **tomorrow**.*'

*She told me (that) **she** would phone **the next day**.*

Other common examples of adverbs of time include:

now → *then*   *yesterday* → *the day before*

Adverbs of place also change. For example:

here → *there*   *this* → *that*

Note: When we report what someone said on the same day, or if a person says something which is still true, we can often retain the verb tense used in direct speech.

'*We **launched** the site in 2012.*'

*He told me (that) they **launched** the site in 2012.*

*He told me (that) they **had launched** the site in 2012.*

Reported questions

- When reporting **yes/no** questions we often use **ask + if/whether**, then change the verb tenses, pronouns and adverbs of time and place if necessary.

  '*Do you enjoy the work?*'

  *I **asked him if/whether** he enjoyed the work.*

  '*Have you been back to Harvard?*'

  *I **asked him if/whether** he had been back to Harvard.*

- When reporting **Wh- questions** we **use the same question word**, then change the verb tenses, pronouns and adverbs of time and place if necessary.

  '*What do you like most about being an entrepreneur?*'

  *I asked him **what he liked** most about being an entrepreneur.*

  '*Why has the business been such a success?*'

  *I asked him **why the business had been** such a success.*

  Note: We do <u>not</u> use question word order or question auxiliary verbs in reported questions.

6.5 Order of information in sentences

Topic words and known information

We usually begin a sentence with the topic word or known information. This is followed by new information and ideas about the topic. For example:

***George Johnson** started making toys for his children.* (*George Johnson* is the topic word or known information so it comes at the beginning of the sentence.)

*George Johnson started **making toys for his children**.* (*Making toys for his children* is the new information and therefore comes at the end of the sentence.)

Common changes

Often other words in a sentence may change. These include:

- **pronouns**.

  ***These toys** were very popular with other parents.* (*These toys* refers back to 'the toys made by George Johnson'. These specific toys are now the topic of this sentence and known information.)

  ***They** wanted to buy the toys.* (*They* refers back to 'other parents'. This was the new information in the previous sentence and is now the topic of this sentence.)

- **using a noun form instead of a verb form**.

  ***Managing finances** carefully from the start is fundamental.* (The topic of this sentence is *managing finances* so we need it at the beginning of the sentence.)

Grammar reference

7.2 Past tenses: Past Simple, Past Continuous and Past Perfect Simple

Past Simple

We can use the **Past Simple**:

- to talk about **finished or completed actions/situations in the past**, or **past events that happen one after the other** (consecutive events). The events may have happened recently or in the distant past.

  I **asked** what the music **was** and he **told** me that it **was** Indian mantra music.

  During my first year of working abroad, I **learnt** the language. In the second year I **got** to know the culture better.

- with **time expressions** such as *ago, yesterday, last week/month/year*, etc. These usually go at the end of the sentence.

  I came here **last year**.

  We started this business venture **a few months ago**.

  There weren't many students in class **yesterday**.

Past Continuous

We can use the **Past Continuous**:

- to talk about **past actions/events that were in progress or happening at the same time**. We often use the Past Continuous together with the Past Simple and with *when* or *while*.

  When I started working, I **was still living** with my parents.

  While I **was living** in Kenya, I discovered that optimism is highly valued.

- to give the **background situation in a story**.

  They **were doing** a course in cultural awareness to improve their communication with international partners.

  The entrepreneur **was running** a village shop at the age of eight but **went bankrupt** twice before he was eighteen.

Past Perfect Simple

We can use the **Past Perfect Simple**:

- to talk about **a finished or completed past action/event that happened before another action/event in the past**. It is often used with the Past Simple.

  Before working as a cross-cultural consultant, she **had lived** in many countries.

  They admitted that they couldn't meet the deadline, although they **had** previously **agreed** to it.

- to talk about **life experience before a point of time in the past**. We often use the adverbs *ever, never, already, yet* and *just* with this usage.

  I had **never** seen this kind of thing before!

  The meeting had **already** begun when we arrived.

- with **time expressions** such as *by the age of, by the time*, etc.

  He had set up his own business empire **by the age of** twenty-five.

  By the time I had learnt about differences when working in Saudi Arabia, it was time to go home.

7.5 First and second conditional

First conditional

We use **first conditional** sentences to talk about **potential consequences of actions**. The usual structure of a first conditional sentence is:

If + present simple, *will* + main verb.

The two clauses can appear in either order.

If people **are** not familiar with the differences, then language problems **will become** more complicated.

He**'ll think** you're rude **if** you **start** with the business chat immediately.

Unless

We can use *unless* in first conditional sentences to mean *if not*:

Unless training is arranged with immediate effect, some projects will probably suffer. (= **If** training is**n't** arranged, ...)

He'll think you're rude **unless** you start with small talk. (= ... **if** you do**n't** start with small talk.)

Second conditional

We use **second conditional** sentences when we are **less certain of potential consequences**. In these situations, we consider the action more difficult to achieve and so less likely to happen. The usual structure of a second conditional sentence is:

If + past simple, *would* + main verb.

Like the first conditional, the two clauses can appear in either order.

If team members **visited** other members in their own countries, they **would be able to** get to know each other better.

We **would arrange** for everyone to meet in Rome **if** we **had** more money.

Note: If you begin a conditional sentence with *if* or *unless*, then you need to put a comma after the conditional clause. You do not need a comma if you start with the main clause.

Grammar reference

8.2 Relative clauses

We can use relative clauses to add extra information to a sentence.

- **Defining relative clauses** add information which is essential.

    David is the one **who/that** won the competition.

    The newspaper **which/that** she likes most is the Financial Times.

    London is **where** they have their company headquarters.

    Nine o'clock is **when** we are meeting them.

    It's Tracey **whose** computer isn't working.

- **Non-defining relative clauses** add information that is extra and not essential.

    Note: We use commas before and after these clauses.

    David, **who** is highly competitive, likes to win.

    The Financial Times, **which** she reads every day, is her favourite newspaper.

    London, **where** we went last summer, is in the Southeast of England.

    At weekends, **when** most people can relax, it's busy at the call centre.

    Tracey, **whose** sister works with me, is the HR Manager.

We usually introduce a relative clause with a **relative pronoun**. The most common relative pronouns are **when, where, which, who, whose** and **that**. The relative pronoun we use depends on whether we are talking about **times, places, things, people** or **possessions**.

- In **defining relative clauses** we can use **that** instead of **who** to talk about people.

    She is the author **who** wrote the book.

    She is the author **that** wrote the book.

- In **defining relative clauses** we can use **that** instead of **which** to talk about things.

    The course **which** starts tomorrow is about leadership in the 21st century.

    The course **that** starts tomorrow is about leadership in the 21st century.

- In **non-defining relative clauses** we can only use **who** to talk about people.

    David, **who** is highly competitive, likes to win. ✓

    David, **that** is highly competitive, likes to win. ✗

- In **non-defining relative clauses** we can only use **which** to talk about things.

    The Financial Times, **which** she reads every day, is her favourite newspaper. ✓

    The Financial Times, **that** she reads every day, is her favourite newspaper. ✗

With **both types of relative clauses** we use:

- **when** to talk about time.

    Nine o'clock is **when** we are meeting them.

    At weekends, **when** most people can relax, it's busy at the call centre.

- **where** to talk about place.

    London is **where** they have their company headquarters.

    London, **where** we went last summer, is in the Southeast of England.

- **whose** to talk about possession.

    It's Tracey **whose** computer isn't working.

    Tracey, **whose** sister works with me, is the HR Manager.

Omission in defining relative clauses

If the relative pronoun refers to the object of the verb, we can omit it in defining relative clauses only.

She is the neuroscientist **who/that** I spoke to at the conference.

She is the neuroscientist I spoke to at the conference.

This is the book **which/that** he recommended to me.

This is the book he recommended to me.

That was the day **when** we first met.

That was the day we first met.

Note: If the **relative pronoun** refers to the **subject of the verb**, we **cannot omit** it:

She is the author **who/that** wrote the book. ✓

She is the author wrote the book. ✗

8.5 Reduced relative clauses

Relative clauses usually have a **relative pronoun** and a **full verb**. For example:

It was decided that all directors **who are serving on the board** should have hands-on experience.

This is a summary of the decisions **which were reached at the meeting yesterday**.

However, sometimes, relative clauses can be reduced. There are various possibilities:

- If the **verb in the relative clause is active**, we can **omit the relative pronoun** and the **auxiliary verb *be*** and **use the** present **participle**.

    It was decided that all directors **serving on the board** should have hands-on experience.

- If the **verb in the relative clause is passive**, we can **omit the relative pronoun** and the **auxiliary verb *be*** and **use the** past **participle**.

    This is a summary of the decisions **reached at the meeting yesterday**.

- If the relative pronoun and the verb *be* are **followed by a prepositional phrase**, we can also **reduce the relative clause**.

    The debate **which was about the disconnect** was lively.

    The debate **about the disconnect** was lively.

    The file **which is on the table** belongs to the boss.

    The file **on the table** belongs to the boss.

125

Additional material

Lesson 1.2 ▸ 2B

Tall organisations have lots of management levels. There is generally more bureaucracy and decision-making is slow and centralised in the top levels of the hierarchy (top-down decision-making). A criticism of tall organisations is that they are slow to innovate and therefore are less competitive. However, there are also many opportunities for promotion. Large complex corporations with a lot of staff are typical examples of tall organisations.

Flat organisations are less hierarchical. There are few levels of middle management. Decision-making is more decentralised and therefore quicker. The lines of communication between staff and senior managers are more direct and two-way (top-down as well as bottom-up). Flatter organisations are said to be more creative and innovative. However, with fewer management levels, there are fewer chances of promotion. Managers can have more responsibilities and stress. Start-ups with fewer staff are typical flat organisations.

Lesson 2.3 ▸ 10A

1. Your company is in the city centre, a 20-minute bus ride from your home. However, it now plans to move to a new industrial estate over an hour away by car. There are always traffic jams getting there because there are no public transport links yet. Ask your father/mother what you should do.

2. You have moved to a new country to improve your language skills and job prospects. You had no idea how lonely you would feel after six months. Your colleagues at work do not socialise outside the office and you have found it hard to make friends any other way because your language skills are still quite basic. Should you just give up and go back to your country? Talk to your flatmates about what to do.

3. You have recently been promoted at work. The job involves managing staff, which you have never done before. Ask some senior managers for their top tips on how to manage staff – a lot of whom are older than you.

Lesson 1.5 ▸ 3A

a Going to conference.
b But may be late Friday.
c Can go Friday.
d Sorry.
e Thanks for email re induction day.
f Dentist appointment at 8.30 that day.
g I'm not free Thursday.

Lesson 1.4 ▸ 5A

Role cards

Read through the information and prepare for the roleplay. You can include any additional information you want.

Student A

Visitor role (Scenario 1)

PROFESSIONAL
Name:	Use your own name
Job:	Sales assistant
Location:	Australia – office in Sydney
Local manager:	Bruce Mansen
Time in company:	7 months
Length of visit:	One week
Number of times in London:	Once before
Project experience:	Zero

PERSONAL
Background:	Originally from Canada
Travel:	Have visited fifteen other countries
Studied:	At university in Canada and Australia
Weather back home:	Wonderful
Plans for the evening:	No plans

Host role (Scenario 2)

Welcome your guest to the meeting and make small talk to put your guest at ease. You can ask questions about your guest's role in the company (e.g. job title, location, manager, experience), how long he/she is in town, whether he/she has been to your city before, where he/she comes from, travel, where he/she studied, the weather and his/her plans for the evening.

Observer role (Scenario 3)

Observe the meeting and notice how the host and guest make small talk. What areas do they perform well in? How could they improve?

Lesson 3.4 ▸ 6B

Interviewers

1. Decide on the structure and working environment of your company. As the interviewer, which parts of the job are your priority?
2. Read the audioscript of the interviews on page 147. Think of four questions to ask the interviewee. Include questions about their qualifications, experience, attitude and personal qualities. Include both open and closed questions.
3. Think about questions the interviewee may ask you and how you will answer them: e.g. *How big is the company? Is the work environment formal or informal? What are the working hours?*, etc.

Additional material

Lesson 2.5 ▶ 3A

To: Kiran Kaur Pannu
Cc: Marisa Shields
From: Ted Vesely
Subject: Re: Exhibition preview sponsored by C&P Partners

Hi Kiran

Thanks for the invite. I'm sorry but I can't come on 22nd November. I'll be away that day.

But this event sounds great and my colleague, Marisa Shields, is interested in coming instead of me. Can you put her name on the guest list?

Cheers! Hope it goes well.

See you soon!

Best

Ted Vesely

Lesson 3.2 ▶ 3

1. What do you like doing at the weekends?
2. Did you have any trouble finding us?
3. Have you ever been in hospital?
4. Do you prefer working independently or in a team?
5. Are you prepared to work long hours?
6. What were your favourite subjects at college/university?
7. Do you plan to have children in the near future?
8. Do you prefer tea or coffee?
9. Tell me about a successful project you've worked on.
10. What is your greatest passion?
11. What's your proudest achievement?
12. Where did you go on holiday last year?
13. What do you know about us / our company?
14. Who was a mentor for you at university / in your previous job?
15. Why don't you eat meat?
16. I'd like to know why you didn't include any references in your CV.
17. Can you give me the phone number of your best friend?
18. Can you tell me about a time when you worked well in a team?
19. We'd like to know why you left your previous job.
20. If you were an animal, what kind of animal would you be?

Lesson 3.4 ▶ 6B

Interviewees

1. Look at the job information and define your transferable skills, in case you don't have everything the company is looking for.
2. Think of the questions the interviewer might ask and prepare your answers: e.g. think about your experience and qualifications, your transferable skills, your personal qualities, etc.
3. Review the expressions and questions in Exercise 5. Prepare three or four questions to ask about the organisation (e.g. its size, location, etc.), the working environment (e.g. if it is formal or informal), the job (e.g. working hours, how performance is measured, etc.) and any other information you would like to know.

Lesson 3.2 ▶ 11A/B & Lesson 3.5 ▶ 1

SALES INTERNS NEEDED FOR IMMEDIATE START

Do you have a degree in business studies or sports education? Are you competitive? Are you looking for an internship with a dynamic, international employer?

At Surfing Technologies we need graduates who are highly motivated, organised and communicative. You must be prepared to learn quickly about the latest trends in surfing and you will be responsible for selling to key clients.

Surfing Technologies are based in Sydney and we have a proven track record in offering our successful interns an exciting career in sales with opportunities to travel around the world. This position is for 3–6 months. No previous experience is required and working hours are flexible.

If you think you have the necessary skills and are passionate about surfing, please send your CV with a covering letter to our Head of Recruitment at hr@surftechnologies.au.

Successful candidates will be called for an interview. We would love to hear from you!

> **Additional material**

Lesson 1.4 ▶ 5A
Role cards

Read through the information and prepare for the roleplay. You can include any additional information you want.

Student B

Observer role (Scenario 1)
Observe the meeting and notice how the host and guest make small talk. What areas do they perform well in? How could they improve?

Visitor role (Scenario 2)
PROFESSIONAL
Name:	Use your own name
Job:	Works in Human Resources, team member
Location:	Germany – Frankfurt office
Local manager:	Peter Mann
Time in company:	One year
Length of visit:	Two weeks
Number of times in London:	Never
Project experience:	Zero

PERSONAL
Background:	Originally from Germany
Travel:	Have visited two other countries
Studied:	At university in Switzerland
Weather back home:	Very good
Plans for the evening:	Would like to see a musical

Host role (Scenario 3)
Welcome your guest to the meeting and make small talk to put your guest at ease. You can ask questions about your guest's role in the company (e.g. job title, location, manager, experience), how long he/she is in town, whether he/she has been to your city before, where he/she comes from, travel, where he/she studied, the weather and his/her plans for the evening.

BUSINESS WORKSHOP 5 ▶ 5B

Kin, the representative of Bot-automation, the Japanese supplier

You are the supplier from Japan. You have quoted an approximate figure of 6.4 million zloty for the delivery and installation of three robots. Considering the size of your client's warehouse, it would be much more efficient with four robots: each robot costs 2.1 million zloty, although you are prepared to negotiate a discount for the after-sales service for this contract. The final price of the deal will depend on the terms and conditions you negotiate.

- Prepare some questions to get to know your client better.
- Explain why they should buy from you. Give examples of good relationships with other clients and referrals.
- Answer the client's questions about payment and delivery terms: confirm it is 50 percent on signing the contract, and 50 percent on delivery and installation. During installation, two engineers adapt the system to the client's needs.
- You offer one installation period as you find this is more efficient for you and the customer.
- You work with very reliable transportation companies. If the robots are damaged in transit, your company is responsible for replacing damaged goods.
- Explain your guarantee terms, i.e. if there is a major technical failure, you will send a maintenance technician to repair it within 36 hours. This work is outsourced to a robotics specialist in the client's country.
- You provide hands-on training in English during installation so that staff learn how to operate the robots and basic maintenance. But this service is provided at an additional cost of 43,000 zloty. The training is normally done by two specialist engineers.

BUSINESS WORKSHOP 4 ▶ 4A

Student A

Mulberry's

Mulberry's is one of the main players in the UK with 16 percent market share. It has 1,370 grocery stores including 760 convenience stores. In recent years it has suffered a decline in sales and its market share has fallen due to competition from the discount supermarkets.

In the last decade the chain invested heavily in building 'big box' outlets away from town centres selling everything from clothes to electronic goods. Analysts argue that the chain needs to focus on its core business and sell off other businesses, such as in-store cafés. The chain's self-service checkouts have cut staff costs. Its online shopping service only makes 1p on every pound because of delivery costs on its minimum order of £25. It stocks 25,000 product ranges including 1,500 own-brand products, which keeps distribution costs high and overwhelms customers. According to Kantar Retail, the average household buys only 400 products a year, with just 41 items in their weekly shop.

Lesson 4.2 ▶ 10

Sample PEST analysis

Introduction
Lagartijo is a small Spanish-based company founded in 2006. It produces handmade leather bags, shoes and accessories and sells these in high-street shops. The products are made with Spanish leather but manufactured in Indonesia, which has cheaper labour costs, and then the finished products are imported back to Spain. Lagartijo also imports products made with rare animal leather, such as shoes, bags and belts made from python and alligator skin.

Political factors
- Spain and Indonesia have good trade relations.
- Spain has a minority right-wing government.

Economic factors
- The Spanish economy is recovering from a long economic crisis and is growing slowly.
- Spain has a long tradition of making leather goods but the industry has mostly closed down.

Social factors
- People's attitude to the use of rare animal skins in consumer products.
- Consumers in Spain are prepared to pay for reasonably priced leather goods.

Technological factors
- Similar products can be manufactured more quickly and more cheaply in Asia.
- More people are shopping online these days.

Conclusion
By outsourcing manufacturing to Indonesia, Lagartijo has been able to keep costs low while at the same time producing high-quality leather goods. It is clearly missing an opportunity to sell its goods online both in Spain and to other countries which value Spanish leather goods as well as luxury products made from more exotic animals. However, there is a threat that conservation movements may begin campaigning against the use of python and alligator skins, which would affect Lagartijo's business. To reduce the risk, the company needs to find out if there is a conservation problem about using these skins and decide whether it wants to continue with these product lines.

Lesson 5.4 ▶ 6B

ATAX (Seller)
ATAX has had a very successful year and is planning to produce more coats (40 percent more next year), and is opening a new factory in southern Turkey. LAURA is an important customer for you. You see the potential for medium- to long-term cooperation, so you want to sign a new contract for next year.

You have five areas to negotiate, with different options in each area:
- number of coats (units) • number of colours
- number of designs • level of discount • terms of payment.

Each area has a number of associated points. If you score over 25 points, you win a personal €5,000 bonus.

	Comments	Points
Number of coats		
2,000	Want to sell maximum number possible.	4
3,000		6
5,000 or more		8
Number of colours		
3	More colours means higher production costs, so a lower number is better.	6
7		4
10 or more		2
Number of designs		
3	More designs means higher production costs, so a lower number is better.	6
6		4
10 or more		2
Discount		
15%	You are growing, so you have some flexibility on price.	6
20%		5
25%		4
Terms of payment		
30 days or below	Managing cash flow is important, so you prefer to have speedy payment of invoice.	7
45–60 days		5
Above 60 days		3

Don't forget to plan the process and who says what in the negotiation.

Lesson 7.5 ▶ 3B

Situation on cross-cultural teams

Staff don't get on – projects delayed / misunderstandings

Suggest/Advise
- get feedback from each team member
- more training
- arrange meeting with whole team
- move members to other teams

Recommendation

Lesson 8.2 ▶ 1

a the process of gradually becoming bigger, better, stronger or more advanced
b someone's general attitude, and the way in which they think about things and make decisions
c determination to do something that you have decided to do, even if this is difficult
d careful thought, or an idea or opinion based on this
e the ability to understand other people's feelings and problems
f the things that a person or animal does

Additional material

Lesson 3.5 ▶ 3A

Do you have a degree in media? Are you very competitive and looking for a fast-paced job working with a small highly motivated team? Then you might be the person MolMedia is looking for.

We want someone who is very ambitious, has excellent communicative skills and is career-focused. Intensive training is given by our Senior Sales Executive so an ability to learn quickly is vital.

The job involves sourcing and developing new client relationships, initially by cold-calling, so good telephone skills are necessary and the hours are flexible.

If you think this is you, send a CV to: marcslater@MolMedia.com

---

To: Marc Slater
From: Tim Worthy
Subject: Re:

Dear Mr Slater

I'm writing about your job. I attach my CV.

I've got a degree in media and need to find a job as quickly as possible.

I like talking on the phone and working flexible hours. My friends tell me that I'm very good at selling things so I think I'll be good at this job.

I look forward to working with you.

Bye
Tim Worthy

Lesson 4.5 ▶ 3B

Problem	Reason	Result
customer complaints	(1) can't contact customer service by phone (2) staff rude and unhelpful	customers cancel contracts
phones not working	raw material supplier	replace handsets
poor network service	not enough phone masts	phones useless in some areas

Lesson 5.5 ▶ 3A

Problem	Details	Demand
late payments	month overdue	immediate payment / court
damaged goods		
wrong goods		
invoice incorrect		
inferior quality		
late deliveries		

BUSINESS WORKSHOP 5 ▶ 5B

Tadeusz (Ted), Company Director of Meble BDB

The Japanese supplier has quoted a figure of 6.4 million zloty for the delivery and installation of three robots. A fourth robot will cost an additional 2.1 million zloty but your maximum budget is 7.7 million zloty. As Company Director, you don't think a fourth robot is necessary for now. The final price of the deal will depend on the terms and conditions you negotiate. You also have to consider the costs of training existing staff or hiring new staff to use the robotics technology.

- Ask the supplier for examples of client satisfaction or referrals.
- Check payment and delivery terms, e.g. they have quoted 50 percent on signing the contract, and 50 percent on delivery. You prefer not to pay the final 50 percent until after a trial period of six months.
- Check how the robots will be transported. They must not be damaged in transit. If they are damaged, or parts are damaged, the item has to be replaced immediately.
- Ask about guarantee terms, e.g. if the automated system breaks down, you want the supplier to send a maintenance engineer to repair it within 24 hours.
- Check the terms for training and after-sales service. You want free maintenance to be provided in the first two years. Training should be given in Polish.

BUSINESS WORKSHOP 1 ▶ 7

To: Clara Jensen
From: Angela Martinez
Subject: Hot-desking* policy

Hot-desking was introduced a year ago when we moved into the new headquarters as a way to make more flexible use of workspace. It has had a positive effect and encourages new relationships and connections. However, there are a few issues:

1. Many people can feel really strongly about where they sit and as a result, most of our hot desks are informally allocated to the same individual on certain days of the week.
2. The organisational hierarchy is reflected in who always gets the best desks. This can cause resentment among staff who feel less valued.
3. People tend to leave personal possessions around on these desks.
4. There is a rush every morning for the best remaining spots.

I recommend we introduce a few principles that can improve our current hot-desking procedures.

*****hot-desking:** a way of saving office space and reducing costs. Staff do not have their own desks. They use an available desk when they are working in the office.

Lesson 7.5 > 3A

Hi Josh

I've just get your email about the supplier problem. Have you tried talk to Salvador Greco, the boss, about the delivery problems? You ought speak to him immediately. However, make sure that you aren't too direct about the business. He'll probably will ask about general things first. He'll think your rude if you start with the business chat immediately.

Unfortunately, unless the problem continues, you will have to find a new supplier. We don't afford to delay production anymore. You'd better to start looking for alternative suppliers if you can't speak to Salvador.

Lesson 5.4 > 6B

LAURA (Buyer)
ATAX is an important supplier for you. The products are generally popular, and you believe you can sell more if you have more colours and designs. You have five areas to negotiate, with different options in each area:
- number of coats (units) • number of colours
- number of designs • level of discount • terms of payment.

Each area has a number of associated points. If you score over 24 points, you win a personal €5,000 bonus.

	Comments	Points
Number of coats		
2,000–2,500	You want a slight increase on last year.	7
2,501–3,500		5
3,501 or more		4
Number of colours		
3	More colours means better sales opportunity, so a higher number is better.	3
6		5
8 or more		7
Number of designs		
3	More designs means better sales opportunity, so a higher number is better.	2
5		3
6 or more		6
Discount		
15%	If you have more designs and colours, you can be flexible on price.	7
18%		6
21% or above		5
Terms of payment		
30 days or below	Managing cash flow is important, so you prefer to have slower payment of invoice.	3
45 days		5
60 days or above		8
Don't forget to plan the process and who says what in the negotiation.		

Lesson 8.5 > 3A

Hi Jose

Sorry you missed this morning's sales department meeting. Just to let you know what was decided. Firstly, we all agreed that Sylvie du Martin should chair the International Sales Managers' meeting next month. We thought she was the best person for this.

Regarding better communication between Production and Sales, we couldn't agree about regular joint meetings, I'm afraid. It seems Production will continue to complain that we give out the wrong information, or accept orders that are too large.

Finally, we've arranged a social event for Friday evening next week because we thought it was a good idea to try and sort out a few problems informally if we could.

BUSINESS WORKSHOP 7 > 2B
Student B

2 Directness vs. indirectness
Being direct is a concept that is often admired in cultures such as the USA and parts of Europe, but not necessarily in the UK. Being polite means different things to different cultures. Being courteous and indirect is a characteristic of many Asian cultures. In China and Japan, for example, people find it very difficult to say 'no' as this would offend the other person, in their eyes, especially when speaking to a person in authority. On the other hand, American, Spanish, German and Polish speakers might appear very direct, even rude to Asians. The concept of being (in)direct can therefore cause friction in business. Remember, not everyone believes you should 'say what you mean'. In practical terms, it is always good business practice to check and confirm what you have understood to avoid ambiguity and misunderstandings, especially concerning delivery dates, or terms and conditions of contracts.

3 Individualism vs. collectivism
The concept of the individual is very strong in Anglo-American cultures, whereas other cultures believe what the 'collective', or group, thinks or does, is more important than an individual's opinion. In the business world, the idea of team-building, for example, is highly valued, where the 'collective' works together as a team with common goals.

> **Additional material**

BUSINESS WORKSHOP 3 ▶ 4A
Student A: Human Resources Manager

Amalia Attwood-Azinheira's CV

Profile
- An experienced Marketing and PR professional
- A creative team player who's highly skilled at problem-solving
- Excellent written communication and language skills

Employment History

Jan 2014–present Communications department of a coffee shop chain
My duties include writing promotional copy and press releases, working with the Communications team in all communications for both social media and the traditional press.

2012–2014 Assistant Store Manager (part-time) of an international coffee shop chain
My responsibilities included the following:
- *Managing the day-to-day food and beverage operations*
- *Ensuring all customers are provided with excellent service*
- *Ordering supplies, inventory control and relationships with suppliers*
- *Organising, training and motivating staff*
- *Assisting the General Manager*

2007–2012 Hotel receptionist, working for an established hotel chain in Lisbon, Paris and London.

2006–2007 Travelled abroad

Education and Qualifications

2012–2014 MA in Communications and Public Relations
2002–2006 BA Degree in Marketing, University of London
2000–2002 A-levels* in French, Spanish, Portuguese and Business Studies, Wandsworth Sixth Form College, London

Computer skills
I am familiar with most office software packages.
Interests
Cinema, classical music, reading, hiking and yoga
Additional information
I have a clean driving licence.

Referees: available on request

*****A-levels:** public exams that students take in England and Wales when they are 17–18

BUSINESS WORKSHOP 1 ▶ 5A
Student B

Employers are enticing staff with informal workspaces

In Poland today leading companies, competing for the most talented employees, want to attract and retain their staff with work environments a cut above traditional offices.

Many Polish millennials – those born in the 1980s and 1990s – like their counterparts in other European countries, are adopting a different approach to their careers. They value teamwork and creativity and are not used to strict hierarchical management. A small but growing number of office developers are attempting to capture this spirit.

The less formal approach to workplace design, now common among high-tech companies in the USA, is a new phenomenon in Central and Eastern Europe. Companies there are now mimicking Google and Facebook. Their offices include areas designed for different types of work, such as creative spaces with walls for writing notes; 'silence boxes', where people can concentrate in peace, as well as relaxation rooms with games consoles and spacious kitchens with full fridges.

The office has to support creativity, conversations and teamwork. Companies have noticed that their workers are much more efficient if no one imposes where they have to work.

Last year KPMG moved its offices to the brand new Gdanski Business Centre. KPMG's website stated that the move was 'not only a change of address but also a step forward in thinking about the company as a workplace'. Indeed, its Warsaw employees brag about having new spacious kitchens, modern conference rooms and a large rooftop terrace.

Standard facilities in modern office blocks today in Warsaw include restaurants, hotel-like lounges in the reception, cycle racks and showers. The new Warsaw Spire, the second tallest building in the Polish capital, offers renters not only 100,000 sq metres of office space but also a green area with ponds, an amphitheatre, art galleries and cafés.

BUSINESS WORKSHOP 3 > 5

18th November

Re: Application for Social Media Manager position

Dear Sir/Madam,

I am writing to apply for the position of Social Media Manager at Media Solutions, as advertised on your website. I believe I would be a real asset to your company: I have a degree in marketing and an MA in Communication and PR. In addition, I have worked in a variety of sectors, from the hotel industry to telecommunications. I'm currently working in the Communications department of a well-known coffee chain.

I consider myself to be reliable, flexible and I have excellent communication and language skills. I speak Portuguese, as well as Spanish and French and I am currently learning Chinese.

Please find a copy of my video CV enclosed.

I look forward to hearing from you with regard to a possible interview.

Regards

Amalia Attwood-Azinheira

To: jobs@mediasolutions.com
From: birtebernsen@yahoo.com
Subject: job as Social Media Manager

Hi!

My name is Birte, and i'd love to work for *medium solutions*. I've seen your web and it looks really intersting. i'm a 'people person': i love social media and spend all my time doing it. I'm not only sociable, but also really creative and I'd get on well with all the team and the clients. My english teacher always said I was great at writing stories, so I'm sure writing reports won't be a problem. Also, I love all kinds of team sports and I'm a martial arts expert. See my video!! It's a bit longer than a minute – sorry ...

Looking forward to hearring from you soon.

Birte Bernsen

📎 ▶ 1.2MB

To: jobs@mediasolutions.com
From: cindycas@gmail.com
Subject: Social Media Manager post | 📎 MOV 1MB

To whom it may concern:

I would welcome the opportunity of working for your company as a Social Media Manager. I have recently completed a degree in business administration and have worked as an intern in the marketing department for local government.

Currently, I'm working as a Customer Service Manager in a call centre. This is a challenging position as I am responsible for a large team, although I enjoy dealing with people and problem-solving on a daily basis.

In addition, I have always kept up-to-date with current social media trends. Please find attached my video CV where I describe my key qualities and skills. I am confident that my skills will prove useful for this post.

I would very much appreciate the opportunity of an interview to find out more about the position and demonstrate how I can be of value to your company.

Best regards

Cindy Castro

BUSINESS WORKSHOP 4 > 4A

Student B

White's is an upmarket retailer with 350 stores and online delivery. It has largely ignored the price war between the major players and discount retailers. Instead of competing on price, it differentiates itself by offering premium food, specialist products and well-staffed stores. The retailer, with a strong reputation for not compromising on quality, had its best results ever last quarter by capturing 5 percent of the UK grocery market. Many consumers go to the discount supermarkets for the essentials, such as tinned goods and cleaning products, and White's for fresh and organic produce, especially meat. White's also has a range of gourmet meals-to-go which are popular with busy customers who don't want to eat out and want to treat themselves. Although they already stock over 10,000 products, the store needs to keep innovating with its own brand products to meet the changing preferences of demanding consumers. Its larger supermarkets are not as profitable as its convenience stores.

> **Additional material**

BUSINESS WORKSHOP 3 > 4A
Student B: Head of Communications

Cindy Castro's CV

PERSONAL SUMMARY

A talented, well-organised and strong performer who has a proven track record of achieving excellent results. I am passionate about raising standards and am committed to furthering my professional development in an organisation that can provide me the opportunity to develop my skills and knowledge in social media.

WORK EXPERIENCE

April 2017 to present	Customer Service Manager in a call centre for a national telecom company. My responsibilities include: • managing a large team • problem-solving and dealing with difficult customers • communicating management directives to staff • ensuring excellent results, according to monthly targets
July to December 2016	Internship in marketing for the Department of Transport in local government in the Philippines – this was a six-month position.

EDUCATION

2014–2018	Degree in Business Administration, Hamburg Business School, Germany – this included a one-year Erasmus exchange programme with the University of Copenhagen
2012–2014	International Baccalaureate*, Santo Tomas School, Manila, the Philippines

SPECIAL INTERESTS

- Captain of the women's hockey team at university
- I sing and play lead guitar in a local rock band.
- I won an award for public speaking while studying for the International Baccalaureate.

Contact information
Email: cindycas@gmail.com   Mobile phone number: +49 40 706 8221

*International Baccalaureate: international school-leaving certificate that students take when they are 17–18

Lesson 6.5 > 3A

Business advice for entrepreneurs

George Johnson gives entrepreneurs advice about setting up a business and says it is different for everyone. His first point is that they must believe passionately in their product or service and love it or they won't be able to sell it. After that, the first thing they should do is conduct extensive market research and listen to feedback. He also says that good planning is vital, especially time management, and that this plan should act as a map for the business. The best piece of advice someone gave him was to be open to advice but to remember that not all advice is helpful and that he should ignore any advice that doesn't feel right. However, entrepreneurs should be ready to ask for advice when they need it. Another important thing is to manage their finances carefully so that they know exactly what their money is doing and this becomes even more important as the company and the amounts of money get bigger. Since he has worked with retailers, George knows that it's very important for entrepreneurs to value their product and not to sell it to retailers at prices which are too low. They need to know exactly what is the best unit price for themselves and keep to it. But without customers a company is nothing, so developing customer relations is very important because without customers a business will fail. Another thing which is important to remember is that it can be frightening when an entrepreneur suddenly discovers that he is a leader and is managing a company. His advice is to learn to trust key people and to delegate work appropriately. This is hard for someone who has been responsible for everything. Finally, it's important to know how hard it is to succeed and that they will probably work harder than they have ever worked.

BUSINESS WORKSHOP 5 > 5B

Tony, the representative of Novarobot, the Singaporean supplier

You are the supplier from Singapore. You have quoted an approximate figure of 6.4 million zloty for the delivery and installation of three robots. Considering the size of your client's warehouse, it will be much more efficient with four robots: each robot costs 2.1 million zloty, although you are prepared to negotiate the price of the fourth one for this contract. But the final price of the deal will depend on the terms and conditions you negotiate.

- Prepare some questions to get to know your client better.
- Explain why they should buy from you. Give examples of good relationships with other clients and referrals.
- Answer the client's questions about payment and delivery terms: confirm it is 20 percent on signing the contract, 30 percent on delivery and 50 percent on final installation. During installation, an engineer adapts the system to the client's needs.
- You offer two installation periods as this allows more flexibility for the client.
- If the robots are damaged in transit, your company is responsible for replacing or repairing damaged goods. However, the goods must be unloaded with care.
- Explain your guarantee terms, i.e. if there is a major technical failure, you will send a locally sourced maintenance technician to repair it within 48 hours.
- You provide training in English during installation so that staff learn how to operate the robots and basic maintenance. This service is provided at an additional cost of 21,000 zloty. The training is done by a specialist engineer. You expect the company to provide their own interpreter.

BUSINESS WORKSHOP 7 > 2B

Student C

4 Linear-active, Multi-active or Reactive cultures

According to cross-cultural expert, Richard Lewis*, Italians, Spaniards, Latin Americans and Arabs are 'multi-active'. They are generally talkative and lively and do many things at the same time. These cultures are known as 'polychronic'. In contrast, the Germans and Anglo–American, are 'linear-active', meaning they have a linear vision of time and action. They like to plan and organise and do one thing at a time – they think this way they are more efficient. These cultures are called 'monochronic'. 'Reactive' cultures are those that value respect and courtesy, as reflected in most Asian cultures. Reactive cultures prefer to listen rather than talk, and take their time to consider proposals carefully.

5 Authority and hierarchy

Behaviour regarding authority can mean that in China the most important or senior person is treated with a great deal of respect, while Anglo–American countries and the Netherlands tend to be less formal with people in authority. These cultures will also have companies with flatter and less hierarchical organisational structures. Nevertheless, we've found it depends on the sector, so an IT company anywhere in the world will usually have a less formal culture than say, a bank or financial institution.

If you bear in mind these five areas and remember the way we do things in our culture isn't the only way, you will connect with other cultures more successfully when doing business around the globe.

* Richard D. Lewis, cross-cultural communication consultant and author, 'When Cultures Collide: leading across cultures'.

Lesson 2.1 > 9A

- In your analysis of the advertisement, first describe the product and the advertisement. Which marketing channels are used? e.g. print, TV, online, product placement, celebrity endorsement (with a famous person promoting the brand).
- Describe the advertising campaign in more detail. Think about these questions: How often does the logo appear? What is the slogan? Who is the target market? Is the product part of the brand's core business, or an example of brand stretching?
- When you compare your analysis with another pair, describe your personal emotional response to the advert and the findings from your class survey.
- Remember to say why you think the advertisements are effective or ineffective. Are your classmates a possible target market? Did people respond emotionally to the advert? How was the advertising campaign memorable?

Lesson 8.5 > 3B

Decisions from Monday's sales meeting	
Point discussed	**Decision**
need customers' view of new product range	ask them to do online survey + offer incentives?
replacement team leader for national sales	John Hedges – previously regional team leader – 2 years
new sales staff lack of training	contact training company immediately to arrange
conference dates	to be confirmed
conference venue	Plaza Hotel or Grand Moon

Additional material

BUSINESS WORKSHOP 7 > 2B

Student A

1 Time

Different cultures have different attitudes to time. In countries such as Germany and Switzerland, people like to be punctual to the minute and will often dedicate specific speaking times in meetings. Certain cultures view time as linear, for example, in Germany, Switzerland, Scandinavia, the UK, the United States and the Netherlands. In Dutch there is the proverb. 'Stay a while, lose a mile'. The idea is not to waste time. However, in Southern Europe, Latin America and the Middle East, relationships and the event are what count, and schedules are less relevant. Time is flexible because of the business relationship. Although it's good to be punctual for business meetings, be aware that meetings might start late and/or over-run in cultures with a flexible attitude to time.

In most Asian countries, people see time as cyclical, as with the life-death cycle. This cyclical, or circular and repetitive, view of time affects the way people make business decisions and may cause conflict in business communication. Westerners, for instance, often want to make a quick decision. Asians, however, always think long term: opportunities and risks need to be assessed carefully, and they need to consider what has happened in the past. We cannot assume business decisions in other cultures will be made in the same way as in our culture. As any person working in sales will tell you, in order to strike a deal, we need to make a connection.

BUSINESS WORKSHOP 5 > 5B

Anna, Logistics Manager of Meble BDB

The Singaporean supplier has quoted a figure of 6.4 million zloty for the delivery and installation of three robots. A fourth robot will cost an additional 2.1 million zloty but your maximum budget is 7.7 million zloty. As Logistics Manager, you think a fourth robot will be a very good investment. The final price of the deal will depend on the terms and conditions you negotiate. You also have to consider the costs of training existing staff or hiring new staff to use the robotics technology.

- Ask the supplier for examples of client satisfaction or referrals.
- Check payment and delivery terms, e.g. they have quoted 20 percent on signing the contract, and 30 percent on delivery. You prefer not to pay the final 50 percent until after a trial period of six months.
- Check how the robots will be transported. They must not be damaged in transit. If they are damaged, or parts are damaged, the item has to be replaced immediately.
- Ask about guarantee terms, e.g. if the automated system breaks down, you want the supplier to send a maintenance engineer to repair it within 24 hours.
- Check the terms for training and after-sales service. You want free maintenance to be provided in the first two years. Training should be given in Polish.

BUSINESS WORKSHOP 3 > 8A

Amalia

This candidate had relevant qualifications, spoke several languages, demonstrated good writing skills and showed a passion for social media; they found she posted photos and articles on social media sites every day. Unfortunately, Amalia was nervous in both the video CV and the interview, so both the Head of Communications and the HR Manager thought she would be better suited to a different kind of position in the company. They were worried she would not come across well when communicating face to face with clients. The HR Manager has kept her CV on file in case a more suitable position comes up in the near future.

Birte

The Head of Communications at Media Solutions wanted to hire Birte because she was very personable, enthusiastic and came across well in the video CV and the interview. However, the HR Manager thought her writing was awful, that she would have difficulty when writing reports and also thought some of the team would find her a little irritating. In addition, they looked into her social media profile and found she had posted some inappropriate videos and posts about her personal life. Birte has since become a very successful personal trainer and YouTuber with a huge fan base.

Cindy

When the company checked Cindy's social media profile, they found she wrote a regular blog about marketing and PR trends. She has now been hired. Why do you think that is?

Lesson 1.4 ▶ 5A

Role cards

Read through the information and prepare for the roleplay. You can include any additional information you want.

Student C

Host role (Scenario 1)
Welcome your guest to the meeting and make small talk to put your guest at ease. You can ask questions about your guest's role in the company (e.g. job title, location, manager, experience), how long he/she is in town, whether he/she has been to your city before, where he/she comes from, travel, where he/she studied, the weather and his/her plans for the evening.

Observer role (Scenario 2)
Observe the meeting and notice how the host and guest make small talk. What areas do they perform well in? How could they improve?

Visitor role (Scenario 3)

PROFESSIONAL
Name:	Use your own name
Job:	Financial officer
Location:	Canada – office in Toronto
Local manager:	Pauline Jones
Time in company:	Nine months
Length of visit:	Six days
Number of times in London:	Never
Project experience:	One small project at university

PERSONAL
Background:	Originally from San Francisco, USA
Travel:	Have visited three other countries
Studied:	At university in the USA
Weather back home:	Cold at the moment
Plans for the evening:	Wants to go to see a soccer game in London

BUSINESS WORKSHOP 3 ▶ 4A

Student A and B

Birte Bernsen's CV

1 _____

birtebernsen@yahoo.com
Skype name: birte.bernsen

2 _____

I have just completed a degree in marketing and event management, specialising in advertising events and consumer analysis. I am an enthusiastic team player with excellent communication and leadership skills. I enjoy working with others and am always ready to take on new challenges. I am looking for the chance to work for a dynamic international organisation.

3 _____

• Taekwondo instructor for children aged 5–12

• Monitor on a summer camp, responsible for organising sports and other activities for children.

• Volunteer work for a charity that provides help for people with eating disorders.

4 _____

2014–2018 BA Degree in Marketing with Event Management, University of Copenhagen

2011–2013 School-leaving Certificate

5 _____

Social media (I write my own blog), martial arts, black belt in Taekwondo, sports and health, dancing Lindy Hop and travelling.

BUSINESS WORKSHOP 4 ▶ 4A

Student C

C&C is a leading discount supermarket chain with 650 stores in the UK. It sells a very limited range of items – under 800 mostly packaged products – and offers no services, such as home delivery or online shopping.

For the first time ever the company gained a 6 percent share of the grocery market last year and sales reached a record £7.7 billion. However, profits fell as the price war ate into the retailer's profit margins. Its strategy is to sacrifice short-term profit margins in order to gain a bigger market share. Analysts believe C&C's cheapest price guaranteed strategy will not allow it to grow in the future.

A recent survey of 50,000 customers revealed general dissatisfaction with older store design, signage, lighting, cleanliness, cramped aisles and check-out areas. Customers also want more fresh food options which would involve investment in chilled space.

Videoscripts

1.1.1
P = Presenter   A = Arti   N = Nick
J = John   M = Melanie   R = Ray

Presenter: The structure of an organisation is key to its success. It is important that individuals and teams understand their roles and responsibilities within the organisation. Business leaders have to ensure that different departments and operations coordinate and work together. The principle of clear structure applies to all companies – start-ups, small and medium enterprises as well as multinationals.
This company is one of the world's leading news organisations. It creates and distributes news and information on television and digital platforms, 24 hours a day, 7 days a week. Its teams operate all over the world.
The newsroom is the hub of the operation. Staff here are responsible for coordinating the teams gathering news.
A: My name is Arti Lukha and I'm a news editor. My job involves news-gathering for a major news organisation in Britain. I'm in charge of our daily news-gathering operations. I am responsible for how we deploy our reporters, our producers, our cameras and our satellite trucks.
P: When Arti decides to follow a particular news story, she gives a reporter the task of covering it. The reporter is then in charge of the team that produces a report on that story.
N: Hello, I'm Nick Thatcher and I'm one of the general news reporters here and I work to the main bulletins that go out throughout the day. It's all about teamwork. If you're working with a camera operator then together you're making sure you're getting the right pictures on the ground. Back at base you're being supported in ensuring that if you need pictures from the library – from file if you like – then those are available to you in good time as well. And those conversations are ongoing all the time between you and the editor to make sure you're telling the story in the best possible way.
P: The news bulletins are broadcast live.
J: My role as programme director is to lead the production team and to be responsible for the technical and creative execution of the programme. Teamwork is absolutely crucial in the build-up and during the programme. There is no real one role who can do it by themselves, so we are very tightly coordinated. My role as director is to be conductor of that orchestra.
P: In a large organisation like this there are a number of departments working behind the scenes to ensure the company runs well. Managing the staff is a key function.
M: I'm Melanie Tansey and I'm the director of human resources. So I'm responsible for running the human resources team, making sure that we're delivering on all our strategic and operational priorities for the company.
P: The finance department is another important part of the organisation.
R: I'm Ray Snelling and I'm the finance supervisor. I look after all of the billing for our customers and also collection of debts and maintaining customer queries and making sure our customers are happy. It's important that we make sure the payments are coming in on time – it can impact on payments we are making to our suppliers. So if we've got a lot of costs we're incurring on a specific project, we need to make sure we're getting cash in to support that. So it can affect us quite a lot.
P: These are just some examples of the roles in some of the departments in the company. There are many more such as marketing and support all working together to ensure the organisation runs smoothly and successfully.

1.3.1
M = Matt   S = Stefanie   J = James   A = Alistair

M: Pro Manage is a global company, providing project management training qualifications. I'm Matt Farnham, head of UK operations ... based here in London. We're in the middle of launching some new online project management courses ... I'm the project lead, but the team are in Germany, India, Japan, Mexico ... it's an international effort. Pro Manage is a great place to work, great people. I suppose you'd describe me as the boss, but I don't like people to think of me that way ... I try to be quite open and flexible in the way I do things. I'm pretty informal really ...
S: I'm Stefanie Hatke and I run the Pro Manage German office ... based mainly in Cologne, but I also work from time to time in Switzerland. We're in the middle of a very important product launch and as the main technical expert, I've been asked to travel to London to meet with the project lead. We're very busy at the moment ... which is positive. I consider myself to be efficient and effective, I like to be well organised and focus on getting the job done – that's what the company pays me to do.
M: Morning, boys.
J: Oh, Matt, hold up. I've got a hard copy of the prospectus that needs approving. It's just a sample, but if you could let me know that the layout's basically OK ...
M: Sure, have to wait until later though, Stefanie from the German office is coming in this morning ...
J: Ah, Stefanie! I know her, she's excellent.
A: She's rude, if you ask me. Everything's urgent with her; she's always on the phone demanding – never asks how you are or has a human conversation.
M: That's a bit alarming, she doesn't sound very much like a team player.
J: I get on fine with her. She's just very work focused, that's all, but she gets results, she's a good person to have on your team.

1.3.2
M = Matt   S = Stefanie

M: Stefanie, hi, I'm Matt.
S: Hello.
M: Coffee?
S: What?
M: Can I get you a coffee?
S: Oh, no, thank you. Do you have power?
M: Listen, why don't you come with me? I can show you the office and introduce you to a few people.
S: But I've got everything ready to discuss ...
M: Yeah, but it'll only take a few minutes ... do you know the design guys?
S: No. Well, yes, a bit, I met James in Germany.
M: Great, well, let's go and say hello. So ... first time in London?
S: No, I was here several times.
M: Great. Good trip over?
S: Yes.
M: Great. Ah, here they are. Guys, this is Stefanie. You've met before, right?
J: Yes, in Cologne, *Guten Tag*, great to see you again.
S: Hi.
A: I'm Alistair. Good to finally meet you in person.
S: Ah, yes, hello Alistair. Excuse me.
M: No worries.
J: How's it going so far?
M: Hard work, to be honest. She's been very quiet, a bit ... serious. You need people skills for a job like this.
A: Told you.
J: Honestly, I wouldn't worry about it, she is a bit serious, but just needs time. She's actually very nice, just very results focused.
M: I was trying to be informal, friendly, positive ... you know, focus on relationships first. But Stefanie really didn't seem very comfortable at all. As it turns out, though, I think she's starting to understand how we do things at the London office, she sent me an email to say that she really enjoyed the visit.
S: It was a bit unclear and confusing for me at the beginning, I'm used to getting down to work, not socialising in the office. But I do see that having strong relationships is a benefit when working on a project like this ... I'm planning on moving to London for three months, it will be good to get to know the team better and know more about Matt's way of working.

1.3.3
C = Charlotte   M = Matt   S = Stefanie

M: Stefanie, hi. I'm Matt Farnham, Head of UK Operations. I'm glad we could arrange this meeting.
S: Yes, me too.
M: OK, shall we make a start? You've only got two hours – is that right?
S: Yes, that's right.
M: OK well, let's focus on getting up to date with the project, there are a few issues I'd like to discuss.
S: Very good.
M: If we have some time at the end, I can introduce you to a few of the team. I've prepared a short agenda, if that's OK?
S: Ah, excellent.
M: Let's start with India; as you can see, we might be about to run into a problem ...
S: By when did you say?
M: 24th of November ....
C: Sorry to interrupt.
M: No, that's OK.
C: Taxi's waiting outside.
M: Thanks, Charlotte. OK, so we need to leave it there. I'll email you all those dates later on and we can continue on the phone tomorrow.
S: Thank you. Sorry to be in a rush like this.
M: No, don't worry ...
S: I need to organise another visit to meet everyone ... maybe we could discuss that tomorrow?
M: Yes, let's do that. Thanks for coming and ... have a safe trip!
S: I will, thank you.
I very much enjoyed my trip to London, yes. I had a very productive meeting with Matt. I think that we'll work well together.
M: She seemed fine, but I can't say that I learnt anything about her. She's clearly very capable, but I'm not sure that she's the right person to take on a project like this ... I need to get to know her better as a person ... We won't have a chance to meet again for at least a couple more months so, no, it's not ideal really.

1.3.4
So, we've seen that people have very different ways of managing first meetings. One is not better than the other. In fact, both have advantages and disadvantages depending on the situation. With the relationship style, you can start to build trust; but it can look unprofessional to be too friendly for too long. With the work style, you can be more efficient more quickly. But maybe you can look rude or impolite to others.
So, to handle first meetings is not easy. But there are a few things you need to think about.
Firstly, know your own communication style; know how you like to do things.
Secondly, understand the communication style of the other person. You can do this in different ways. You could ask someone who knows the person in advance of the meeting, like Matt did. Or, just observe carefully when you meet the person – what they say, what they do.
Finally, think about and decide on the best communication style to have a positive impact on the other person.

2.1.1
J = Jean-Christophe Babin   S = Silvio Ursini   P = Peter York

J: To pave the way for growth we needed to speak to a-, a broader and aspirational base of clients, which probably with jewellery would come much, much later, and so we have added products at a much lower price point as you would ever dream for a piece of jewellery.
S: At the end of the '90s the company had jewellery, watches, accessories and fragrances. And then we-, we thought about uh how can we interact uh in a more intimate way with our customers. And uh this idea of doing a very small collection of ultra-luxury hotels came about. I was in a taxi, and an artist who's a friend of mine gave me a call and said, 'You have to see this

place,' so I turned the taxi around and it was love at first sight. The area used to be monasteries and cloisters, and adjacent to our garden is the Botanical Gardens in Milan, which is a hidden gem in–, in the city. There was a building which used to be a convent, uh part of it uh very old, from the 1600s, part of it more recent from the 1970s, and uh we set about uh redesigning it, completely changing its image.
J: In London we have a 25-metres pool that you would never expect uh from a hotel that small, so in that way uh you create, I mean, a sequence of unexpected experience which eventually will create uh a unique emotional memory when you get out of it.
P: There's a lot of bad history about brand extensions. If you over-extend your brand, you spread it thin, you go into areas where you're less credible. At the end, if you overdo it, your brand is devalued. I think the brands which are most careful have the longest future.
S: The most frustrating thing in this project has been um the fact of uh finding so few locations that were appropriate. My strongest advice would be do something only if you have something to say. If you see an opportunity to do something in novelty and relevant, then that's a–, you know, that's a beautiful energy that will make it into a success. If you sit cold-blooded and start saying, 'OK, let's venture into this business, and what are we gonna do? Let's copy the competitors,' for me the customer ultimately will read between the lines and–, and punish you.

2.3.1 M = Matt D = Dan S = Stefanie P = Paula

M: It's a busy time, we're right in the middle of launching a new series of online project management courses ... exciting, but also very challenging ... International projects can complicate life in so many ways ... everyone working separately and in different time zones ... for me, the number one priority at this stage is to create a real team ...
D: I've got October 12th, 24th and then November 8th, so if those are the dates that you have ...
S: One minute Dan, Matt has arrived.
M: Hi, Dan.
D: Hey there.
M: Not late am I?
S: No ...
D: Not at all, we're just running a bit ahead of time.
P: Hello! It's Paula!
M: Hi Paula.
M: Hi Paula, it's Matt, we've got Dan and Stefanie with us.
P: Hi. Hi, everyone.
M: Excellent, everyone's here. So this is our first meeting as a team. As I'm sure that you all have seen on email, most of the programming work for the Mexico part of the project will be handled by our U.S. IT department. We're having a call with them next week so I thought we could have a brief chat today to plan our priorities for that conversation. Dan is from the US, and knows the people in IT, and is on the call because I would like his advice. But, Stefanie, do you want to start? Priorities for you?
S: OK. I've worked on similar online projects to this in Germany, also working with the US sometimes, I think that we need to be careful about time and budget. These are the top priorities; making sure that they respect the schedule and don't go over budget; we can discuss other things as the work moves forward. But we need the US to deliver on time and on budget for Mexico.
P: That sounds like great advice. This project is really exciting for Mexico as online learning is starting to become big here ... I've never worked with the US so I really think your experience can help us, Stefanie.
D: Totally disagree. I respect your experience, Stefanie, yes, budgets and timing are important, but I was actually an IT lead over here in the past;

I've delivered over a hundred projects to the U.S. market and in Mexico; and I'm telling you, our focus should absolutely be on quality. If you get the quality wrong, you've got very unhappy customers. And we want happy customers.
P: Mmm, a high standard of final product is very important for us ...
D: It's key. Quality should be your number one priority.
S: But I think that we have to focus on timeline and costs. We can evaluate the work later ...
D: Sure, but they're not the main thing ...
M: OK. Look, I think we can all agree that standards are important, but delivering on time is important too, budgets for projects are very tight at the moment so ...
D: Quality is what wins customers, quality is what will get their attention.
M: ... So, Stefanie, let's take a look at your proposed schedule and costing, and then we can discuss quality. Is that OK?
Right then, thanks everyone, we'll all meet again at the same time next week. Bye.
P: Thank you.
S: I'm not sure, I'm really not sure.
M: About what?
S: Dan. He's just so arrogant. 'Quality', 'quality', 'quality'. I'm not sure that I can work with him.
M: Look, this is the first time you've talked. I'm sure you'll find a way. Why don't you just try?
S: Could *you* manage the U.S. IT side of things? I'd prefer to work with Paula and the Mexico roll-out. I really like Paula.
M: Well, hang on, let's take some time to think about this ...

2.3.2 S = Stefanie M = Matt

S: But how can we be a team if we don't listen to each other? I'd be happier if I could take Mexico and leave you to deal with Dan and the US.
M: Look, Dan's a strong character ... but I know him pretty well and can handle him. Maybe it would be better for you to just focus on Mexico and let me worry about Dan. It'll be easier if you work with Paula, the two of you get on well.
S: We do. Thanks Matt, I just think that Dan and I are too different, you know, sometimes personalities just clash a bit.
M: OK, let's do that ... I'll call Dan and explain.
S: Thanks, Matt.
Oh, Matt, do you have a moment?
M: Sure, what's up?
S: I have a problem with the project.
M: What is it? Problems with schedule or costs?
S: Not exactly. It's quality. And I know, I know, this was Dan's big concern. He was right, the quality isn't good enough.
M: Have you tried talking to him?
S: I spend all my time with Mexico.
M: Do you want me to set up a call?
S: Please.
M: OK. You need to be able to keep in touch with Dan yourself, we're all on the same team, don't be afraid to ask his advice where you need it.

2.3.3 S = Stefanie M = Matt

S: But how can we be a team if we don't listen to each other? I'd be happier if I could take Mexico and leave you to deal with Dan and the US.
M: I'm not comfortable with that ... I think it's important for you to work with Dan.
S: We're just so different.
M: Yes, you are, but that's why I think you'll make a strong team, you have different skills. C'mon ... why don't you try?
S: ... It's just always all about him.
M: Look, I agree that he sometimes communicates a little ... strongly. But he knows what he's talking about ... and it would be a great opportunity for you to learn about the U.S. market ... y'know, that could be career-changing for you ... As you move up it's important to show that you can manage different kinds of people, different personalities. Look, if you need any help, I'm here to support you.

S: OK. Sure. I'll try.
M: I think it's the right decision. Let's have another chat with him, I'll organise a call.
Stefanie!
S: Good morning.
M: Just wanted to ask how things are with Dan.
S: Hmm. It's OK. I find it much easier working with Paula, we get on really well together. It's a bit more difficult with Dan but, to be fair, I am learning from him.
M: Oh yeah?
S: Yeah, we did end up having some issues with quality control. There are some delays.
M: Ah.
S: Yes, as Dan said ... but he's really on top of it, and with the two of us working together ... we'll be fine, I'm sure.
M: Great, let me know if you need anything from me.
S: Will do.

2.3.4

Successful teamwork depends on many things: a clear task, competent people, enough resource, and different people with different skills. But it's not always so easy to work with people who are different from us. So what do we need to do to make a diverse team really work?
Firstly, we have to make an effort. When Stefanie worked with Dan in Option B, she found it really challenging and she didn't like Dan's communication style at the beginning. She had to work really hard to build that relationship. She needed to be patient and make an effort, but in the end, she learnt a lot and the team did much better.
Secondly, people will need advice and support when working in an international team with different people – it can be really tough. So we need to be there for others with support, sometimes advice, sometimes just listening – either as a manager or as a colleague.
And finally, if you're giving colleagues advice about dealing with other people, you can advise them to be safe – to just work with people like them – as Matt allowed Stefanie to do in Option A – it's easier in a way. My own advice would be to encourage people to think positively about diversity, and try to engage with different types of people – it's more challenging, but may be a better learning experience and may be better for teamwork.

3.1.1 P = Presenter JC = James Caan
S = Simon Dolan E = Esther J = John Lees
I = Interviewer

P: The job market is very competitive. People who want to progress their career need to stand out from the crowd. Usually, the first thing a potential employer sees is a CV or a résumé. This is the jobseeker's opportunity to advertise experience and skills, and also to show an employer their character or personality. So, what do the experts say about writing the perfect CV or résumé?
This is Esther. She is a nineteen-year-old student. She is applying for internships to gain experience in the business world.
James Caan is an entrepreneur who founded a successful recruitment business. He has agreed to help Esther.
JC: I think one of the biggest problems, I think when you're young, is that everybody says 'But you've got no experience, how do you add any value?' I think what you've got to be able to do is present yourself as somebody who can walk in and make a difference now.
P: But James doesn't think that Esther is selling herself well with her CV. Esther needs to sort out her CV. Simon Dolan is a very straight-talking entrepreneur. Esther goes straight to Simon's office. The first thing Simon notices on Esther's résumé is a spelling mistake.
S: What's the main thing that strikes you on here? So, if we've got ... this second line down, have a look there. That word. What is it?
E: Intermediate.

Videoscripts

S: If you can't spell that right, what hope have I got employing you and expecting you to get your first few emails and go through the door to a client?
P: The next key point is staying focused in what you say on the CV or résumé.
S: I don't really care about the fact that you enjoy socialising with your friends, you go to the gym. What I care about is how you're going to help me run my business better.
P: Expressing personality is a key to getting employed. Companies look for so-called soft skills like commitment, flexibility and imagination, as well as hard skills like knowledge and diplomas. Next stop for Esther is a careers coach who can help her get that kind of soft information across. John Lees has read thousands of CVs and résumés and knows all the mistakes.
L: I saw a CV where the candidate listed under interests, 'I enjoy eating pizza'. It's not impressive.
P: The next challenge is how to stand out from the competition.
L: Graduate CVs make the same mistakes over and over again. They use clichéd language. So everyone says 'I'm a team player', 'I'm a self starter', 'I'm highly motivated'. And if you use the same language as everyone else, all that shows is that you are exactly the same as every other candidate.
P: Esther has taken all the advice and presents her reworked CV back to Simon.
E: I would very much appreciate the opportunity of an interview to find out more about the role and to demonstrate how I believe I could be of value to your company.
S: Perfect. That's better than 99.9 percent of the CVs that we get in. You would definitely, definitely, definitely get an interview, here or anywhere. Really good job.
P: Two weeks later Esther's new CV has already had an effect. She has an interview for an internship. It has gone well.
I: I thought Esther came across as very well prepared for the role and I'll certainly be recommending her to my partners for a second interview here.
P: Getting a job is a job in itself. You've just got to get out there and make it happen.

3.3.1 P = Paula M = Matt A = Alistair J = James

P: I flew into London from Mexico City yesterday. The first thing in my diary is to meet with Matt, who wants to go over the Mexico launch of our new online courses.
Matt sounded a little tense when we spoke on the phone, but British people always sound tense! I'll tell him exactly what I feel about how things are going – I can focus on results when I need to, but we Latin Americans like to always express our feelings first. You need to be honest in life, don't you?
M: I bumped into Paula's old line manager at an international event recently and quite frankly I have some concerns. Paula's over in the UK this week so I've asked her to come in and see me. He mentioned issues raised around Paula's ability to meet targets and perform as part of a team … I'm a little worried about it so I need to understand what's gone wrong … if I need to replace her, I need to do it soon.
P: Hi!
A: Paula! Where did *you* come from?
P: Mexico, of course … I came all the way …
J: How long are you here for?
P: … just to bring you these! I'm just here for the week, but I have to see Matt now and I'm already late. Let's catch up later, bye … Good morning!
M: Good morning, how are you?
P: I'm good thanks.
M: How was the flight?
P: Long, but good. And I'm excited to be here in London.
M: Excellent, come on, let's go and get a coffee and catch up.

3.3.2 M = Matt P = Paula

M: I wanted to talk to you this morning about the online courses launch. Obviously you know how important it is.
P: Of course. We're working really hard every day to make sure that it's a success in Mexico. And everywhere else too.
M: I know. How about timing? Do you think you're going to have everything ready by the deadline?
P: Yes. Everything's fine.
M: Confident about that?
P: Yes. Where's this coming from?
M: After you. I recently bumped into Julio Gonzales, and he mentioned something about deadlines on your last project. Is there anything I need to be concerned about?
P: Oh, not this again. Julio's incompetent. Totally incompetent. And he likes to blame other people for his mistakes.
M: But … Do you want milk?... It *is* true that you missed all of your deadlines last quarter, isn't it?
P: That wasn't *my* fault. I wanted to take extra time to make sure we weren't rushing a complicated project. Julio didn't want to listen to me. Everything got delayed and so we missed the target, yes.
M: Right. So you had a disagreement with your manager and held up the project?
P: Er … no, that's not what I said. And I don't see what it's got to do with the online launch in Mexico.

3.3.3 M = Matt P = Paula

M: I wanted to talk to you this morning about the online courses launch. Obviously you know how important it is.
P: Of course. We're working really hard every day to make sure that it's a success in Mexico. And everywhere else too.
M: I know. How about timing? Do you think you're going to have everything ready by the deadline?
P: Yes. Everything's fine.
M: Confident about that?
P: Yes. Where's this coming from?
M: After you. I recently bumped into Julio Gonzales, and he mentioned something about deadlines on your last project. Is there anything I need to be concerned about?
P: Oh not this again. Julio's incompetent. Totally incompetent. And he likes to blame other people for his mistakes.
M: OK, why don't you tell me a bit more? You say he's incompetent. How would you describe a competent manager?
P: Well, a good manager should support their team and listen to their team. If someone thinks that something should be done differently, maybe they're right.
M: OK … Do you want milk? … So it's important for you, as a team member, to be involved in decision-making, right?
P: Yes, of course. We missed those deadlines because I wanted to take extra time to make sure we weren't rushing a complicated project, and Julio didn't want to listen to me, so everything got held up.
M: Why? Why did you have concerns about the project being rushed?
P: There were too many things that all had to happen at the same time, it was just moving too quickly. It was obvious that we were going to miss things.
M: What do you mean by 'too many things'? Do you think you might have managed a bit better if there had been greater planning or more support, for example?
P: Probably. It was just too much at the time.
M: OK, that's useful to think about. I'm sure we'll make a success of this project … you know I like to involve the team in decision-making, so I'm trusting you to let me know if there's anything we need to change or do differently for Mexico. Thanks for the chat. I think it was important to talk this through.
P: No problem. I think it's good that we can talk like this and, yes, I'll let you know my thoughts on how things are progressing in Mexico.

3.3.4

Listening actively isn't easy. We often focus too much on facts and potentially miss key information that's being communicated about feelings. On the other hand, if we focus too much on listening for feelings, we might miss important facts.
There are a number of things we can do to become more effective listeners.
Firstly, we can listen carefully to identify those key words in a sentence which can give us more information about how someone is feeling and what's important for them. So when Paula was talking to Matt she used words like *incompetent* and *rushing* and said they were trying to do *too many things*.
Following on from that, once we've identified these key words, we can try to understand what the person really feels by asking clarifying questions, such as 'Why do you say "too many things"?'
Another point to make is that it's very useful to summarise and to check our understanding before moving on, like Matt did in Option B when he said, 'So it's important for you, as a team member, to be involved in decision-making, right?'
And finally, be open. Truly listen to what the other person is saying. If we only focus on what <u>we</u> want to talk about, we might miss something important.

4.1.1 P = Presenter J = Joel Hills I = Irene Rosenfeld

P: When business leaders develop strategies to tackle problems, they often have to take risks. Nobody can predict the future, but businesses do have to anticipate it and make judgements. The Kraft Heinz company based in the US is a major player in the food industry. Over 90 years, Kraft built up a portfolio of well-known food brands including confectionary, biscuits, snacks and dairy products. In the first decade of the 21st century, Kraft's performance was poor. Markets lacked confidence in the company's growth prospects. Its profits were disappointing. Kraft's products were less appealing to a new generation of consumers.
J: It was seeing demand for the processed food and drinks that it manufactured from Dairylea all the way to Oreo biscuits decline. And that the profit margin – the amount of money it was making for every unit of sales – had been squeezed almost to the thinness of a piece of paper.
P: This was only the first of Kraft's problems. The second issue that Kraft had to tackle was that it relied too heavily on its home U.S. market. That meant it was missing opportunities in fast-growing emerging markets around the world. The company's third problem was that its costs were too high. That meant it was not making enough profits on its sales. Kraft's management came up with a bold plan to tackle these issues. It started with a takeover bid for the chocolate maker Cadbury. Cadbury had a 200-year history of making chocolate in the UK. Its products were well established around the world, especially in emerging markets.
J: There was clearly an attraction of having an even larger portfolio of internationally recognised brands that they could seek to take into different markets. So inevitably attracting a bigger international audience was part of Kraft's interest in Cadbury's.
P: Kraft took a gamble that combining the operations of two established companies would be successful and solve another one of its problems.
J: Kraft's primary interest in Cadbury was it enabled it to – because it became a bigger company – essentially cut costs. Where there was overlap between the two companies it found a way of saving money and increasing therefore the profit margin that it was able to get from each one of its products.

P: The second stage of the strategic solution was a merger. Kraft merged with another food giant – Heinz – and became the Kraft Heinz company. The merger created the world's fifth-largest food company. As with the Cadbury deal there was an opportunity to cut costs. There were other potential advantages which helped to solve Kraft's problems. Heinz was considered more innovative in its development of new product lines that met changing consumer preference.
The immediate results were positive. The Kraft Heinz company's share price rose seventeen percent on news of the merger. The combined company has been successful in cutting costs. Looking at the Kraft story it is clear the solutions involved considerable risks. Takeovers and mergers do not always work. Irene Rosenfeld was Kraft's chief executive. She was responsible for the company's strategy.
I: I think there were a number of folk that were questioning our acquisition of Cadbury. We said it was going to be important to us to expand our portfolio, to expand our footprint, particularly in developing markets. And it's played out that way. We're very much on track with the integration. It's enabled us to outperform our peers around the world.
P: For Kraft Heinz it seems that the risks paid off. But finding solutions to large corporate problems is not straightforward and taking risks can lead to business failures as well as successes.

4.3.1 K = Kenji   A = Alistair   M = Matt   J = Jack
A: Good morning.
K: Good morning, how are you?
A: Yeah, fine thanks, you alright?
M: Life is very busy at the moment. There's just so much to do and coordinate. Here, Germany, Mexico, Japan. I spend half my time on the phone these days, dealing with the project … it's like my workload just doubled overnight. Plus, as project lead, I have to host the regional managers when they come to London. We had Paula in from Mexico recently and now Kenji's over from Japan … it must be tough on Paula and Kenji, they're completely new to international projects.
J: Knock, knock … are you not answering your phone today?
M: Jack. Sorry. Was that you a few minutes ago?
J: You look a bit tired mate, what's up? Having fun with the new markets project?
M: No. I mean yes. Overall, so far so good. I've just got loads of work and I'm getting more and more concerned about what's going on in Japan.
J: What do you mean, 'concerned'? Isn't Kenji here at the moment?
M: They're running about three weeks behind schedule, and I just don't see how we're going to make up the time.
J: Three weeks is not a concern, it's a disaster. What's going on?
M: Well, hold on. It's complex. Kenji doesn't have a great deal of experience, Stefanie is busy with Mexico, so no time for Japan and, yeah, we're behind.
J: Three weeks behind.
M: I'm going to talk to Kenji about it later.
J: I suggest you go over there and have some strong words sooner rather than later. Tell him that he needs to perform or he's out. A bit of straight talking wouldn't do any harm.
M: I know, I know. But it's Japan, you can't do 'straight talking' or you'll offend everyone.
J: Matt, you can't stereotype like that. Kenji's a professional. You need to tell him to his face what you expect and when you expect it.
M: Look, you may be right … but the guy's trying. Shouting at him isn't my style; I think I'd prefer to take a more gentle approach.
J: Yeah, but being gentle often gets you nowhere. If you don't fix this soon, you're going to have senior management complaining. Anyhow, it's your call … you know what I would do.

4.3.2 M = Matt   K = Kenji   J = Jack
M: Kenji, I need to have word.
K: Yes?
M: I'll come directly to the point as we need to find a solution. I've been going over our schedules this morning and the Japan side of this project is running more than three weeks late. It's a major delay, I'm not happy about it.
K: Aha, OK, I understand it is not ideal but I am working very hard to put things right. It's not necessary to worry.
M: I do worry Kenji and, no, it's not simply 'not ideal', it's a serious problem. As I'm sure you've seen since you've been over here, we have a lot of resources dedicated to Japan. If you delay, there's a planning impact here.
K: OK, I understand your concern, but we don't have all the required resources in Japan.
M: I don't agree at all. We discussed resources in detail at the start of the project and it's very late in the day to be having this kind of discussion. I've had a word with Stefanie and I'm going to send her over to Tokyo for a couple of weeks. I think that you could benefit from her experience. If we don't resolve this now, we are risking the whole project.
K: OK.
M: Right. Stefanie has been briefed and she will talk to you about this tomorrow and make arrangements.
K: OK. And thank you … see you later.
J: Hey.
M: Oh, hi, how're things?
J: I was thinking about you, how did that Japan business go?
M: It wasn't easy. I took your advice and was pretty tough on Kenji.
J: Tough guy. And?
M: He was pretty quiet, actually, didn't say much. I sent Stefanie over there last week and I've spoken to him since then, he seems very grateful, said it was strong feedback but that he'd learnt from it. He said that he'd try to be more open about issues, going forward.
J: Good stuff. What did I tell you?

4.3.3 M = Matt   K = Kenji   J = Jack
M: Morning Kenji, how are you doing? How's the family?
K: Very well, thank you.
M: Listen, Kenji, have you got a few minutes for a quick chat?
K: Certainly.
M: I know that you're very busy, and I hear that things are going very well in some areas, but I think it's good to update on the project. It's a very demanding situation for you and there's a slight delay on your part of the project, right? Just over three weeks.
K: Yes. We are struggling a bit with resources. There are some other projects that management in Japan wants to take priority, it's difficult to balance.
M: I understand. Look, how do we go forward to get back on track. Any ideas?
K: Er … I think we can manage.
M: I'd like to help. Is there any further support from our side which can help?
K: Maybe Stefanie, is she available? Her expertise would be very helpful, but I understand that she's in Mexico.
M: Not a problem, I can ask her to travel to Japan for when you get back, stay for a week or so until things are back on track? Would next Friday be good for her to visit?
K: Yes, that would be good.
M: Excellent, so we are in agreement. In fact, why don't you call Stefanie and arrange for her to go over, and we can talk again in a couple of weeks? I'm sure that we can get things back on track.
K: OK, I'll call her. Thanks for the support, Matt, I appreciate it.
J: Hey.
M: Oh, hi, how's things?
J: I was thinking about you, how did that Japan business go?

M: Good. I tried to keep things positive.
J: Oh yeah? How did that go?
M: Slowly. Kenji was supposed to coordinate with Stefanie, but didn't. I had to pick up the phone and ask – very nicely again – if he *could just please* call Stefanie.
J: And?
M: He did. She's there. It's going well, I think we're back on track, team spirit is high.
J: You're too nice. You know, Kenji's lucky I'm not managing the project.

4.3.4
It's important to be aware that people communicate differently depending on their culture, as well as their personality.
So firstly, be aware that a direct style can be useful and effective. It makes things clear – it's honest and fast, and some people actually like it. So we see Matt in the first video, partly on the advice of Jack, say very clearly that he's not happy and what needs to happen, and he gets Kenji to understand the situation quickly; that's useful for the team. But, we all know, a direct style can be dangerous. It can close down conversation; it can even cause conflict.
Indirect communication can also work; it's more polite for some, but it can take longer to be effective. So, in Option B, Matt asks Kenji to take the next steps to call Stefanie. However, Matt has to step in again later and make the call himself as Kenji was slow to do it. So in the end, the same result is achieved as Option A, but with the indirect style, but Matt possibly has a happier team without any conflict.
In the end you have to decide. Choose the style which best fits the situation, and not simply the style you prefer.

5.1.1 P = Presenter   AL = Allen Lyall
JR = Jukka Rosenberg   JM = Jim McAuslan
P: Online shopping is now a major part of the retail sector. It's convenient and often cheaper than buying in traditional stores. E-commerce operators have invested heavily in their logistics systems so that consumers receive a quick and efficient service. An online shopper only has to make a couple of clicks on a website. It is so easy. But behind the scenes, retailers rely on complex logistics operations to fulfil orders. Systems have to handle millions of orders efficiently. Many of the operations in Amazon's giant warehouse are automated. Each order is placed in a separate yellow container. The containers are tracked with their own barcodes. It is a complex operation.
AL: My role is to make sure that the fulfilment centres and the thousands of people we employ in the UK are busy making sure that our orders are delivered on time.
P: Allen Lyall is Amazon's Vice President of European Operations. He explains the scale of the work that the warehouse is capable of.
AL: We dispatched on our busiest day 2.1 million items. There was a truck leaving this building, one every two minutes thirty seconds last year. There was a thousand one hundred tonnes of equipment on that peak day.
P: The orders then have to be packed. This stage in the process is still done by hand. Good packaging is essential to prevent goods getting damaged in transit. With the orders packed they are ready to leave the warehouse and begin the next stage in the process – delivery to the customer. Delivery can be undertaken by the postal service or by courier companies. Frequently, customers are able to track the progress of their package online. Consumers enjoy the convenience of having goods delivered to their homes. But of course customers are not always at home to receive their package. One solution is to use these. They are called collection lockers. Packages can be left inside and the customer can pick them up at any time by entering a PIN number. The logistics that e-commerce relies upon are developing all the time. In the future

141

Videoscripts

we may see some changes in the way our online shopping is delivered. This robot has been designed to deliver packages. Customers can arrange to collect their goods from the robot via a mobile app. Some companies are also considering using drones to transport goods to customers. This drone is being developed by the postal service in Finland. Jukka Rosenberg is the Project Director.
JK: This is part of the testing of new technologies in our parcel delivery and post deliveries and this could be an opportunity which we are now testing.
P: Amazon says that in the future, customers could order goods and they would be delivered by drone in as little as thirty minutes. However, are all these changes really for the better? There are concerns about the widespread use of drones. For example, will they create congestion in the sky? Airline pilots are worried about the safety issues raised by drones. Jim McAuslan is a spokesperson for commercial pilots.
JM: There is an issue about the safety of their operation. But our bigger concern is where this technology is going for the future. We're not against the technology but we want it to be properly regulated.
P: As drone technology develops, issues like safety and congestion will need to be balanced against the convenience of delivery by air. It is a discussion that is certain to continue.

5.3.1   S = Stefanie   M = Matt
S: Another day in paradise?
M: We're going round in circles here. Unbelievable.
S: Been talking to Raj?
M: No, IT downstairs. Trying to get some understanding of an email I received from Raj this morning. Of course, they were very happy to point out that if it was *their* responsibility in house, and not 'my expensive external provider', there wouldn't be any of these issues. They told me to cancel the contract with Raj and let *them* handle the project.
S: They may be right.
M: I know they're right. But it's still not very helpful.
S: But I thought you discussed this with Raj last week.
M: I did. We had, what was it, a three-hour conference call? Look, I know they have their issues, Raj is under a lot of pressure over there in India, but he made promises about where we'd be by now. And then he suddenly went very quiet ... and then I get an email this morning that there are these issues, and they need more time ... more money ... You know, maybe it's cultural, Raj didn't feel that he could say no to me in the first meeting, when I asked him if he could solve things.
S: People love to go on about cultural differences but it's too simple, just stereotyping. To be honest, I think it's you. I think you're too soft on Raj. If the platform is not ready, and the project is going over budget, you need to put some pressure on him. He needs to make *us* his number one priority. Call his manager.
M: I don't know ... bringing in management ... it changes the atmosphere. I don't want to make it more difficult to work with Raj.
S: It's a waste of time, Matt. You need to get tough. We're the customer here. Demand some action.
M: Raj is pretty sensitive; he might not react too well to that kind of thing. Look, I have a call with him later, I'll try and negotiate some kind of solution on the pricing at least. Costs are getting out of control. What?
S: Nothing ...

5.3.2   R = Raj   M = Matt   S = Stefanie
R: Hello?
M: Raj, it's Matt Farnham.
R: Hi, Matt. Good to hear your voice. How are you?
M: Not great actually, Raj. I got your email this morning, it wasn't exactly what I wanted to read. There are now really significant problems with increased cost and no clear timeline to sort out the technical problems. We can't run the project like this. Things have to change.
R: OK, I'm surprised to hear this. You know we're talking about a complex project and we have many other contracts happening over here.
M: Raj, you need to deal with these issues. There's a risk we have to delay the pilot to customers ... that means we might even lose customers. And my management is going to complain about these costs. Basically, what I need is for you to cover the extra costs for additional work on the project. What you're billing us is unacceptable ... these costs are just out of control.
R: But not all the technical problems that we have were discussed at the beginning, this is a lot of extra work for us.
M: Look, this is how it is: we have a contract, we're not going to accept an open budget. If that's a problem for you, then we need to involve your management. You have to bear the costs, all these delays aren't our problem, we shouldn't pay for them.
R: Erm. OK. Look, let me have a look at the numbers.
M: OK, fine. Send me something by this evening.
R: OK.
M: Right, I have to go to a meeting, I'll talk to you tomorrow.
R: OK.
S: Hello.
M: Hi.
S: Did you speak to Raj?
M: Yes, we had a chat yesterday. Wasn't easy at first. But he was pretty open in the end, and we had a very direct conversation. I had a chat to his manager as well.
S: And?
M: No extra costs on the project ... so the money is back under control ... we've agreed to have a phone call every day, just to track and manage the fixes. We should be OK in about a week.
S: Good.
M: It *is* good, yes, but I still had to go over Raj's head and talk to his manger ... he doesn't seem very happy about it.
S: It's not about making people happy, there's a job to do.
M: That's one way of looking at it, but he's told me he's struggling with a young family and all these problems are a bit demotivating. And if he gets demotivated and decides to walk off the project, we'll have a major, major problem on our hands. To be honest, I'm a bit worried that he's going to walk.

5.3.3   R = Raj   M = Matt   S = Stefanie
R: Hello?
M: Raj, it's Matt Farnham.
R: Hi, Matt. Good to hear your voice. How are you?
M: I'm good thanks but, to be honest, we've got some difficult issues to discuss, Raj, this project is really challenging for everyone at the moment.
R: Yes, it's a real headache.
M: But I want to work with you to resolve things. Now, I appreciate that you're working very hard to deliver, but as we talked about a week or so ago, all these delays are creating financial and commercial issues for us ... first there's the cost, all this extra work, and also there's going to be a problem for our customers.
R: You mean being late with the pilot phase?
M: Exactly. Now I want to work with you to resolve this, I don't want to be the bad guy, but I think we need to negotiate on your fees. This is really down to you, not us, so I think it is reasonable to ask to split the costs, we'll take 10 percent, OK?
R: I don't think it's fair to blame us in this way, your team changed some of the requirements, added things, that meant more work, more people from our side ...
M: OK. Could I suggest something? What about, if we help from our side and give you one of *our* IT guys, and then *you* should have everything that you need to clear this up quickly.
R: OK. With an extra resource from you, that would be a good solution, I can agree to that.
M: Good stuff. I'll give you another call tomorrow.
R: OK, talk to you tomorrow.
M: Have a good one.
S: Hi. Did you speak to Raj?
M: Yes. We spoke yesterday.
S: And?
M: Good, I think. He's very cooperative. I agreed to take 10 percent of the extra costs ... so that should bring the money back under control ... I also suggested we send someone from IT *here* to work on this. There's a young guy down there, Mike I think it is, seems keen. He could also help track things a bit in case this happens again ...
S: That makes sense.
M: We need to work with these guys, keep them on our side. You know, we need to think about the big picture ... there are more countries on the horizon, and my boss is already talking to Raj's boss about the next contract, so ...
S: Good thinking.
M: You see, I'm not just a pretty face ... Anyway, let's see. I want to keep things positive at this stage. The only thing I have to do now is convince my boss about the extra costs on our side ... not going to be easy.

5.3.4
There are a number of learning points in these videos about collaborating with people outside of your team.
Firstly, in professional life, it's important to be demanding sometimes with external partners, to get to a result which is good for your team and your organisation. In Option A Matt communicates powerfully to get Raj's company to pay extra costs. A good result financially. But demanding has risks. Raj is demotivated and might leave the project. An alternative to the demanding style is to use a supportive approach – external partners can respond very positively to this; they support the solutions and they remain very motivated. But, you may need to invest time and money to achieve an outcome that is acceptable for everyone. Matt found this in Option B – he reached an agreement with Raj, but to do this he had to provide extra money and resources.
When communicating internationally, be flexible, and choose the style that best fits the situation.

6.1.1
The phone is really, really you know core element of our everyday life, but on the other hand we don't know anything about it. We didn't start as a company, we started as a campaign and the campaign question was how can we give visibility to er the situation in Eastern Congo?
Millions of people died in, in, in wars related to the mining of these minerals we use in, in our mobile devices. So what we thought is, and you know with my background as a designer, is that you know what, why don't we make a device, make a phone? We've been announced the, the fastest growing start-up, tech start-up of Europe by *The Next Web*, which says something about the, the speed in which we grew. We grew from two people to over forty people in two and a ha, two years. Uh we made, in the first one and a half years of our existence, we made a turnover of sixteen million euros. First actually was through crowdfundings, and then in three weeks more than 10,000 people bought the phone. So we had over three and a half million euros on the bank account, we didn't know how to make a phone, you can imagine me laying in bed at night crying and my wife, you know, going at me like, 'Bas, come on! You can do it, you, you started this so you have to, you really have to go for it now,' – it's a success.
All components are actually uh, built up as modules, and people can actually exchange those modules, repair those modules themselves. We work with mines, local mines, in Eastern Congo and where we get our tin, our tantalum, from, so we

contribute to the actual economic situation in the Congo instead of, you know, avoiding the country which a lot of companies are doing. If you produce phones, you produce waste, right? And by doing that, you know, by making a Fairphone you're already kind of in the paradox. So what we said is we want to take back phones as well to source minerals. So we've collected over 60,000 phones in the, you know, in the Ghana and we er, we, we got them back to er, Belg, to a Belgian refinery to, you know, to take back to, the minerals to be used in the supply chain again. I might call myself an idealist but I also know, you know, that the world works in a certain way and you have to, you know business is, is an important mechanism to actually create change, um you know that's why we set up Fairphone –that's why we started a company instead of, you know, doing art projects for example. And um, you know a fellow er designer of me, er of mine has, has once said, you know, we're all hippies with business plans. The mechanism we use to change things is a commercial model, and by being part of the economic system and a market mechanism, we are able to actually, you know, put those idea, idealist kind of values into the core of what moves the world. So we're not in it to become, you know, the biggest phone company in the world, but by doing what we do we show that there's a market, we grow demand and if the demand grows the market will follow –that's the way the world works, right?

6.3.1 P = Paula   M = Matt
P: I think I'm quite good at influencing people. I'm usually able to make a strong argument, backed with good reasoning. We have some potential buyers from a Mexican chain of business schools coming to London this week.
M: When will they be here?
P: About twenty minutes. … They want to look at partnering with online training and education providers from the UK and I'll be pitching … I expect to get what I want, I haven't failed yet!
M: Remember not to be too pushy … go easy on them.
P: Stop worrying! I've thought of everything, really. Remember we've designed this just for them.
M: I know, I know … but Pedro likes to be involved in decision-making, he's quite a collaborative guy and likes to give input.
P: I'm sure it'll be fine.

6.3.2 Pa = Paula   M = Matt   S = Susan   Pe = Pedro
Pa: So that brings me to the end of the presentation. I'm sure that you've been able to see the many, many benefits that partnering with us and introducing our online courses will bring to your business schools. I'm sure that you'll agree that our courses are among the best currently available in the global marketplace. Their success and quality are demonstrated by the fact that a number of other business schools and universities in other countries already use them.
M: Well, I'm sure we'd love to hear your thoughts.
S: Yes, I'm really impressed. I like the approach, it feels very new … I can see how it would fit very well in our business schools.
Pe: Hmmm … I'm not sure, I think that there are a lot of technical matters to think about. Who will manage it? How long will the platform take to integrate? We're already quite busy for the rest of this year at least … there's also money to think about … it's the same story with our budget.
Pa: I totally understand your concern. We put together this proposal just for you, so this doesn't relate to anyone else's institution – just yours. We've done an analysis of your business schools and we're aware of the challenges that you mention, but that's why we're so confident that it will be a great success …
Pe: Maybe, but there's a difference between analysing on paper and how things are in practice, this year is …
Pa: Sure, but that's why there's provision for us to support the platform, it's not all just left to you …
Pe: Yes I understood that in your pitch, but …
Pa: And you just won't find a better price anywhere on the market. Not for something like this, nothing more competitive exists.
Pe: OK. Well, I think Susan and I have a lot to think about. I think we can have a discussion over the next few weeks … and we'll get back to you.

6.3.3 Pa = Paula   M = Matt   S = Susan   Pe = Pedro
Pa: So that brings me to the end of the presentation. I'm sure that you've been able to see the many, many benefits that partnering with us and introducing our online courses will bring to your business schools. I'm sure that you'll agree that our courses are among the best currently available in the global marketplace. Their success and quality are demonstrated by the fact that a number of other business schools and universities in other countries already use them.
M: Well, I'm sure we'd love to hear your thoughts …
S: Yes, I'm really impressed. I like the approach, it feels very new … I can see how it would fit very well in our business schools.
Pe: Hmmm … I'm not sure, I think that there are a lot of technical matters to think about. Who will manage it? How long will the platform take to integrate? We're already quite busy for the rest of this year at least … there's also money to think about … it's the same story with our budget.
Pa: Pedro? Sorry, the most important thing for you is not to have to spend a lot of time integrating the platform and managing the implementation?
Pe: Yes.
Pa: OK, well we can help with that. We can take on the work of looking at your set-up and creating an implementation plan. On top of that we'll also fully manage implementation … and support it. And of course we'll make sure that any disturbances will be kept to an absolute minimum. Would that be a good solution for you?
Pe: That sounds fine, but there's also cost … I just don't think it's going to work financially.
Pa: Can I ask why you don't think the finances will work out?
Pe: Cash flow. Cash flow and the fact that we allocate budget a couple of years ahead … most of what we have over the next year is already assigned.
Pa: I understand. That doesn't have to be a problem. We would be able to plan and test now, but set the launch for next year and spread the cost. So you could go ahead now, but put it into next year's budget and we could probably agree quarterly payments. How does that sound?
Pe: Well that makes a big difference. If we could agree to those conditions … I think we would be happy to go ahead.
S: Let's do it.
Pa: Great!
Pe: Thanks for being so flexible, Paula.
M: Right, let's take you both to lunch.

6.3.4
When we're just being ourselves, we often try to influence people using our own natural style, and this potentially limits our success. We saw this with Paula in Option A – her 'push' style seemed to suit Susan, but it wasn't working on Pedro. He felt frustrated in the end and Paula wasn't able to close the deal.
In Option B, she adapts to a 'pull' approach and asks Pedro questions to find out more about his needs, while still guiding the conversation to a positive result.
Both 'push' and 'pull' are valid and positive approaches. But they each have advantages and disadvantages depending on the situation. Overall, we have a better chance of communicating successfully if we understand the needs and preferred style of others in specific situations. Then we can choose an influencing style which suits the situation and also the person.

7.1.1 P = Presenter   E = Evelyn   R = Rodrigo   M = Marcus   H = Hannah   R = Rennie
P: Working abroad is now a fact of life for many people in business. Multinational companies often require their staff to relocate to offices in different countries or even on different continents. And international experience can be a valuable asset in career development.
The prospect of moving to a new country is exciting. It brings the opportunity to see new places and to get to know different cultures. But going abroad to work is not the same as travelling for pleasure. It brings challenges. Foreign professionals have to learn about cultural issues like customs and etiquette. They may find the way people communicate and interact at work is different.
One of the first things that someone in a new job overseas has to encounter is interacting with co-workers. In different cultures, different standards apply.
E: When you are in Germany people are a bit more reserved to begin with. Once you've broken the ice and got to know them, they will be your friends for life, if they make friends with you. But initially they are a bit more reserved, so don't be put off by that.
P: The workplace culture in Brazil is quite different.
R: When it's time for lunch, you always have lunch with someone – you never have your lunch alone – there's always, usually more than one person. So it tends to be very face value and very friendly, which can be unhelpful at times because you want to do some work and be quiet, but people tend to be interactive, communicative. But at the same time you have a very strong sense of team spirit because everybody's together there doing the same things.
P: Good communication is essential in a work environment. It can present some challenges as Marcus found when he relocated from Sweden to the UK.
M: I thought I was very fluent in English when I, you know, when I lived at home in Sweden. But then when you actually come to live here, you realise (that) the nuances and phrases that you don't know at all. And, you know, doing your mistakes and saying the wrong things at the wrong time, but quickly learning, was fun.
P: The etiquette of communication can also vary. In Poland people tend to be direct when they talk to each other.
H: You might be a little bit shocked that the Poles tend to be more abrupt, or that's how they will come across. The use of 'thank you' and 'please' – it's probably less widely used. The linguistic elements, the cultural element doesn't demand that. So it's absolutely polite if you just say 'yes', 'no' and leave it at that.
P: Many of the rules of a culture remain unwritten. Learning them can be challenging but it is also rewarding and is one of the keys to success in the global workplace.

7.3.1 S = Stefanie   P = Paula
S: Today is a big day for our project. We have some clients coming in who are thinking about making a major purchase for the Mexican market … Paula has responsibility for Mexico, but I'm a bit more experienced so Matt has asked me to lend her some support. The important thing in these kinds of conservations is to make sure that things keep on moving ahead. I'm keen to keep the focus on our launch date, and sticking to the plans that we have between now and then. After that we can worry about group decisions and small details. I think with the important points we should use our expertise and let our clients know what's best.
S: Hi, Paula.
P: Hi, Stefanie.
S: The first thing I'd like to do is go over all the dates we have for the next three months … can we start there?
P: When we're talking about making decisions, I would say that I prefer to try to find consensus … It's a huge project … in Mexico! There are so many

Videoscripts

things to think about … How will we register students? When to register students? What are we going to do about marketing? Are we going to assist with that? We need to ask them all these questions and take decisions together, we can't know everything about everything ourselves … So, yes, for me this meeting is about getting to understand more about how they work … we can think about a launch date later.

7.3.2 St = Stefanie Su = Susan P = Pedro
St: We think that the next step is to decide when exactly we would want to plan the launch.
Su: Yes, I'm happy to have that conversation.
St: Great, well we think that it would be a good idea to keep things moving …
Su: Absolutely …
St: … so I suggest we plan to launch this year.
Su: OK.
St: In our experience it's a good idea to use the summer. When the students aren't around we can implement and test everything … hopefully your IT guys will have a bit more time then … it's just easier to set everything up. So my advice is that we aim for a launch date in September.
Su: I totally agree. Let's do that.
P: OK. That's not far off … I think we should know a little bit more about the process … I just want to make sure that we're all being realistic.
Su: It's realistic. Let's just do it, we can get into the process later. OK great, we're all agreed then.
St: Fantastic.

7.3.3 St = Stefanie Su = Susan Pa = Paula Pe = Pedro
St: We think that the next step is to decide when exactly we would want to plan the launch.
Su: Yes, I'm happy to have that conversation.
Pa: Great, when would be the best time for you? It would probably be a good idea to keep things moving and plan for sometime this year, but we're happy to work around your needs.
Su: September time would be good.
Pe: I think that we should do a pilot first … let's just trial it in one of our business schools and, then, if it all runs smoothly, we can roll it out to the rest of the group.
Pa: We could do that, certainly … sounds logical … have you thought about how and when you'll register your students, or how we're going to market the courses in advance?
Pe: No, not yet … I guess we would need to discuss those things internally to start with … let's keep it flexible for now. You know, sometimes things change, let's keep talking.
Pa: Sure, after all, we're here to facilitate what works best for you.
Su: Thanks, Paula, but I'm sure we don't want to waste your time or ours in meeting after meeting. I'm happy to make a decision now and stick to it … let's say September. If we don't go live in that semester, there'll be another six-month wait, which no one wants. So can we launch in September? And fix an exact date? You can do whatever piloting you want between now and then.
St: Absolutely, that sounds perfect.
Pe: OK.
St: Great, well, we'll start looking at dates.

7.3.4
Everyone's decision-making behaviour is shaped in some way by their culture; it could be national culture, corporate culture or some other form of culture.
Firstly, some people can take a very target-driven approach while others may prefer a more collaborative approach. For example, in Option A, Stefanie and Susan dominated the discussion and were very target-driven, while in Option B we see that Paula and Pedro are clearly more consensus-oriented.
Another difference is how people view time and deadlines. What's fixed for one person may be flexible for another, and this can cause problems.

As we saw in the videos, Stefanie was keen to have a fixed decision on the launch date while Paula was happier taking a more flexible approach.
Thirdly, we can look at attitudes to status and hierarchy. In some places, hierarchies are flat and you can openly discuss and debate ideas with your manager. Elsewhere, status and hierarchy are more important, and you probably shouldn't openly disagree with your manager.
In this story, Susan is ranked higher than Pedro, and Stefanie has more experience than Paula. These factors could have enabled them to push through their decision in both video options.
So, how can we overcome these challenges? We can first observe others, then discuss our preferred approach. This can help us achieve better business results while protecting relationships at the same time.

8.1.1 P = Presenter N = Nadia
PM = Park Manager VS1 = Vet Student 1
VS2 = Vet Student 2 S = Steve Leonard
P: Leadership in business requires a range of skills. These include an ability to make decisions, good communication and knowing when to delegate tasks. Leadership skills such as these are just as important in running a team as they are in managing a multinational. Learning to lead a team can be a challenge.
In *Safari Vet School*, sixteen veterinary students take that challenge and test their leadership abilities in real-life situations with dangerous wild animals. The students have been selected from thousands of applicants to travel to South Africa where they will be supervised by specialists, including experienced TV vet, Steve Leonard.
Nadia is studying at Cambridge University. She's a high achiever – used to getting top grades. The Vet School selectors were impressed by her determination.
N: Failure is not something I cope well with. If you want me to boss you, I will! People can be quite intimidated by me I think. I mean I've had people say they're scared of me, which I don't understand why, but obviously I must be quite 'in your face' maybe. I kind of have one volume and it's 'loud'.
P: Nadia's sense of purpose means that she is chosen as team leader for the first task. An animal must be sedated, treated, put on a truck for transit and then woken up.
As team leader, Nadia has to make key decisions, motivate the group and ensure they all work together. If the animal is not revived quickly, it may be harmed or even die.
It does not run smoothly. Luckily the team manages to administer the reversal drug to wake up the animal. The Park Manager is critical of Nadia's management style in the team debriefing session.
PM: There was far too much chatter going on. And running around. Everyone a bit disorganised. It took you fifteen minutes from when the trailer arrived up to when you actually gave the reversal. OK? Far too long.
VS1: I think we just needed just one person to like kind of control the operation. Because I, literally, didn't know what you guys were doing. I was just on …
VS2: I was just focusing on the heart rate, the lung field …
VS1: I didn't know the trailer was there …
N: Yeah we all got so side-tracked with immobilising it that we forgot the whole point was just to get it on the truck. And I felt that the team was disappointed with how I behaved as the team leader.
P: Nadia receives feedback from Steve, her mentor. She admits that leading and motivating a group is different from motivating herself.
N: I normally cope really well with adrenaline. But looking back I think I cope well with adrenaline when there's just me and I just have to think, 'Right! I have to do this. I'm going to do it'. Whereas when you've got a group of nine people that you're

trying to control and when …
S: You're trying to control nine people?
N: Well … because … it was a group of nine and I was supposed to coordinate them
S: When you look back at this, how many questions did you ask of your team that were advice questions?
N: How do you mean?
S: In terms of 'What do you think we should do?'
N: I can't remember.
S: I didn't hear any. Do you think you'd taken on too much responsibility?
N: Yeah definitely! That was the problem. I was completely out of my comfort zone.
S: You've just got a taste of what it's like to be in charge. How did that make you feel?
N: Awful.
S: Did it? What you experienced was very, very difficult. I don't think you did that bad a job.
P: It has been a tough learning experience for Nadia. She now understands that leadership involves a range of skills – such as motivating all the team members, keeping focused on the main objectives of the task, and communicating clearly.

8.3.1
So this is it … It's been a long journey, but very successful in the end, I think. All that's left now is to wrap everything up with the team. It's always important at the end of long and detailed projects like this to take the opportunity to learn lessons. As project manager, I'm keen to get some feedback from the guys, so we've set up a brief session while they're still all here in London … hopefully it won't be too brutal. Obviously I hope they give me some positive feedback. Everyone likes to feel that they've done well … But it would also be interesting to get some developmental feedback, to hear where they think I could improve.

8.3.2 M = Matt S = Stefanie K = Kenji P = Paula
M: I'd like to ask you all for some personal feedback. As you know, this is one of the first times I've worked on an international project like this so I'm keen to know how you all feel … so don't be shy, who wants to go first?
S: I'm happy to go first.
M: OK great, go ahead.
S: Well, I think you did a very good job communicating with the team and keeping us all informed … once we knew each other's roles it was very easy to work together.
M: Great! Thanks Stefanie, I'm happy you feel that I was able to … pull everyone together, even though we were all in different parts of the world.
K: I agree. And it was good that you asked Stefanie to help out when I had some difficulties.
M: Sure, it just seemed like a sensible idea to me at the time. Paula?
P: I agree. I thought you were a good project manager … thanks for all the coaching you gave me and for the tips about making presentations … I felt like you were there to support me.
M: Excellent. Thanks, Paula. Well, I'm looking forward to the next big project already, thanks guys.

8.3.3 M = Matt S = Stefanie K = Kenji P = Paula
M: I'd like to ask you all for some personal feedback. As you know, this is one of the first times I've worked on an international project like this so I'm keen to know how you all feel … so don't be shy, who wants to go first?
S: I'm happy to go first.
M: OK great, go ahead.
S: Everything was OK in the end and I think the project was a success … but I have to say … I thought it was a bit chaotic at the beginning. I think that it was your responsibility to make sure that we all knew each other and communicated … but I don't think we did have a clear idea of who was on the project or our roles … I think that was a problem.

M: That's interesting ... I thought I had done that. If you remember I sent around some email intros and I set up a virtual conference?
S: You did, but it came too late and was also a bit short ... It was difficult to know how to get started without knowing my role and everyone else's. I think if you could have called each of us *before* the project began, that would have been good.
M: Right, I'll bear that in mind. Anyone else? Kenji?
K: Everything was fine.
M: Are you sure? You looked like you were thinking about something there. I'd like to hear anything that's on your mind.
K: This project was just one of many tasks that I had. I'm always very busy, but I don't think you understood that, you always asked me to do things urgently. I'm sorry that I was not always able to act so quickly.
M: OK. I really had no idea that you had a lot of other jobs on, you must tell me things like that ... otherwise there's no way that I can know ...
P: But I think what Kenji's saying is that you often waited until things were urgent before passing them on, and that puts us under pressure and creates a lot of stress ... it's just a question of being organised. I think in future if you gave us all a timeline or something, that might help us to plan better.
M: OK, I get the point. We've all been under pressure, and it's not like *your* work was perfect, I had to spend a lot of time fixing other people's mistakes. Anything else?

8.3.4
When giving or receiving feedback, we must always remember that our approach to feedback is usually driven by our own personality and preferences. And that no single approach is best. There are a few points that we should keep in mind: When *giving* feedback, firstly motivate others by focusing on things which have been done well. Also, remember to help them improve by focusing on areas in which they can develop. We saw the team do each of these in the videos, but was their positive intention clear in Option B? I'm not so sure. And in terms of *receiving* feedback, remember that feedback is valuable so, when you're not hearing any, you should actively ask for it, as Matt did. Then when you do get feedback, listen to it first without disagreeing or making excuses about any potentially negative points. Then decide later if you want to act on it. Matt may have missed some valuable information when he started making excuses in Option B.
Finally, use a balanced approach to giving positive and developmental feedback. Positive feedback reaffirms someone's actions and position, and is good for their motivation. But, without developmental feedback they may not be aware of areas in which they can improve.

BW3.01
Amalia
Is this webcam on? Oh, right! So, why should you hire me? Well, I have to say I think I'm hard-working, I'm reliable and, and … I'm highly qualified. I have a background in marketing and a lot of experience in different sectors. I also speak various languages, so that will be very useful for an international company like Media Solutions.
I would like to work for you because I think I'm good at communicating, especially writing, and I could contribute to your Communications department with my ideas and improve the presence of your clients in social media. Err, … that's all really. Thanks for listening. Oh, and please call me if you'd like me to come in for an interview.

Birte
Why should you hire me? Because I'm a 'people person': I'm not only sociable, but also really creative and if you hired me, I would give 110 percent and I would get on with all the team and the clients, too. Another thing you should know about me is I'm really into sports and martial arts, as you can see. You can check out some of my videos in social media on how-to-do sports training. I love social media and dedicate a lot of time to it. It's the way everyone communicates nowadays.
What else? I've got a degree in marketing. I did an internship at my dad's company and I learnt *a lot*. I'm a fast learner. I don't have lots of experience but I think it's more important to have the right attitude and just get out there and do it! Why should you hire me? Because I'm worth it! Call me for an interview and please give me the chance to tell you more.

Cindy
So, you'd like to know why you should hire me? That's a good question. Looking at my CV you might think I don't have any relevant experience but I *do* have experience in managing people. I have to communicate in my job every day, where I'm responsible for a team of forty people, talking to different departments and dealing with difficult customers. I'm good at working under pressure, so you can depend on me to write those reports on time!
Err, just a minute …. Another consideration is that I'm a big fan of social media. I write a blog in my free time, although I don't have that many followers yet. I'm also studying marketing online in the evenings. So, if you hire me, I will help you to find the best solutions for you and your clients and improve their online presence with the contributions of key opinion leaders and influencers.
Thank you for considering my application and I look forward to your call!

BW6.01
Ben Fischer
Hi guys! I'm Ben Fischer and my award-winning theatre company performs at events and festivals all over the world. We bring the works of famous German writers and dramatists, such as Bertolt Brecht, to audiences across the globe.
In true dramatic style, our latest production of Brecht's *The Good Person of Szechwan* has just been hit by disaster. An electrical fire destroyed the arts centre where we were performing in London and took with it all our costumes and equipment. Fortunately, nobody was in the building at the time and nobody was injured in the fire.
We know one day the insurance company will eventually pay the compensation to rebuild and replace everything, but we need to complete our world tour now and can't wait around for the money to arrive.
Can you help us? We need to raise €10,000 in the next few weeks to replace everything. I promise all donations to our cause will be repaid when we receive the insurance payout. Not only that, depending on the size of your donation you will receive discounts on tickets and even free tickets to see our play in any city of your choice on the tour. Just see our website for more details.
As Brecht himself once said, 'Everyone needs help from everyone.' By contributing to our disaster fund, you will be doing your bit to support community arts and help our young theatre group to literally rise from the ashes. Thank you!

Alison Chadwick
My name's Alison Chadwick and this is my story. I started my T-shirt business, Alison's Tees, back in university as a hobby. Friends and fellow students used to ask me where I got my T-shirts from and when I told them I designed them myself everyone said that was cool.
Then I thought, you know anyone can design their own T-shirt. It's simple, it's fun and it's creative. On my website you can choose the colour and style but more than that, you can have any design or logo you like printed on it including photos to make your very own unique T-shirt. Friends will be amazed. Before we finally produce the T-shirt, you'll receive a photo of the design for final approval.
No more shopping for hours looking for something you actually like. No more low-quality shop-bought products. All our T-shirts are 100 percent organic cotton and ethically sourced. We're helping independent cotton farmers. We work hand-in-hand with our suppliers to ensure highest-quality tees.
Thanks to previous crowdfunding our business has been a big success. Now we need your support and your money to help us develop our mobile app so our users can design and order their own tees on their smartphones, anytime, anywhere.

Marcos López
If you like travelling, you'll love our new tour guide mobile app. It's like an audio guide but on your mobile phone, so you carry it with you all the time. I'm Marcos López and I'm one of the founders of Holidapp. It's the ultimate travel companion. It's like having an audio guide but on your smartphone. You'll never want to buy another guidebook or tourist map again in your life. You'll find out about the places you're visiting whenever you want in a new, original and entertaining way. Our app is free to download and quick and easy to use. Enter the desired location and for just €10 you will get an expert guide to one of over 30 destinations in Europe and the USA. And the list of places is growing longer each month.
The guide features audio tours by experts in their towns, from qualified tour guides to local storytellers of all ages with a passion for the place where they live. Our platform is free to our guide contributors and they receive 70 percent of the revenues generated by their guides.
Each travel guide on our app comes with high-quality photographs and can use your geolocation to help you get the most from your guide.
We need your backing to help us cover the cost of production, audio recording, programming and photography. We'd also love to hear what you think of the guides so we can keep improving our service.

Audioscripts

1.01 DR = David Robinson JW = Janet Wood

DR: In this part of the show I'm talking to organisation consultant, Janet Wood. Janet, the tall organisation structure is still typical in companies today, isn't it?
JW: Yes, and this traditional pyramid hierarchy has many problems.
DR: Such as …
JW: Well, decision-making is generally slow. This type of company can be very bureaucratic and inefficient. It's slow to change and innovate, which is a real danger in today's world.
DR: But is there really any alternative in a large corporation?
JW: Yes, there are examples of successful innovative organisations which do things differently. One of the most famous is W. L. Gore, a multinational manufacturing company.
DR: W. L. Gore is probably best known for the fabric Gore-Tex, isn't it?
JW: That's right. Bill and Genevieve Gore started the company in the USA back in the 1950s with a flat structure. Today, the company still has no traditional organisational chart. Gore believes that if people are passionate about their work, they're going to be highly self-motivated.
DR: So, how does the company operate?
JW: Well, there are over 10,000 employees in 30 countries divided into teams of 8 to 12 people, who work on projects and products together. The staff at Gore are actually called 'associates'. They don't have job titles. And they don't have managers. Instead they choose to 'follow' leaders. Basically, you decide what you are going to contribute to the team and you establish your own work and pay.
DR: I hear the associates actually *elected* the company's chief executive, Terri Kelly.
JW: Yes, she's one of the few people at the company who has a job title.
DR: There's been a lot of talk in the business news recently about a concept called 'holacracy'. Can you tell us what that is exactly?
JW: Yes, the expression comes from the Greek word *holos*, meaning 'whole'. Holacracy is essentially a system with no bosses at all.
DR: How does this manager-free system work in practice?
JW: Well, it's probably too early to know. Just two years ago Zappos, the U.S. online shoe and clothes store which was started in 1999, introduced 'holacracy'. Now all the functions of the company have been delegated to teams called 'circles'. Zappos has about 1,600 employees distributed among some 500 circles. Each circle has a 'lead link' who has a similar role to a project manager.
DR: Does this person, the 'lead link' decide who does what tasks?
JW: No, circle members decide their roles and responsibilities in meetings. Larger teams have circles within circles. Staff can either start a new circle or join a circle depending on the type of work they'd like to do.
DR: Sounds complicated.
JW: Yes, the CEO of Zappos, Tony Hsieh, says it could take another two to five years to complete the transition. In fact, Zappos has a training session next week, called a 'Culture Camp', and I'm flying to Las Vegas tomorrow for that.
DR: I'm sure that's going to be a very interesting experience. Janet, thank you for coming into the studio today.

Ext1.01

1 Well, decision-making is generally slow.
2 This type of company can be very bureaucratic and inefficient.
3 … there are examples of successful innovative organisations which do things differently.
4 W. L. Gore is probably best known for the fabric Gore-Tex, isn't it?
5 Today, the company still has no traditional organisational chart.
6 … she's one of the few people at the company who has a job title.
7 Now all the functions of the company have been delegated to teams called 'circles'.
8 Staff can either start a new circle or join a circle.

1.02

A: Hi, Juliana. What time does the department meeting start tomorrow?
B: At 10 o'clock as usual, but I think I'm going to be about fifteen minutes late. I have a dentist's appointment.
A: Are you going to be able to talk after your trip to the dentist's?
B: Yes, it's just a check-up. In fact, I'm giving a presentation on the company restructuring.
A: I'm sure that's going to be interesting. Is it true we're moving to offices outside the city?
B: I'm not going to tell you anything before the meeting. You know that.
A: Well, I'm going to sit right at the front. I don't want to miss anything.

1.03

First meetings in an international business setting can often be difficult. Two strangers come together. Often, they both have to speak a foreign language, English. So you have strangers who aren't sure what to say to each other. And they aren't sure how to say it. The result is pretty predictable: a difficult silence. Now, silence isn't necessarily bad. In some cultures, silence is good; it's positive because it signals respect. But for me, if you want to get to know someone, to understand them as a person and as a professional – which is essential for doing business together – then silence is a risk, because you stop this process.
If you want to learn about the other person, and build a relationship, you need to ask questions. And this is the real value of asking questions – you learn stuff about the other person.
So … Which questions do you ask? I would say, in terms of style, keep it short and simple, just ask simple starter questions. If you are meeting a visitor, you can say things like, 'Did you have a good trip?' Is this your first time here?' These kinds of questions are good because they allow an easy answer, they're not too personal, but they can quickly break the ice and get the conversation flowing.
You know, sometimes the specific questions don't really matter; you just ask a question to get the ball rolling. And then it's important to ask follow-up questions – if you don't, small talk can feel very mechanical.
In terms of what you ask about in those first few minutes, I think in business you need to have a mix of personal and work topics. On the work side, asking about roles and responsibilities is good, and the organisation behind the person, and where people work and travel … all these questions are easy to answer and give you useful background. And if you listen to what people tell you, you'll find more ideas for other questions.
And all this asking questions, well, it builds understanding and in the end … trust. Remember, it's impossible to trust someone if you don't know them well. And how can you know them well? You've got to ask questions! Oh, one final thing: if possible, find something you have in common with the other person – maybe you visited the same place, you like the same food, the same music or sport. When you and the other person have similar interests, the conversation often goes better.

1.04 P = Paul E = Eva

P: Hi, is it Eva?
E: Yes.
P: Hi, Eva. Nice to meet you. Welcome.
E: Thank you. It's nice to be here.
P: Did you have a good trip? Hotel OK?
E: Yes, no problems. I haven't seen the hotel yet. I came straight here from the airport.
P: OK, well, follow me. My office is just through this door. So, here we are. Can I take your coat?
E: Thank you.
P: Good. Take a seat. Can I offer you something to drink? Coffee? Tea?
E: Just water would be nice, thanks.
P: OK. Here you go. So, is it your first time here in the London office?
E: Yes, it is. But I've been to London once before.
P: OK. For work?
E: No, just a holiday that time.
P: So, where do you work exactly? Are you in the Zurich office at the moment?
E: Yes, I'm responsible for sales support there. I work 20 percent in Geneva, though.
P: OK, and, do you report to Paul Blaettner?
E: Yes, I do. You know him?
P: Yes, I worked with him on a sales project last year. I was thinking of inviting him to join us later. Are you free for dinner this evening?
E: Yes, that would be nice.
P: Fine, so I'll organise that. And, funny, you know I also worked in Geneva. When did you join the company?
E: End of last year.
P: OK, then I just missed you. I moved to this job here in October. So you know, I'm now Head of Customer Service, and also this new international project around Service Excellence, which is why we're here.
E: Yes, I'm really looking forward to this project. It's going to be a lot of work, but I'm ready.
P: It's really good to have you on the project. So, shall we make a start? I know you have a busy schedule and lots of other people to meet.

2.01

1 Good morning, everyone. My name is John Hawkins, and what I want to do today is give you a short introduction to the company. I won't take more than ten minutes because we have a lot to get through today. But if you have any questions, please feel free to interrupt.
2 I would like to start by offering a very warm welcome to everyone here today. Thank you very much for coming. I know many of you have travelled a long way to be here. As you know, I'm Pam Ellis, Managing Director here. What I want to do today is give you an introduction to the company. Firstly, a little information on operations; secondly, more about the people; and finally, the culture we have here. But to begin, I want to look at operations.
3 Good morning. I'm Paolo Orlandi, Managing Director of Production here. Er, sorry for my poor English. But I must, before we take a tour of the factory, give you an introduction to health and safety, so that everyone is safe here. Please, do ask questions if there is anything you don't understand. I know some things I say may not be so clear. But, it's important everyone understands what to do and what not to do in the production area. So, please, ask me questions. Any questions, any time, if anything is not clear. I'd like to start with some rules on where you can walk and where not to walk. As you can see …

2.02

1 So, before I begin and tell you why I am here, I would like to start with why you are here. And how can I know that? Well, I asked a couple of you during coffee this morning. Jackie, over there, yes, she wants to learn about which countries we are active in, as she wants to work abroad one day. Good, I'll talk about that. Peter, he's a finance guy and wants to know more on the numbers. Are we profitable? Important question, Peter, and I'll talk about finance too. And Samir, the interest there is how to become a leader as quickly as possible. And I will talk about that too – what kind of organisation we are, and what kind of people do well here.
2 To begin, before I say anything, I'd like to ask you a few questions, find out what you know about this organisation. Who knows how many people work here? OK … put your hand up if you know the

answer to these questions. Which countries are we active in? ... OK. What are our main products? ... Hmm, so, not so many of you. That's fine. That's why I'm here. My name's Pam Ellis and I want to tell you a little bit about ...

3 Now, to start, I'd like to share a story with you, about a young man, around twenty years ago, who was sitting right where you are standing, new to the company, a little nervous on the first day, not knowing what to expect. Well, that was, as you can probably guess, me all those years ago. On that day, I listened, and I continued to listen and learn, and now I'm Managing Director. So, welcome.

2.03 JH = John Hawkins
Au = Audience member

JH: So, let's begin with the most important part of the company, and that's its people. And there are three important points I want to make here. Firstly, we're a very young company. It was set up only three years ago and the average age is only twenty-nine. This means we're fresh and energetic and we really like innovation, which is our main strength. Secondly, we're a small company, with only fifty-six people at the moment. This is also important because we want to stay personal; people know each other here, we have a family atmosphere, which our customers also feel and love about us. And finally, and as I said earlier during lunch to some of you, we are very international. In fact, we now have twenty different nationalities in the company, working in five countries. For me, on a personal note and speaking very openly, this is important as I believe very much in being international and the value of working across different cultures. So, if you can take a look at this slide, you will see the nationalities in the company. I hope I haven't missed anyone. Truly international. Great. Yes, a question?

Au: Is the company growing? Getting more international?

JH: Great question. Really good question, in a number of ways. Yes, we are growing, probably to around sixty-five people this year. But I don't want to grow much more or we become too big, too much a large corporation. So, yes but no. We are small. We want to be small. And we plan to stay small. But I'll say more about that a little later. Are there any other questions now on that? So, I'll close there. Thank you very much for listening. And I'll hand over to Paul to tell you something about products and services.

3.01
1 What are your strengths and weaknesses?
2 Are you working at the moment?
3 How long have you worked as a chemical engineer?
4 Do you have any experience in green technologies?
5 Why would you like to work for us?
6 What would you do on your first day at work?
7 Do you have your original certificates with you?
8 Where do you see yourself in five years' time?

3.02
1 You've told me about your strengths. Can you tell me what your greatest weakness is?
2 Could you tell me about your work experience?
3 You write in your CV that you have good leadership skills. Can you tell me about a time when you showed leadership skills?
4 Although you have the right qualifications, you don't have much work experience in this sector. I'd like to know if you've ever done any voluntary work.
5 Could you tell me how you would add value to our company?
6 This job involves visiting waste-water facilities around the country. I'd like to know if you are prepared to travel for the job.
7 Right. Finally, I'd like to know who I should contact for a reference.

3.03 I = interviewer C = candidate
1
I: You've told me about your strengths. Can you tell me what your greatest weakness is?
C: I'm not sure, but my friends tell me I'm quite demanding.
I: Are you a bit of a perfectionist?
C: I don't know. Sometimes perhaps.
I: Anything else?
C: Erm, err ...
2
I: Could you tell me about your work experience?
C: I'm afraid I don't have much experience, but I have a PhD in waste water management.
3
I: You write in your CV that you have good leadership skills. Can you tell me about a time when you showed leadership skills?
C: Sure. I was responsible for a large team of researchers while I was doing my PhD in the States. And in my last job I was the assistant project manager for a waste water facility. That was a temporary position because someone was on maternity leave.
4
I: Although you have the right qualifications, you don't have much experience in this sector. I'd like to know if you've ever done any voluntary work.
C: Erm, let me think now ... Well, when I was at university, I did voluntary work visiting schools. I was working on a project together with teachers and children, raising awareness about water consumption and waste water processes.
I: I see.
5
I: How would you add value to our company?
C: Sorry, I didn't catch that.
I: Could you tell me how you would add value to our company?
C: That's a difficult question. As I said before, I think I'm highly qualified for the job, I'm a fast learner and I'm really passionate about green technologies. It isn't just a job. It's a lifestyle.
6
I: This job involves visiting waste water facilities around the country. I'd like to know if you are prepared to travel for the job.
C: Yes, of course. That will be very interesting.
7
I: Right. Finally, I'd like to know who I should contact for a reference, in case we decide to offer you the job.
C: References? Well, there are two or three contacts. I'll need to check and get back to you. Is that all right?
I: Fine. Do you have any questions for me?

3.04
1 S = Sue M = Max
S: Thanks for coming in today, Max. ... So tell me, why do you think you're the right person for this job?
M: Well, I'm hard-working, ... I'm flexible, ... I'm good at working with colleagues and customers, and I have the relevant experience and skills.
S: OK. That all sounds good. Have you ever worked in a regional sales team?
M: No, I haven't.
S: Oh, OK ... Do you have a driving licence?
M: Not yet.
S: I see. If you get this job, you will need to have a driving licence. So ... You've told me about your strengths and experience. Can you tell me about your weaknesses?
M: Hmm. Well, ... I'm not very organised, like with paperwork and other things.
S: I see.
M: So, what are the next steps? When can I expect to hear from you?
2 S = Sue J = John
S: Thank you for coming in today, John. I invited you here because Anna has told me a lot about you and your abilities.
J: That's great. Thank you for your time today.
S: Of course. So tell me, why do you think you're the right person for this job?
J: Well, I'm hard-working, I'm flexible, I'm good at working with both colleagues and customers, and I have the relevant experience and skills.
S: OK. That all sounds good. Have you ever worked in a regional sales team?
J: That's a good question. I haven't, but I do have many transferable skills. I've worked in different local offices of the same company, so I understand the balance between local and regional priorities. So, while my experience is local, I have a good awareness of the sales focus from regional perspectives too. I've also indirectly supported a regional project with local information.
S: That's good. Anna told me about the project you worked on. So, moving on ... Do you have a driving licence?
J: It's good you asked that. I'm currently learning to drive, and I have my test in two weeks' time.
S: OK, that's good. If you get this job, you will need to have a driving licence. Now, you've told me about your strengths and experience. Can you tell me about your weaknesses?
J: Well, I'm very good at dealing with people, which as you know is essential in sales, but I sometimes struggle with the administrative work and paperwork. I am aware of this, though, and I'm working on it so that I can improve.
S: OK, it's good that you're working on this. Do you have any questions for me?
J: Yes, I do. Could you tell me what a normal day or week in this job would be like?
S: Sure, it would start at about 8 o'clock and initially what you'll be doing is ...

4.01
Why is it difficult for companies to plan for the future? Because it isn't easy to know what's going to happen in this complex world we live in. How can a business ever know what will have an impact on its performance and success? In today's session we'll look at a popular tool to plan business strategy called PEST analysis. That's P-E-S-T. PEST is an acronym and the four letters stand for the different types of external factors that a business has to face and generally has no control over. By external factors I mean influences outside a company that can however impact a business. So, what do the letters P-E-S-T stand for? Well, P stands for 'Political' as you might guess. E means 'Economic'. S stands for 'Social factors' and finally T refers to 'Technological factors'. I should mention there is also an extended version of PEST analysis called 'PESTLE' – that's P-E-S-T-L-E, which puts 'Legal' and 'Environmental' factors into additional categories. Anyway, going back to PEST, let's look at some examples we can put into each category so you get a clearer picture. Then later I'll get you to apply PEST analysis to a company you know well. You don't have to take notes as all of this information is on the intranet.

4.02
So, examples of political factors are the stability or instability of governments in a company's markets which will affect business growth. Another example is the employment laws in each country, which are obviously decided by politicians, and thirdly corporate taxes, also decided by government. Economic factors are often closely related. An economic recession is clearly going to affect demand for a company's products. High inflation is going to affect costs and prices. A third example is exchange rates, which will affect exports and imports. Social factors, as the name suggests, are about people and society. For example, changing consumer preferences and the age demographics of the population can affect demand for products. Also, is the population growing and how fast? As for technological factors, we all know the impact technology has on our

Audioscripts

lives. Businesses have to analyse the possible uses of emerging technologies, for instance automation on production lines. Another example is the impact of the internet, such as online shopping, and thirdly the smartphone revolution which allows a company to reach customers faster than ever.

4.03
Obviously, a PEST analysis is not only about collecting lots of data. The next step is to prioritise the most relevant factors and identify any business opportunities these offer. For example, can a new technology improve production processes and reduce costs? It's also crucial to identify any significant risks, or threats, to the business. For instance, if consumer demand is falling in one part of its market, should the company develop new product lines? Finally, managers have to go beyond analysis into action. A company mustn't miss any opportunities for the business so these must form part of the business plan. If there are significant threats, the company must come up with a strategy to deal with these risks too. I should mention that PEST is used with other tools which also analyse internal factors, but we won't go into that today. OK, let's look at a PEST analysis of a well-known footwear company.

4.04 R = Roel B = Bibi P = Peter A = Annette
R: OK, let's get started. Good morning, everyone. Great to see you all here today. Now, what I want to look at today is a problem, a nice problem in a way, but a problem, the fact that we're now getting a lot of telephone and email enquiries from new countries: Belgium and France, and Germany, of course, but also the Czech Republic, Poland and Hungary. I think the new website is helping; it's very attractive and it's generating traffic. But it is creating a problem.
B: Can you explain again what the problem is, exactly? New customers – that isn't a problem, is it?
R: No, the problem is that in many of the emails that people are sending, particularly, but also some phone calls, people are not using English; and we don't have the skills in house to deal with customer enquiries in Polish and Czech, etc.
P: OK, so the real problem is a lack of language competence here in the company, which we need to solve or we will lose potential customers. I guess that's the point.
R: Exactly. So, I wanted to take a few minutes of your time to discuss this. Any ideas?
P: Um, would it be possible to train our people here to use the different languages? It's a cost, but it's a solution.
R: OK, intensive training could be a solution. I'll note that down, thanks. What else can we do? Bibi?
B: How about using a call centre service for different languages? People who call us, they can choose the language they work with, and we contract a call centre to handle first contacts, and then they contact our sales staff.
R: That sounds like a possible solution.
A: OK, but I'm not sure how that would work. If we do that, it will just increase our costs.
R: Let's just stick with ideas for the moment. So Annette, anything to add?
A: Maybe we recruit some people with the languages we need.
R: I think that's a nice idea; simple and doable. I don't know the cost, but I like the fact that we might be able to do it relatively quickly.

4.05 R = Roel B = Bibi P = Peter A = Annette
R: So are there any more ideas? No? Well, I think recruitment is the best option.
B: Why do you think recruitment is the solution?
R: Well, we are looking for new salespeople anyway, at least two. And so it's a very easy thing to just add languages to the profile required.
B: I'm not sure that it's the best solution. I prefer training.
P: Bibi, just building on Roel's idea, I think it's easier to hire someone than train them in language skills. For our staff to learn Czech or Hungarian, it would take a very long time … years!
B: You may be right.
R: OK, then I think we need to look at recruitment as the quick solution. Agreed?
B: OK, I can live with this.
P: Yes.
A: Agreed.
R: Shall I take this on, or do any of you have time to do this? Annette, you normally handle people topics.
A: Do you want me to do that? I'm happy to take it on.
R: Great. So if you could get a job description done by the end of this week for us to discuss, then we can advertise next week, maybe hire by the end of the month. Problem solved in … what, three weeks?
B: If you need any help with this, just ask, Annette. It's quite a lot of work.
A: Great, thanks.
R: Great. That's what I love about you guys – such a great team.

5.01 A = Anne And = Anders
A: Anders. Good to see you again. Are you well?
And: Not bad. Just back from a weekend to see family in Copenhagen.
A: Very nice. We're just in here. Please, take a seat. Coffee?
And: No, I'm fine with water, thanks.
A: Please, help yourself. So, firstly, I should apologise for pushing. I really needed to have this meeting this morning. So, sorry about the very short notice but we have some new financial objectives in the company, from the board, so I have a lot to do on this end by the end of the month – all very urgent.
And: No problem. We need to discuss next year, anyway.
A: We do. So, as I said in my email to you, I think there are some important things we need to talk about. What I'd like to discuss today is, firstly, of course, price of service. Secondly, our cancellation policy. We have more and more cancellations, and we need to discuss how to handle this.
And: OK.
A: Thirdly, quality. You know, we've had a few issues with late taxi pick-ups, some hotels have been a little below standard.
And: OK, very happy to talk about that.
A: To start, I'd like to hear from you first. We talked about these topics last time we met, was it the end of last month? And you said you would have some discussions with your management. So perhaps it's useful to update first on how that went, and you can give me your first ideas on these topics.

5.02 And = Anders A = Anne
And: Yes, we did have some discussions. So, OK, firstly let me just check here, yes, OK, on the pricing side, my proposal would be that we go with an inflation-level price rise, which means just 2 percent, because I think we both appreciate that the economic situation is difficult, so I think this is probably fair to both of us. On the cancellation side, the policy is currently that you need to inform us eight hours before a taxi or a flight needs to be cancelled, or we will charge you for the booking. This is something we want to keep. We think eight hours is reasonable. And then, on the quality side, well, which is more on hotels, we only book as per your instructions, three- or four-star hotels, and we use the national rating system as a guide. The problem we find with hotels and experience of hotels, some people like one hotel and some people another. I realise some people are unhappy with some of the three-stars, but some are happy. So we would recommend no change here.
A: We've had some very unhappy executives.
And: I realise that, but as I said, in some of the same hotels, we have happy executives, even from your company. So, I think this is more around what some people like and don't like, and it's not really a quality issue. So, how does that all sound to you?
A: Thanks for that. So, going through the three points … Just to clarify, do you mean a 2 percent increase on both taxi and hotel accommodation prices?
And: Yes, that's right.
A: OK, I think the 2 percent, that's a little high; we were hoping for something lower. Would you consider 1.5 percent? That is more or less in line with the current company policy on vendor prices. Before you answer that, on the flight cancellation side, because business is less and less predictable, and more and more trips are being cancelled, we need to agree a different policy on this; we're paying for too many cancelled flights. My proposal would be that we go to three hours pre-warning of a flight problem from our side. I think that would really help us. Most trips are cancelled the morning of travel, so three hours would deal with this fine.
And: But three hours is very short notice.
A: It is. But it's reality. So we need to find a way around this. On the hotel quality side, I think we need to change how we do things and just go for four-star instead of three-star. Assuming we did this, we would want a three-star price on all our bookings; I think this is justified by the volume of bookings.

5.03 And = Anders A = Anne
And: OK, thanks for this. I think this is very fair, overall. On pricing, I can agree to 1.5 percent. We will need to review it again in the future but for next year, fine. On the flight cancellation problem, your proposal is very difficult for us to accept. If we make a flight booking, and then cancel it, we have a cost. This isn't something we can accept.
A: OK, but then you need to negotiate with the airlines.
And: We do talk to the airlines, of course, but they're not always so flexible. And any negotiation on this takes time; so it's very difficult for me to accept this shift to three hours. We could maybe go to six.
A: Six? OK, that might work. It's better than the eight – it makes it easier to cancel on the day of travel … so let's agree to that.
And: OK, good. And then on hotels, I think we can do this but we will need to limit the range of hotels. That will help us to be more flexible on price. You have a big choice of hotels in some locations. Can we change this to two hotels per location, for example?
A: That seems reasonable. OK, fine. Two hotels per location. I think we have six in some cases. And that's too many.
And: OK, good. Yes, so two hotels per city location, and we have a deal.

5.04 And = Anders A = Anne
And: So, is that everything?
A: Yes, I think that we have an agreement. We said that prices would go up by 1.5 percent. We agreed to change flight cancellation time without penalty to six hours before scheduled travel.
And: Correct.
A: And we are going for four-star hotels at three-star rates, but with just two hotels per location.
And: Yes.
A: What do we agree as the three-star rate?
And: That's actually going to be difficult because the rates actually vary a lot. Can we take the average three-star hotel rate in that location, just to use as a benchmark?
A: Fine. Great. So, thanks very much, Anders. If you confirm that in an email to me, then I will get agreement internally with my manager. Then we can draw up a new contract.
And: Very good. I'll email you by the end of this week.
A: Excellent. Well, that was quick and efficient. We have a little time for you to tell me all about your weekend in Copenhagen.

6.01
1 What do you like doing in your free time?
2 I like hanging out with friends.
3 Do you have any previous work or voluntary experience?
4 I take the dog for a walk every day.
5 What do you think you'll be doing in five years' time?
6 I've never thought about that.

Ext6.01   S = Susana   D = David
S: I think there are some unique challenges for young entrepreneurs like me.
D: What do you think they are?
S: Um, I had to find finance, which is harder because I had no experience. And I had to learn how to manage a team and be a good boss.
D: Do you think it's stressful?
S: It can be, but I have learnt ways to deal with it.

6.02 and 6.03
Part 1: the overview
In this next part of my presentation, I'm going to tell you more about the target market for our new company as well as market growth and our forecast for the next quarter. As you know, we produce specialist and high-end cases for mobile phones, tablets and laptops in a range of sizes for each product line.
On this slide you can see three charts. This pie chart shows us the age demographic of our target customers. You can see which ages the colours refer to on the right. You'll notice that the 18- to 25-year-old age group is our biggest target group. Next, you can see the growth of our market in terms of annual revenue on this line graph. The main point is that the mobile case sector is both our largest and fastest-growing sector.
Finally, on this bar chart, you can see the stock levels we have and our forecast for the next quarter year. At the end of Q4 we'll have this much stock and you can see from our projected sales that we're not going to have enough. We'll need more stock to be able to fulfil the orders that will come in. For that reason, we need a short-term loan so that we can buy more stock. I'd now like to hand over to my colleague, who will give you more details.

Part 2: the details
So coming back to the growth development graph. It is significant that the growth of the tablet product line has been slow and the laptop line has fallen slightly. On the other hand, you can see that the mobile sector has risen sharply and is projected to continue. These details confirm that mobile devices, in general, are outselling both tablets and laptops combined.
I'd also like to show you something on the customer age demographic pie chart. Although our cases are high-end and not exactly cheap, it's interesting to see that almost half of our customers are in the 18-to-25 age group, and almost a quarter are in the 25-to-30 age group. This means that around 70 percent of our customers are in the 18-to-30 age group and are willing to pay high-end prices for our cases. This fact proves that our cases are highly desirable for this age group and they're willing to spend, even though they might not have a lot of disposable income.
The last thing I want you to think about is our current stock levels. The stock is the quantity of product we have ready to sell in our warehouse. Looking more closely at the bar chart, you can see that we have greatly underestimated the growth of the mobile sector. For that reason, we don't have enough stock to meet the demand. We need more, but we'll need money, like a loan, to be able to buy more stock. If we can secure this loan, we will be investing in further stock, especially mobile cases. We see mobile cases as the big winner for the next two years at least.

6.04
Good evening everyone, I'm George Johnson and I started my business, GJWoodToys, while I was still working at my full-time job at an estate agent's, selling houses. Although I quite liked my job, ever since my kids were born I'd been making wooden toys for them as a hobby. But then other parents saw the toys and wanted to buy them and kept telling me that I should set up my own business. I started by selling the toys at craft fairs and they sold out every time. My target market was enormous: parents and their children, because kids are usually the ones to persuade the parents to part with their money. Parents like something that is well made, durable, reliable and above all safe, and the bright colours and versatility of each piece appeals to the children. It looked like we were onto a winner.
I continued making the toys in my garage for a while but then, when a couple of local stores approached me, I realised that I needed funding to expand my production and move into slightly larger premises. In order to do this and invest in more tools and employ more people, I had to use family savings and remortgage my house, which was a big risk because I could've lost all their money.
However it wasn't long after this that a big department store became interested in the toys after one of their directors had bought some at a craft fair. They started talking about placing an order for 50,000 units. It was at this point that I realised I had a potentially very successful product on my hands. However, this next step would require a huge investment and I just didn't have the money. With the promise of the order from the store I tried pitching to various potential backers to find the funding. The bank wasn't interested, so I started looking at the possibility of crowdfunding, although I eventually decided against this. I also talked to business angels. I was very lucky to meet a business angel who'd been looking for a start-up to invest in and he brought not only the investment needed but a wealth of experience, too.

6.05
So I know you're interested to hear any advice I can give you about setting up your own business. I think it's different for everyone but there are some common points you need to focus on.
Firstly, in the early days it's very important to believe passionately in your product or service. If you don't believe in it, you won't be able to sell it. You have to love what you do.
Once you know that you love the product, conduct as extensive market research as you can and listen to people's feedback. It's no good trying to take a product or service to market if nobody's going to be interested.
Thirdly, I think that good planning is key, especially time management, but also planning every step of the journey. A good plan acts as a map for your business. And if something fails, you can go back to the drawing board and redraw that map.
The best piece of advice someone gave me at the beginning was to be open to advice, but remember that not all advice will be helpful so, if it doesn't feel right for you, ignore it. And don't be afraid to ask for advice or help when you need it. Remember you're not an expert in everything.
Another vital thing is to manage your finances carefully and make sure you know how your money's being used, how much you're spending and earning at all times. As you get bigger and the amounts of money involved get larger and the money is no longer just yours, this becomes even more important, so start off as you mean to go on. And talking about money, if you end up working with large retailers, like me, don't let them beat you down on unit prices as they'll always try to push the price down as far as they can. When you know what price works for you, stick to it. If the retailers want to sell your product, you know it must be good so don't give it away.
With everything else that's going on, don't forget your customer. The customer is the source of your inspiration and rewards, so developing close customer relations is absolutely vital. As soon as you start forgetting the customer, your business is likely to begin to fail.
Furthermore, the frightening thing is that suddenly you become a leader and managing a company and its personnel is not easy. So my advice to you here is to learn to trust your key people and delegate work appropriately. When you've been the only one responsible for everything for so long, I think this is the hardest thing to do – handing it over to others.
And finally, above all, never underestimate how hard it is to succeed. You'll probably find yourself working harder than you've ever worked in your life.

7.01
1 Let me tell you about my experience of working abroad. At the time, I was working as the Regional Financial Director of a construction company with a division in India. Part of my job consisted of meeting senior bank executives to arrange bank guarantees and credit facilities. Once, I went to a meeting with the chairman of a bank in Mumbai and when I went into his office, I was surprised to see a shrine set up on the table where discussions were going to take place and incense was burning in the room. After the customary greetings and introductions, the chairman then turned on some chanting music. I asked what the music was and he told me that it was Indian mantra music to help create a good atmosphere in the meeting. The Indians believed it encouraged a positive outcome. It was quite a different experience to doing business back at home. I had never seen this kind of thing before!
Another thing is that in countries like India, employees will hardly ever tell their bosses that something is not possible. Saying 'no' is often considered 'loss of face'. By 'loss of face', I mean embarrassing a person in front of others, or offending them, and this can of course lead to problems in the workplace. While I was working in India, I often experienced this problem first hand. For instance, employees didn't report problems because they didn't want to give a bad impression to their bosses.
2 While I was living in Kenya, I discovered that optimism is highly valued in Kenyan society. It's reflected in the popular catchphrase 'Hakuna matata', which means 'No worries'. This idea of 'Hakuna matata' sometimes caused conflict at work and led to missed deadlines, you know, people didn't finish a task or a report by a given time.
When I was working in the office in Nairobi, workers preferred to agree to deadlines without questioning them. Later, they admitted that they couldn't meet the deadline, even if they had previously agreed to it. I found it very frustrating. On the other hand, being surrounded by optimistic people helped lighten the office atmosphere and often diffused stressful situations. So, that was the positive side of 'Hakuna matata'.
3 While I was working as a supervisor in a call centre in Delhi for a multinational, I had to report to my boss in Los Angeles. It was very stressful working in customer service. We had to deal with complaints on a daily basis. The last week of the month my American boss was insisting on me sending a report with our latest figures for resolving complaints, and I had promised to send them to him. But then we got very busy. A lot of my co-workers had fallen ill with a virus that was going round and I was working really hard: I was going to work early and I was leaving late at night to cover for them. So I didn't have time to reply to my boss. It was unlucky because he had wanted the figures by the end of the month, but I had to prioritise. Then he started sending me urgent emails with red flags and written in big, capital letters and that was the equivalent of shouting at me. He had also copied in my colleagues. I mean, he shouldn't have written in capital letters, right? He should have picked up the phone and talked to me. Of course, that wasn't easy because of the time difference. And I know Americans are stricter

Audioscripts

about time, but he didn't have to shame me like that! Thinking about it, I wanted to create a good impression because the company culture was very competitive, so I didn't explain all the problems we were having. That was my mistake. But the worst thing was he had copied in all the team – it made me look really bad. It was so embarrassing. I couldn't work there after that, so I quit my job. I didn't go in the next day.

7.02 T = Tadashi   Pe = Peter   Pi = Pilar
T: Hello.
Pe: Hi, I'm Peter. I'm from D2 Logistics.
T: I'm Tadashi.
Pe: Nice to meet you, Tadashi. So … I'm a finance specialist. What do you do? Are you working on any interesting projects?
T: I'm in marketing. I design marketing campaigns.
Pe: Oh. … Er, so what do you think of the elections? Who do you think will win?
T: I don't know.
Pe: But you must have an idea. What do you think?
T: I'm not sure.
Pe: Oh.
Pi: Hi, I'm Pilar.
Pe: Hello Pilar, it's nice to meet you. I'm Peter.
Pi: It's nice to meet you too, Peter.
T: Hello, I'm Tadashi.
Pe: So, Pilar. What do you do?
Pi: I'm an accountant during the day and I play in a local band at weekends … in Mexico City … that's where I live at the moment … We practise a lot during the week which doesn't give me too much time with my family. I have two brothers, and we all still live at home.
Pe: You're an accountant. Really? I'm a finance specialist. Who do you work for?
Pilar: Oh, er … I work for ACC Products. I'm a property accountant.
Pe: OK. I … er … don't know much about property. Well, I think I'll go back to the buffet to … get some more …

7.03 Pe = Peter   T = Tadashi   Pi = Pilar
Pe: So, Tadashi, you're in marketing. What sort of campaigns do you design?
T: I'm working on one at the moment for a hotel chain. We're making ads that will run in planes, on the little screens. Er, is that OK?
Pe: Er, sure. That project sounds really interesting. I saw ads like that the last time I flew on holiday.
T: Maybe they were my ads.
Pe: Yeah, maybe … It's a very good place to run ads, everyone on the plane sees them.
T: Yes. We try to make the ads specific to the country, if possible, and we always try to put in a little humour.
Pe: Yes, flying and going through airports can be stressful. It's good to have a little humour.
Pi: So Peter, where did you go on holiday?
Pe: I went to Brazil. It was a very long flight, but I had a really nice time with my family. It was a special trip for my father's 60th birthday.
Pi: Great!
Pe: You know, I also have two brothers, like you. One older and one younger.
Pilar: So you're in the middle, then?
Peter: Yes, that's it.

7.04
That was a really nice evening. At the beginning it felt a bit awkward, it wasn't that easy to talk to Tadashi or Pilar. I thought that Tadashi's English wasn't very good and that he was shy and insecure. But I was making assumptions and I was wrong on both points. He was quite fluent, and very enthusiastic when we were talking about things he likes and he's good at. He thinks a lot about what other people say before he reacts. When I realised that, I stopped talking so much. Then he had more time to think, and he spoke more too. And Pilar? I didn't really take her seriously at first; I thought she just wanted to talk about her free time. But when I stopped talking about work and talked about my family and travel, the conversation really developed. We connected more, and then it was easier to find out more about her job and what she does. I guess first impressions can often be wrong, especially with people from different cultures. Anyway, I'm glad I adapted my approach and got to know them a bit better.

8.01 J = John   P = Philippe   B = Bettina   A = Angela
J: Thanks, everyone, for coming to this special meeting today.
P: No problem. Happy to be here.
B: Sure.
J: There is a management meeting at the end of the month and I have to present a short update on our team and our current project. I called this meeting because I need your help to prepare the presentation, and I want to give the most accurate update, while also representing the successes our team has had recently.
A: OK, how can we help?
J: Well, ideally, the goal for this meeting is to decide which information we want to present to senior management, and which tasks each of you will do to prepare.
P: OK, sounds good.
J: So, we have one hour. Let's start by first focusing on our goal in a little more detail. Then, I'd like to collect your ideas on what we should present. After that, we can discuss your ideas and mine. Next, we'll choose the best options, and then finally we can assign tasks for each of you to do in advance of the management meeting. Does that process sound alright?
All: Yes.
J: OK, let's begin by thinking about the management meeting and what our goal actually is.

8.02 A = Angela   P = Philippe   J = John   B = Bettina
A: So I think we should include some information about the delay in finishing the new designs as that has had a …
P: No, we shouldn't do that. We don't want to draw attention to our mistakes. I think we should focus on different facts of the …
J: Philippe, I understand what you're staying is important, but please let Angela finish. We can come to you next, OK?
P: OK, sure, fine.
J: OK, Angela, back to you. Could you try to limit your overview to about two minutes? We need to keep an eye on the clock.
A: No problem. Thanks, John. So, as I was saying, I think we should at least explain that there were delays because they had an effect on the next steps of the project, which meant that we all had to work overtime to get back on track.
J: Yes, that's a good idea, I'll need to explain the increase in costs due to overtime. OK, back to you Philippe.
P: Thanks, John. Well, as I was trying to say, we need to be careful about the negative information we present. We don't want to focus on the negative elements of the past, risk getting in trouble or even worse, we could have our budgets cut.
B: Wait a minute. Who said anything about budgets being cut?
P: Don't interrupt me, Bettina.
J: OK, OK, you two, take it easy. I know you're both passionate about this, but we need to allow each other time to speak.
P: Yes, I agree. And I am not finished. I just wanted to say that I think we should instead focus on the fact that we ran into some difficulties, but we got the designs finished and the project is now running smoothly.
J: OK, thanks, Philippe. Good idea.
B: I need my budget to pay for the market research we already agreed on.
J: Bettina, I understand your concern, but the market research has already been commissioned and the results are also expected back next week. No one has said we need to reduce the budgets. The market research results aren't on today's agenda, so can we talk about that when the results come back in? In the meantime, can you give us a brief update on what you'll be working on in the project for the next couple of weeks?

8.03 J = John   P = Philippe   A = Angela   B = Bettina
J: Thanks, everyone. This has been a very productive meeting. It was useful to talk through both our successes and areas for concern. I need to be able to present a realistic, but positive, picture of our team's activity at the management meeting.
P: Thanks, John. Yes, it's been good to talk through everything.
J: OK, so the action points from this meeting are: Angela, you'll prepare two slides on the designs update. I'll mention that there were delays that we are now on top of, but the main focus should be on the positive outcome of the designs and the next steps.
A: Right.
J: Philippe, you'll prepare an overview of the media campaign we're planning and the timeline for what will happen.
P: OK.
J: And Bettina, you'll prepare an overview of the market research results. Hopefully they'll confirm what we think about the market and give some further information.
B: Sure. I hope to have them on Wednesday, so that will give me time to review them and send you the most important points.
J: Great. So, is everyone OK with their tasks?
All: Yes./Sure.
J: Does anyone have any questions about what they have to do? Or need any support?
All: No.
J: OK, great. And I'll prepare some brief information on the overall timeline and where we expect to be in the next two months. Let's meet again to finalise everything at 2 p.m. on Friday next week. Please send me your completed tasks before close of business on Thursday.
A: Sure.
P: No problem.
B: Fine.
J: OK, thanks, everyone.

BW1.01
1 As the company's grown we've squeezed more and more people into the same space. It's just so cramped now. And people have different work styles. I don't like being tied down to a desk all the time – moving around helps me to think, like when I'm talking to people on the phone. But this open-plan office makes this impossible for me to do without disturbing other people. Likewise, it's sometimes difficult for me to do any work where I really have to concentrate due to noise levels and visual distractions.
It'd be great to have a more flexible work environment – more meeting rooms, you know, breakout spaces for teamwork and quiet zones where you can work alone and really focus.
2 There isn't anything special about our current office space that differentiates it from any other office right now. It doesn't say anything about our business. We say we're innovative, fun-loving and tech-savvy so that message should be loud and clear in our office design, in the furniture and in the artwork on the walls. Let's make sure potential clients and recruits see and feel what we're about when they walk through the doors.
The company values work–life balance for staff and I'd like more flexible working hours and the chance to work from home a few days a week rather than the current presenteeism, so I can pick my young son up from school every day.
3 The kitchen is a tiny, windowless room with grey walls. Nobody wants to spend more time there than strictly necessary. Then there are

vending machines in the corridor but no seating areas. I'd provide free fruit in public areas and let's get away from people eating at their desks. Apart from anything else, it's smelly!

The best ideas aren't going to come when sitting in front of your monitor, but from those chance interactions and exchanges between staff. We need to create welcoming public spaces, such as a kitchen/dining room where staff from different departments can actually mingle and communicate. Let's make sure to have plenty of space for socialising and collaboration. How about a ping-pong table and attractive outside spaces as well?

BW2.01

1 So, you're asking about window displays? Well, I think this is something the company could improve. Kloze-Zone's design and quality are great, but I'd like to see more innovation in the window displays because it's what makes you go into a store when you're walking down the High Street.

2 We have some special offers and promotions, but our competitors, for example, organise special days in their stores every season, with clothes at 50 percent off. That attracts a lot of interest. I know this heavy discounting doesn't increase sales that much, but it works really well to raise brand awareness. We did have a special event for the store opening – it was a lot of work, but it was great; there was a local band playing and staff gave out free T-shirts to customers. Another thing is, I think we should organise some kind of promotional event in months like November and February, to promote the store. Those months are very quiet for us.

3 I think fast-fashion retailers do a lot to market their clothes at mostly women. I get bored with seeing the same kinds of adverts that are targeted at girls. I think they should aim their campaigns at guys, too. For example, I like going shopping with my girlfriend. Also, when men go shopping, we often buy two of the same thing if we really like it, so that's good business. Perhaps they need more engaging marketing campaigns for guys?

4 What do I think of their customer service? Well, shop assistants sometimes seem too busy to help customers when you're trying on clothes in the fitting rooms. I mean, you might want to try on a different colour or size, and you're not with a friend, so it's difficult. I think they need to employ more staff in the store. But I love their mobile app and it's dead easy to use. The design is really cool because you can check out the clothes and mix and match them online before you come to the shop.

5 Well, I work in the Berlin store. It's difficult because there are a lot of High Street fashion stores in Berlin – it's very competitive. But we work really hard. When we first opened, it used to be fun, then a couple of my colleagues left last month because of the long working hours. We have to work from nine to seven, and Saturdays, too. And even some Sundays. I don't know about Japan – I think they only get two weeks of holiday every year there. But in Germany workers expect a break and longer holidays, you know?

6 What could we improve at Kloze-Zone? The main problem I have as a store manager is that staff turnover is pretty high. Some young people start working in fashion thinking it's going to be good fun, trying on clothes all the time. They don't realise you're on your feet all day and you have to be polite to the customers all the time – even when they complain and return items. I need staff who understand fashion, although, to be honest, a lot of the people I interview aren't even aware of our brand. They confuse us with other High Street stores! I think we need to improve brand awareness to attract both more customers and staff.

BW3.01

Amalia
Is this webcam on? Oh, right! So, why should you hire me? Well, I have to say I think I'm hard-working, I'm reliable, and … I'm highly qualified. I have a background in marketing and a lot of experience in different sectors. I also speak various languages, so that will be very useful for an international company like Media Solutions. I would like to work for you because I think I'm good at communicating, especially writing, and I could contribute to your Communications department with my ideas and improve the presence of your clients in social media. Err, … that's all really. Thanks for listening. Oh, and please call me if you'd like me to come in for an interview.

Birte
Why should you hire me? Because I'm a 'people person': I'm not only sociable, but also really creative and if you hired me, I would give 110 percent and I would get on with all the team and the clients, too. Another thing you should know about me is I'm really into sports and martial arts, as you can see. You can check out some of my videos in social media on how to do sports training. I love social media and dedicate a lot of time to it. It's the way everyone communicates nowadays.
What else? I've got a degree in marketing. I did an internship at my dad's company and I learnt a lot. I'm a fast learner. I don't have lots of experience but I think it's more important to have the right attitude and just get out there and do it! So why should you hire me? Because I'm worth it! Call me for an interview and please give me the chance to tell you more.

Cindy
So, you'd like to know why you should hire me? That's a good question. Looking at my CV you might think I don't have any relevant experience but I do have experience in managing people. I have to communicate in my job every day, where I'm responsible for a team of forty people, talking to different departments and dealing with difficult customers. I'm good at working under pressure, so you can depend on me to write those reports on time! Oh sorry, just a minute …. another consideration is that I'm a big fan of social media. I write a blog in my free time, although I don't have that many followers yet. I'm also studying marketing online in the evenings. So, if you hire me, I will help you to find the best solutions for you and your clients and improve their online presence with the contributions of key opinion leaders and influencers.
Thank you for considering my application and I look forward to your call!

BW3.02

Amalia
My proudest achievement? Oh, err … that's a difficult question. I think it was the time when I graduated from university … no, sorry, I think my proudest moment was when I organised a charity event for homeless people in my town. It was a lot of work, but the response from the public was tremendous and we raised over £4,000. I was responsible for organising the social media campaign and talking to the press. I think I did a good job and my family told me they were very proud of me. It was a brilliant experience that made me want to work in social media.

Birte
My proudest achievement has to be when I started a social media campaign about young people with eating disorders. I started posting a video every day with tips for having a healthy diet but it was all about feeling good, not making life more difficult for yourself. There's a lot of contradictory advice about health tips on the internet. You know, people say different things and that confuses people. Then I suddenly got thousands of followers on social media and I realised that my videos and advice on doing exercise and having a healthy diet were making a difference. To give you an example, I received one post from a young woman who was in hospital at the time and she wrote saying that I was an inspiration to her. And that made me feel really proud of what I was doing, my blog was really helping people, you know?

Cindy
That's an interesting question. I'm not sure … I think it was when there was a problem while I was still working as an intern. There was a public transport strike and lots of people were phoning the department and complaining. There was a lack of information and we were getting very negative comments on social media and from the press and a lot of my colleagues didn't seem very interested. Then we had a crisis meeting and the team decided to work hard until late at night to solve problems and to deal with all the emails and phone calls from the public. But I took the initiative to start writing replies to the negative posts on social media, so we improved our company image and my boss thanked me in front of the whole team. And because of me, the department started taking social media more seriously. I felt really proud. I was just the intern.

BW4.01

As the supermarket wars continue we take a look at three major supermarket chains to find out about their strategies.

Upmarket food retailer White's has introduced a loyalty scheme to provide better value to members rather than lowering its prices and entering into a price war with discounters.

It has also expanded its own-brand range and promises 'price matches' with the own brands of other major supermarket chains, like Mulberry's. However, the CEO has announced that it will also continue to invest £400 million each year on weekly special offers and price promotions rather than cutting prices permanently.

She said White's will continue to focus on an excellent in-store service, as well as high-quality product ranges. The supermarket is making a major move into food-to-go to meet the needs of busy consumers.

Food retail giant Mulberry's is still finding it hard to adapt to both increased competition from discounters and changing consumer shopping habits.

Its 'back-to-basics' strategy includes selling off non-core activities, such as in-store restaurants, and it will also stop selling clothes and consumer electronics.

The chain is also spending less on special promotions in order to simplify its strategy and is cutting the number of products to 20,000 to cut costs. Mulberry's smaller convenience stores and its online store have seen good sales growth but falling food prices continue to reduce profit margins. Latest figures show its market share remains flat, at 16 percent.

The discounter C&C has achieved spectacular sales growth in recent years. While the other main players in the retail food market have been closing supermarkets, C&C has just announced its ambitious expansion plan including the construction of fifty new stores.

The chain also said that it will refurbish 150 existing stores over the next three to four years in order to attract more customers. The retailer is also doubling its product range and including more fresh meat and a new own-brand low-price luxury range to rival the main supermarket chains.

With these major investments, it remains to be seen if C&C will also have to change its lowest price strategy.

BW5.01 AW = Anna Woźniak
TW = Tadeusz Walentowicz

AW: So, Ted, what I'm saying is we need automation for selecting and lifting heavy furniture from high shelves.
TW: But we've been doing that with fork-lift trucks for years.
AW: The thing is, there have been more accidents in the warehouse recently because of the increased numbers of orders. Staff are constantly doing overtime, they can't handle the work and goods are damaged, …

Audioscripts

TW: OK, but the items have to be packed carefully and this should still be done manually.
AW: Yes, I agree.
TW: And if we introduce robotics technology to avoid breakage, we have to make sure the supplier provides training. If not, we'll have robots going out of control!
AW: Don't worry, both suppliers say they'll provide training.
TW: So, tell me about these providers. Were they recommended?
AW: Yes, I had recommendations from my contacts in car companies. One here in Poznań and one in Germany.
TW: Good.
AW: One of the providers is a robotics developer from Singapore and the other is Japanese.
TW: Japan, eh? They are going to be expensive.
AW: Both offer quality automation and training. We have to move with the times, Ted.
TW: I know, but I'm worried about costs *and* maintenance. What do we do when the robots break down? What happens if we need maintenance? Are there local people who can fix it, or will they send a guy from Singapore?
AW: Those are good questions. That's why I've arranged interviews with the suppliers tomorrow. You have a teleconference with the supplier from Singapore and I'll talk to the one from Japan. Then we'll compare notes.
TW: All right. And what are *your* main concerns, Anna?
AW: I think there will be some problems with the transition, when we'll have to deal with the old system and the new technology at the same time.
TW: Mmm, Human Resources say there will be a negative reaction from the employees – people are worried about robots taking their jobs.
AW: I know, but we need this automation if we're going to stay competitive. And they'll learn new skills.
TW: Well, Human Resources want to discuss possible job losses. Unfortunately, I don't see all of our workers continuing with robots. But I agree some employees can be retrained. So, tell me a bit more about these suppliers.
AW: Well, Novarobot is based in Singapore. They do industrial automation.
TW: And the Japanese one?
AW: The Japanese supplier is called Bot-automation. They're based in Osaka and also focus on robotics design and …
TW: We are going to be taken over by robots. If my father saw this company now …
AW: Your father would want the company to be successful. It's going to make everything much easier, Ted! Trust me.

BW5.02
Supplier A
TW = Tadeusz Walentowicz   TK = Tony King
TW: So, I understand you are specialists in industrial automation, Mr King. And you have worked with clients in the automotive industry in Germany.
TK: That's right. And we have worked with clients in Poland, too.
TW: Good. That will be an advantage.
TK: As I explained to your logistics manager, I'm sure we can help you manage your logistics more efficiently using artificial intelligence.
TW: So, how do you work? How will the robots be installed?
TK: The way we work is that automation systems are installed in two phases.
TW: Two phases? Why is that?
TK: This allows for an easy …, a smooth transition between manual and automated systems. Your warehouse will have to stop operations for three days during each phase of the installation.
TW: But we can't lose six working days!
TK: We appreciate that, so to minimise the effects on production, this work can be done at the weekend.
TW: From Friday to Sunday?

TK: That's right.
TW: And what happens if something goes wrong? Do you have technicians who can do maintenance, at no extra cost?
TK: Err, … first of all, we offer a *two-year* guarantee. Many robotics companies offer less. There are sometimes technical problems, usually because operators are not used to the system. Any failure will be repaired by Novarobot technicians during this period. We also do a maintenance inspection, free of charge, once a year.
TW: That's good to know. But what happens when this two-year guarantee ends?
TK: Our robots are made to last for years, Mr Walentowicz. But I recommend you contract our after-sales service. That way you can call an emergency hotline and speak to an engineer 24 hours a day.
TW: Mmm, I'll need to talk to our logistics manager. Could you send me the details and costs of your after-sales service?
TK: Yes, of course.
TW: And I'd like to know about training.
TK: Basic training is provided during installation. After that, our technicians deal with any problems via email, or videoconference. You'll also have a maintenance inspection, once a year.
TW: Well, I think we are going to consider your proposal. And then, if we accept your offer, you can visit our warehouse and discuss what we need.
TK: Can I ask, when do you think that will be?
TW: The logistics manager will contact you.
TK: We hope we can do business with you. Thank you for your time, Mr Walentowicz.
TW: You're welcome, Mr King. Goodbye.

Supplier B
AW = Anna Woźniak   KI = Kin Izumi
KI: Thank you for showing an interest in us, Ms Woźniak.
AW: I see your team has won awards.
KI: That's right. We are innovators in robotics design.
AW: But I'd like to know how your company differs from the competition.
KI: Err … If you choose us, we can provide solutions in many areas: mobile robotics, motor control and industrial automation. We are an ISO-certified company.
AW: I see.
KI: And we give customised solutions.
AW: That's good to hear.
KI: And specialist engineers assess your needs and then adapt the mobile robotics to your warehouse.
AW: Great, so you adapt to our specific needs.
KI: That's right.
AW: And what about installation? How will that work? I imagine there will be a transition period when we still operate manually, while the employees learn to use the new system.
KI: Mmm, … not exactly.
AW: Could you clarify that?
KI: Sorry, but we don't have a transition period. We find it causes confusion. We suggest your warehouse stops operations for six to seven consecutive days.
AW: Seven days! That much time?
KI: Err, … we recommend, for example, from Saturday to Friday. This can be done over a public holiday or in the summer.
AW: Well, that's not ideal. And what about training?
KI: Two specialist technicians provide the training after the installation period. Manuals in English are also provided. That way, any basic maintenance can be solved later on by your own staff.
AW: Good. And what about the guarantee?
KI: We offer an 18-month guarantee.
AW: Only 18 months! But what happens after that? Or if the equipment breaks down?
KI: Technicians from Bot-automation can help via an emergency hotline and teleconference. We guarantee our technicians will visit your warehouse in 36 hours if complex maintenance is needed during the first 18 months.
AW: But not after that?

KI: That depends.
AW: Do you mean there will be an additional cost for the after-sales service when the guarantee ends?
KI: That's correct.
AW: Mmm, well, I'd like to discuss your offer with our director, and then we'll get back to you.
KI: Of course. But remember if you order a fourth robot, we will offer you a discount for the after-sales service.
AW: That's good to know. Excuse me. I'm afraid I have another meeting now.
KI: Please contact me if you have any questions, Ms Woźniak.
AW: Thank you, Mr Izumi. We'll be in touch.

BW6.0.1
Ben Fischer
Hi guys! I'm Ben Fischer and my award-winning theatre company performs at events and festivals all over the world. We bring the works of famous German writers and dramatists, such as Bertolt Brecht, to audiences across the globe.
In true dramatic style, our latest production of Brecht's *The Good Person of Szechwan* has just been hit by disaster. An electrical fire destroyed the arts centre where we were performing in London and took with it all our costumes and equipment. Fortunately, nobody was in the building at the time and nobody was injured in the fire.
We know one day the insurance company will eventually pay the compensation to rebuild and replace everything, but we need to complete our world tour now and can't wait around for the money to arrive.
Can you help us? We need to raise €10,000 in the next few weeks to replace everything. I promise all donations to our cause will be repaid when we receive the insurance payout. Not only that, depending on the size of your donation you will receive discounts on tickets and even free tickets to see our play in any city of your choice on the tour. Just see our website for more details.
As Brecht himself once said, 'Everyone needs help from everyone.' By contributing to our disaster fund, you will be doing your bit to support community arts and help our young theatre group to literally rise from the ashes. Thank you!

Alison Chadwick
My name's Alison Chadwick and this is my story. I started my T-shirt business, Alison's Tees, back in university as a hobby. Friends and fellow students used to ask me where I got my T-shirts from and when I told them I designed them myself everyone said that was cool.
Then I thought, you know anyone can design their own T-shirt. It's simple, it's fun and it's creative. On my website you can choose the colour and style but more than that, you can have any design or logo you like printed on it including photos to make your very own unique T-shirt. Friends will be amazed. Before we finally produce the T-shirt, you'll receive a photo of the design for final approval.
No more shopping for hours looking for something you actually like. No more low-quality shop-bought products. All our T-shirts are 100 percent organic cotton and ethically sourced. We're helping independent cotton farmers. We work hand-in-hand with our suppliers to ensure highest-quality tees.
Thanks to previous crowdfunding our business has been a big success. Now we need your support and your money to help us develop our mobile app so our users can design and order their own tees on their smartphones, anytime, anywhere.

Marcos López
If you like travelling, you'll love our new tour guide mobile app. It's like an audio guide but on your mobile phone, so you carry it with you all the time. I'm Marcos López and I'm one of the founders of Holidapp. It's the ultimate travel companion. It's like having an audio guide but on your smartphone. You'll never want to buy another guidebook or tourist map again in your life. You'll

find out about the places you're visiting whenever you want in a new, original and entertaining way. Our app is free to download and quick and easy to use. Enter the desired location and for just €10 you will get an expert guide to one of over 30 destinations in Europe and the USA. And the list of places is growing longer each month.
The guide features audio tours by experts in their towns, from qualified tour guides to local storytellers of all ages with a passion for the place where they live. Our platform is free to our guide contributors and they receive 70 percent of the revenues generated by their guides.
Each travel guide on our app comes with high-quality photographs and can use your geolocation to help you get the most from your guide.
We need your backing to help us cover the cost of production, audio recording, programming and photography. We'd also love to hear what you think of the guides so we can keep improving our service.

BW7.01

1 Oh, when the Dutch managers visited our office, it was very nice. We had good conversations about our respective traditions, our families and food. They loved our Indian food. Regarding business, I would say that we're like one big family here. I have cousins, uncles and aunties in the office working here, and so we work very well together. I realise it's different in Europe but this is how we work in this country. We trust each other. It's just the way it is. Our business relationships are based on trust. The only thing is that they kept insisting about the report for the latest sales figures. And I said, it wasn't a problem, no problem at all. We'll have the report ready soon. I told them not to worry about that. You can't say 'no', or 'that's not possible' to a visitor, can you? That would be terribly impolite!
2 We got on very well with the managers from Betker Finance. It was great seeing them face to face. Perhaps here in the south we're not as punctual as they are. But that doesn't mean we're less productive. In fact I think we're much better at multi-tasking. I find Northern Europeans tend to do only one thing at a time. You know, they're only focused on one thing, which seems a bit limiting if something important suddenly comes up. For example, as the Sales Manager in my region, I have to manage a large team of people and juggle different tasks at the same time. So, it's normal that when I'm in a meeting with a colleague, I might have interruptions, like an urgent phone call, or someone from the office comes in to ask me something. It's the way we work. But I don't think our Dutch colleagues had a good first impression of us. And we're great believers in first impressions.

BW7.02

3 When the sales manager came from headquarters, he just said: 'Hi, how's it going?' and he got down to business right away, talking about figures and KPIs. You know, key performance indicators. Actually, there was no time to reply, or even for me to ask him the same thing. It was very direct and abrupt, which surprised me. I know it's good to be efficient and have a purpose in a meeting, but in our culture, we always make conversation before getting down to business. I often ask the visitor about events in their country, and find out about their interests and maybe their family. It's important to get to know the other person to establish a good atmosphere. I mean, we all want to do business with people we like, don't we?

4 When the sales representative came from Betker Finance, it was quite erm, quite difficult because she talked a lot about the new products which were very erm ... interesting, but I had the impression that she didn't understand our market so well. And at the end of the first meeting, she thought we had finished, we had just begun! She also asked me many questions, which I couldn't answer because I needed to get approval from my boss. So when I said at the end of our conversation that I needed to check everything with him, she seemed a little erm ... annoyed. I felt bad about that. And we thought she was staying for the week, so we would have time to discuss the new products with the team, and adapt them for our market, but she left after a couple of days. Then she sent me an email confirming points that we hadn't agreed on. I tried to explain that we do business as a team, and everything has to be confirmed by my bosses. I hope our next meeting will be more harmonious.

BW8.01   HR = Human Resources Manager
CM = Cris Martinez   AC = Alex Cortés
DL = Danni Lee
1, Cris Martinez
HR: Have you had any thoughts about your current training needs, Cris?
CM: Well, these days I'm responsible for formulating our long-term business plans and, as you know, I report directly to the Chief Financial Officer. I've done a lot of generic training courses in core management skills over the years. Now I need something more practical than sitting down all day in a training room looking at PowerPoint slides and doing roleplays.
HR: I see. So, regular training courses are not of interest to you?
CM: No, no, no. I want to tie my leadership development to my real-world projects. It'd be good to be able to build up a network with other senior managers in Grupo Tula around the world to share ideas, ... and problems and solutions.
HR: So, a support network of peers would interest you?
CM: That's right! We can learn a lot from each other's experiences. One key role of senior executives is managing change and I think we can support each other with this. It would be good to get the perspective of executives with diverse cultural and business perspectives.
HR: At the same time, you have a great deal of knowledge and expertise which you could pass on.
CM: Yes, that's true. Of course I believe that talent development should be a part of a senior manager's job. It's just getting the time to do it, isn't it?
2, Alex Cortés
HR: What type of training would interest you Alex, and why?
AC: My job essentially is to make sure the day-to-day business runs smoothly, which includes overseeing a lot of staff. I know the technical side of my job well. So, I'd like to do something new to improve my leadership skills. I want to help my staff develop, get better results from them, and not just focus on completing the task.
HR: Right. So you want to help your staff improve their performance?
AC: That's it!
HR: Anything else you might like to do?
AC: Yes, well, a big part of my work is negotiating deals with suppliers and clients and more and more of them are outside Mexico nowadays. I can see why the company has adopted English as the official language since the merger, but I don't feel as confident communicating in English as I do in Spanish, particularly in meetings and when I'm giving presentations. I know I'm really going to need to do something to improve my fluency if I'm going to progress through management levels in the future.
HR: Yes, I think a lot of people are going to want more English language training now. By the way, have you been back to Spain recently?
AC: No, but my parents are coming here next month. It'll be good to see them again!
HR: I can imagine.
3, Danni Lee
HR: So, Danni how are you adapting to life in Mexico? A bit different from Wisconsin, right?
DL: It's been great! Everyone's so helpful and friendly.
HR: That's good to hear. Now tell me a bit about yourself. I see you have a degree in business administration and started here six months ago in the sales division. How's that going?
DL: I really love the work, but I'm not always sure what I'm supposed to be doing or if I'm focusing on the right things. I have so many demands on my time and I feel quite stressed by it all. I work really long hours but I don't think that's what I should be doing either because I have no life outside the office at the end of the day.
HR: I see. That's not good. It sounds like you need some help with those issues.
DL: And you know, I don't know why they didn't teach us more practical computer skills at university, like Excel. It would really help me a lot with my job now.
HR: Maybe some on-the-job training would be an idea or an online course?
DL: Yeah, I'm sure I could pick it up quickly enough with some help. I'm really keen to learn as much as I can. At the moment I don't manage any staff but I'm quite ambitious. I'd like to lead a team one day so I'd like to know more about what that involves.

P4.02
1
OK, let's get started. Good morning, everyone.
2
A: How about using a call centre service for different languages? People who call us, they can choose the language they work with, and we contract a call centre to handle first contacts, and then they contact our sales staff.
B: That sounds like a possible solution.
C: OK, but I'm not sure how that would work. If we do that, it will just increase our costs.
3
A: Bibi, just building on what Roel said, I think it's easier to hire someone than train them in language skills. For our staff to learn Czech or Hungarian, it would take a very long time ... years!
B: You may be right.
C: OK, then I think we need to look at recruitment as the quick solution.
4
I'll send Stefanie over to Tokyo for a couple of weeks, OK?

P8.03
1 The workshop, which I was planning to attend, was cancelled.
2 The workshop which I was planning to attend was cancelled.

Glossary

- **adjective** (*adj.*) Headwords for adjectives followed by information in square brackets, e.g. [only before a noun] and [not before a noun], show any restrictions on where they can be used.
- **noun** (*n.*) The codes [C] and [U] show whether a noun, or a particular sense of a noun, is countable (*an agenda, two agendas*) or uncountable (*awareness, branding*).
- **verb** (*v.*) The forms of irregular verbs are given after the headword. The codes [I] (intransitive) and [T] (transitive) show whether a verb, or a particular sense of a verb, has or does not have an object. Phrasal verbs (*phr. v.*) are shown after the verb they are related to.
- Some entries show information on words that are related to the headword. Adverbs (*adv.*) are often shown in this way after adjectives.
- **region labels** The codes *AmE* and *BrE* show whether a word or sense of a word is used only in American or British English.

acquire *v.* [T] if one company acquires another, it buys it

acquisition *n.* [C] when one company buys another one, or part of another one

action point *n.* [C] something that you decide must be done, especially after a meeting or after studying something carefully

advertising *n.* [U] the activity or business of telling people publicly about a product or service in order to persuade them to buy it
advertising campaign *n.* [C] an organisation's programme of advertising activities over a particular period of time with specific aims, for example to increase sales of a product
print advertising *n.* [U] advertising in newspapers and magazines

agenda *n.* [C] **1** a list of the subjects to be discussed at a meeting
2 the things that someone considers important or that they are planning to do something about

angel (*also* **business angel**) *n.* [C] a private investor who puts money into new business activities

application *n.* [C] **1** a formal, usually written, request for something or for permission to do something
2 (*also* **job application**) a request to be considered for a job, usually done by sending in a CV and letter or by filling out a form with information about yourself and your previous jobs
3 a piece of software for a particular use or job

apply *v.* **1** [I] to make a formal, usually written, request for something, especially a job, a place at university or permission to do something
2 [T] to use something, such as a law or an idea, in a particular situation, activity or process

appoint *v.* [T] to choose someone for a job or position

approach *n.* [C] a method of doing something

aspirational *adj.* having a strong desire to have or achieve something, especially something such as a better job or position in society

asset *n.* [usually singular] something or someone that is useful because they help you succeed or deal with problems

associate *n.* [C] someone who you work with or do business with

authority *n.* the power that a person or organisation has because of their official or legal position

autocratic *adj.* relating to a leader who makes decisions and gives orders to people without asking them for their opinion

automation *n.* [C] the use of machines and computers, rather than people, to produce goods or do work

automotive *adj.* [only before a noun] relating to cars or the car industry

backer *n.* [C] someone who supports a plan, person, or company, usually by giving money

backing *n.* [U] support or help, especially financial help
financial backing *n.* [U] money that is given for support or help, especially to start a business or begin making a product

background *n.* **1** [C] someone's past, for example their education, qualifications and the jobs they have had
2 [C, U] the situation or past events that explain why something happens in the way that it does

board *n.* [C] (*also* **board of directors**) the group of people who have been elected to manage a company by those holding shares in the company

boost *v.* [T] to increase something such as production, sales or prices

brainstorm *v.* [I,T] to have a discussion or meeting with other people at work to suggest a lot of ideas for an activity or for solving a problem

brand *n.* [C] a name given to a product by a company so that the product can easily be recognised by its name or its design
brand ambassador *n.* [C] someone, especially someone famous, whom a company pays to use their products and make people more aware of the brand, for example whether they think it is good or poor quality, cheap or expensive, fashionable or old-fashioned. etc.
brand awareness *n.* [U] the degree to which people know about a particular brand
brand image *n.* [C] the collection of ideas and beliefs that people have about a brand, for example, whether they think it is poor or good quality, cheap or expensive, fashionable or old-fashioned, etc.
brand personality *n.* [U] the characteristics that people think a particular brand has, that are similar to human qualities, such as being fun, exciting, healthy, young, etc.
brand stretching *n.* [U] the act of starting to use an existing brand name on a different type of product, hoping that people will buy it because they recognise the name (*see also* **stretch a brand**)

budget *n.* [C] a detailed plan made by an organisation or a government of how much it will receive as income over a particular period of time, and how much it will spend, what it will spend the money on, etc.

bureaucracy *n.* [U] all the complicated rules and processes of an official system, especially when they are confusing or responsible for causing a delay

business plan *n.* [C] a document produced by a company, especially a new company, giving details of expected sales and costs, and how the business can be financed, and showing why the business will make money

candidate *n.* [C] someone who is being considered for a job

cashflow (*also* **cash flow**) *n.* **1** [U] the amounts of money coming into and going out of a company, and the timing of these
2 [C, U] profit for a particular period, defined in different ways by different businesses

centralised (*also* **centralized** *AmE*) *adj.* organised in a way that one central group in an company, organisation or country has the power and control and tells people in other places what to do

chain *n.* [C] a number of shops, hotels, cinemas, etc. owned or managed by the same company or person
discount chain *n.* [C] a number of shops owned or managed by the same company or person that sell goods at lower prices than other shops of the same type
retail chain *n.* [C] a number of shops that are owned or managed by the same company or person
supermarket chain *n.* [C] a number of supermarkets (=shops that sell food or other household goods) that is owned or managed by the same company or person

chairman *n.* [C] (*plural* **chairmen**) (*also* **chairman of the board**) the person who is in charge of a large company or organisation, especially the most senior member of its board

Chief Executive Officer (*also* **CEO**) *n.* the manager with the most authority in the normal, everyday management of a company. The job of Chief Executive Officer is sometimes combined with other jobs, such as that of president.

clichéd *adj.* relating to words, phrases or ideas that have been used so much that they are not effective or do not have meaning any longer

client *n.* [C] **1** someone who pays for services or advice from a professional person or organisation
2 someone who buys something from a seller (= **customer**)
base of clients (*also* **client base**) *n.* [C usually singular] the group of people or companies who regularly use a company's services or buy its products

coach n. [C] someone whose job is to help someone to learn what they should say or do to be successful in a particular situation or in their career
  career coach n. [C] someone whose job is to help people to plan their careers

coaching n. [U] the process of helping someone prepare what they should say or do in a particular situation

commercial vehicle n. [C] a vehicle such as a truck or van, used for taking goods from one place to another

commission n. [C, U] an amount of money paid to someone according to the value of goods, shares, bonds, etc. they have sold

commitment n. **1** [C, U] a promise to do something or to behave in a particular way
  2 [U] the hard work and loyalty that someone gives to an organisation or activity

compensation n. [U] an amount paid to someone because they have been hurt or harmed

competent adj. having enough skill, knowledge, or ability to do something to a satisfactory standard

competition n. **1** [C] an organised event in which people or teams compete against each other
  2 [singular, U] the people or groups that are competing against you, especially in business
  3 a situation in which businesses are trying to be more successful than others by selling more goods and services and making more profit

concept n. [C] **1** an idea for a product
  2 a rule or idea saying how something should be done

consensus n. [singular, U] agreement among a group of people

consolidation n. [C, U] when companies combine in takeovers and mergers, resulting in fewer businesses in an industry

consultant n. [C] someone whose job is to give people or businesses advice or training in a particular area

consumer n. [C] a person who buys goods, products and services for their own use, not for business use or to resell
  consumer base n. [C usually sing.] all the people who buy or use a particular product

contract n. [C] a formal, written agreement between two or more people or groups which says what each must do for the other, or must not do

convenience store n. [C] a shop where you can buy food, alcohol, magazines, etc., especially one that is open for 24 hours every day

core adj. relating to something that is most important to a person, company, etc.
  core business the business that makes the most money for a company and that is considered to be its most important and central one (see also **non-core business**)
  core value n. [C] a principle that you consider to be very important, and which affects all aspects of what you do

corporate adj. relating to a company, usually a large one, or business in general
  corporate tax (also **corporation tax** BrE, **corporate income tax** AmE) n. [C] a tax on a company's profits

cost n. **1 costs** [plural] the money that a business or an individual must regularly spend
  2 [C, U] the amount of money that you have to pay in order to buy, do, or produce something

covering letter BrE, **cover letter** AmE n. [C] a letter that you send with another document or a package, explaining why it has been sent or giving extra information about it

crowdfunding n. [U] a method of getting money to do something, for example make a new film or fund a project, by asking many people to give part of the money needed, often on the internet

customer n. [C] a person or organisation that buys goods or services from a shop or company
  customer engagement n. [U] when customers are interested in a product or company and feel that they have a connection or relationship with that company

customer service n. [U] **1** when an organisation helps its customers by answering their questions and listening to their complaints, giving them advice on using a particular product or service, providing a good quality product, etc.
  2 (also **Customer Services**) the department in a large organisation that deals with questions and complaints from its customers, gives advice on using the product or service it provides, etc.

CV n. [C] (abbreviation for **curriculum vitae**) a short written document that lists your education and previous jobs, which you send to employers when you are looking for a job (= **résumé** AmE)

deadline n. [C] a date by which you have to do something

decentralised (also **decentralized** AmE) adj. organised in a way that moves responsibility, services, or jobs from one central group or place to different groups or places within a company, organisation, or country

decision-making n. [U] the process of making important business, political, or legal decisions

decline[1] v. [I] **1** if an industry or country declines, it becomes less profitable, productive, wealthy, etc.
  2 if sales, profits, production, etc. decline, they become less

decline[2] n. [C, U] **1** when sales, profits, production, etc. become less
  2 when an industry or country becomes less profitable, productive, wealthy, etc.

delegate v. [I,T] to give part of your power or work to someone else, usually someone in a lower position than you

demand n. [U] **1** the amount of spending on goods and services by companies and people in a particular economy
  2 the total amount of a type of goods or services that people or companies buy in a particular period of time
  3 the total amount of a type of goods or services that people or companies would buy if they were available

demographic n. [C] a part of the population that is considered as a group, especially by advertisers who want to sell things to that group
  age demographic n. [C] a part of the population that are a similar age

department n. [C] one of the parts of a large organisation, such as a company or university, where people do a particular kind of work
  department store n. [C] a large shop that is divided into separate departments (= sections), each selling a different type of goods

depression (also **economic depression**) n. [C,U] a long period of time during which there is very little business activity and a lot of people do not have jobs

devalue v. [T] to cause something to lose its importance or value

development n. [U] the growth or improvement of something, so that it becomes bigger or more advanced
  continuing professional development n. [U] the process in which you continue to learn skills and gain knowledge and experience while you are working in a job
  learning and development n. [U] the process of improving the skills and abilities of employees, so that they can perform their work well and meet the needs of the company

disconnect n. [singular] when two people or groups no longer understand or have a relationship with each other

discount n. [C] a reduction in the cost of goods or services in relation to the normal cost
  discount chain n. [C] a number of shops owned or managed by the same company or person that sell goods at lower prices than other shops of the same type
  discount retailer n. [C] a shop that sells goods at a lower price than other shops of the same type
  discount supermarket n. [C] a supermarket that sells food and other goods at a lower price than other supermarkets

disposable income n. [U] the amount of money you have left to spend after you have paid your taxes, bills, etc.

distribute v. [T] to supply goods to shops and companies so that they can sell them

155

Glossary

distribution *n.* [U] the actions involved in supplying goods to shops and companies after they have been produced, for example moving, storing and selling the goods

distributor *n.* [C] a person or business responsible for supplying goods to shops and companies after they have been produced

e-commerce *n.* [U] (**electronic commerce**) the practice of buying and selling goods and services over the internet (= **e-business**)

emerging *adj.* in an early state of development
    emerging market *n.* [C] a country that is in the process of developing its industries, businesses and financial systems
    emerging technology *n.* [C] a machine, piece of equipment, or method that is new and that is likely to have a strong influence on society, a field of study, etc.

employ *v.* [T] to pay someone to work for you

employer *n.* [C] a person or company that pays people to work for them

enterprise *n.* [C] a company or business
    small and medium enterprise (*also* **SME**) *n.* [C] a company that is not owned by another, larger company, and that has a small number of employees. In European countries, companies must have fewer than 250 employees to be called a medium-sized enterprise, and fewer than 50 employees to be called a small enterprise.

entrepreneur *n.* [C] someone who starts a company, arranges business deals and takes risks in order to make a profit

entrepreneurial *adj.* having the qualities that are needed to start a company and arrange business deals, such as the ability to take risks

e-tailer *n.* [C] (**electronic retailer**) a business that sells products or services on the internet, instead of in a shop

ethical *adj.* **1** connected with principles of what is right and wrong
2 morally good or correct
    ethically *adv.*

etiquette *n.* [U] the formal rules for polite behaviour

evaluate *v.* [T] to consider how valuable something is

event *n.* [C] a performance, sports competition, party, etc. at which people gather together to watch or take part in something
    corporate event *n.* [C] an event at which people from a particular company and their guests gather together to watch or take part in something
    promotional event *n.* [C] an event that is intended to advertise a product, company, brand, etc.

exchange rate *n.* [C] the price at which one currency can be bought

expand *v.* [I, T] **1** to become larger in size, amount or number, or to make something larger in size, amount or number
2 if an economy, industry or business activity expands, it gets bigger or more successful

expansion *n.* [U] **1** when something increases or is increased in size, amount or number
2 when an economy becomes more successful, and there is increased economic activity, more jobs, etc.

expertise *n.* [U] special skills or knowledge in an area of work or study

exporter *n.* [C] a person, company or country that sells goods to another country

extend *v.* **1** [T] to make something bigger or longer, or to increase its range
2 extend a brand to use the same brand name for a new type of goods that is similar in some way to the original goods sold under that brand name (*see also* **stretch a brand**)

facilitator *n.* [C] someone who helps a group of people discuss things with each other or do something effectively

factor *n.* [C] one of many things that influence or affect a situation

fall *v.* (*past tense* **fell**; *past participle* **fallen**) [I] to go down to a lower price, level, amount, etc.

fast fashion *n.* [U] fashionable and often inexpensive clothing that is made quickly after being designed, and which often does not stay in the shops for a long time

feedback *n.* [U] advice, criticism, etc. about how successful or useful something is

finance *n.* [U] the management of money by countries, organisations and people

firm *n.* [C] a company or business, especially one which is quite small

forecast *n.* [C] a description of what is likely to happen in the future, based on the information that you have now

function *n.* **1** [C] the purpose for which something is made or used, or the job that someone does (= **role**)
2 [U] the way in which something works or operates, or the way in which it is used

funding *n.* [U] money provided to an organisation, for example in the form of loans, or grants (= money given for a particular purpose)

gain *v.* **1** [T] to get or achieve something important or valuable, usually by working very hard
2 [I,T] to gradually get more of a useful or valuable quality, skill, etc.
3 gain access/admittance to manage to enter a place, building or organisation

global *adj.* **1** including and considering all the parts of a situation together, rather than the individual parts separately
2 affecting or involving the whole world
3 go global if a company or industry goes global, it starts doing business all over the world
    globally *adv.*

goods *n.* [plural] things that are produced in order to be used or sold

government organisation (*also* **government organization** *AmE*) *n.* [C] a group that has been formed to do a particular job or function of the government

grow *v.* (*past tense* **grew**; *past participle* **grown**) **1** [T] to increase in amount, size or degree
2 [T] if you grow a business activity, you make it bigger

growth *n.* [U] an increase in size, amount or degree

guarantee *n.* [C] a formal written promise to repair or replace a product, if it has a fault, within a specific period of time after you buy it

guideline *n.* [C usually plural] rules or instructions about the best way to do something

headquarters *n.* the head office of an organisation

health and safety *n.* [U] the activity of protecting employees from illness or injury at work

hierarchy *n.* [C,U] (*plural* **hierarchies**) an organisation or structure in which the staff are organised in levels and the people at one level have authority over those below them

high flyer (*also* **high flier**) *n.* [C] an extremely successful person, organisation, etc.

hire *v.* [T] **1** to employ a person or an organisation for a short time to do a particular job for you
2 to agree to give someone a permanent job

holacracy *n.* [C, U] (*plural* **holacracies**) *trademark* an organisation or structure in which teams and individuals make decisions about the work they are doing, rather than being told what to do by a manager or executive

human resources (*also* **HR**) *n.* [plural] the department in an organisation that deals with employing, training and helping employees

iconic *adj.* relating to being famous or easily recognised and considered to represent a particular idea, brand, time period, etc.

impact *n.* [C] the effect or influence that an event, situation, etc. has on someone or something

incentive *n.* [C] something which is used to encourage people to do something, especially to make them work harder, produce more or spend more money

in-company *adj.* done within an organisation (= **in-house**)

incompetent *adj.* not having the skill or ability to do a job properly

increase¹ *v.* [I,T] to become larger in amount, number or degree, or to make something become larger

increase² *n.* [C] a rise in amount, number or degree

induction *n.* [C, U] the introduction and training of someone into a new job

industry *n.* [C] businesses that produce a particular type of thing or provide a particular service

inflation *n.* [C] a continuing increase in the prices of goods and services, or the rate at which prices increase

influencing *n.* [U] the process of having an effect on the way something happens or the way someone does something

innovation *n.* **1** [C] a new idea, method or invention
2 [U] the introduction of new ideas or methods

innovative *adj.* **1** an innovative product, method, process, etc. is new, different and better than those that existed before
2 using or developing new and original ideas and methods

in-store *adj.* happening or done within a large shop or store

internship *n.* [C] a job that lasts for a short time, that someone, especially a student, does in order to gain experience

interview¹ *n.* [C, U] **1** a formal meeting at which someone is asked questions to find out whether they are suitable for a job
2 [C] an occasion when someone is asked questions about their views or actions on television, for a newspaper, etc.

interview² *v.* [T] **1** to ask someone questions in a formal meeting in order to find out if they are suitable for a job
2 to ask someone, for example a politician, questions about their views or actions on television, for a newspaper, etc.

invest *v.* [I, T] **1** to buy shares, bonds, property, etc. in order to make a profit
2 to spend money on things that will make a business more successful and profitable

investment *n.* [C, U] when money is put into a business in order to make it more successful and profitable, or the money that is put into a business

investor *n.* [C] a person or organisation that invests money in order to make a profit

invoice *n.* [C] a document sent by a seller to a customer with details of goods or services that have been provided, their price and the payment date

invoicing *n.* [U] the process of preparing and sending an invoice

jobseeker (*also* **job seeker**) *n.* [C] someone who is looking for a job (= **job hunter**)

labelling *BrE,* **labeling** *AmE n.* [U] when a label (= piece of paper with information) is put on something, or the pieces of paper themselves

large-scale *adj.* [only before noun] using or involving a lot of people, effort, money or supplies

launch¹ *v.* [I, T] **1** to show or make a new product available for sale for the first time
2 to start a new company
3 to start a new activity or profession, usually after planning it carefully

launch² *n.* [C] **1** an occasion at which a new product is shown or made available for sale or use for the first time
2 the start of a new activity or plan

lead *v.* (*past tense and past participle* **led**) [T] **1** to be in charge of something such as an important activity, a group of people or an organisation
2 to be the first to do something, especially something good or successful, which is likely to encourage others to do the same thing
3 if you lead a particular kind of life, that is what your life is like

leadership *n.* [U] **1** the qualities needed in order to be a good leader
2 the position of being the leader of a team, organisation, country, etc.

level *n.* [C] **1** the measured amount of something that exists at a particular time or in a particular place
2 all the people or jobs within an organisation, industry, etc. that have similar importance and responsibility

loan *n.* [C] money borrowed from a bank, financial institution, person, etc. on which interest is usually paid to the lender until the loan is repaid

logistics *n.* [plural] the arrangements that are needed for goods, materials, equipment and people to be in the right place at the right time

logo *n.* [C] a design or way of writing its name that a company or organisation uses as its official sign on its products, advertising, etc.

loyalty *n.* [U] the quality of preferring the same brand or shops and using them regularly
loyalty card *n.* [C] a card given by a shop or company that gives regular customers lower prices, money back on goods, etc.

manufacturer *n.* [C] a company that makes large quantities of goods, usually in factories

manufacturing *n.* [U] the process or business of producing goods in factories

margin (*also* **profit margin**) *n.* [C, U] the difference between the price of a product or service and the cost of producing it, or between the cost of producing all of a company's products or services and the total sum they are sold for

market *n.* **1** [C] the activity of buying and selling goods or services, or the value of the goods or services sold
2 [C] a particular country, area or group of people to which a company sells or hopes to sell its goods or services
3 [singular] the number of people who want to buy something
emerging market *n.* [C] a country that is in the process of developing its industries, businesses and financial systems
global market *n.* [C] a country, area or group of people anywhere in the world, to which a company sells or hopes to sell its goods or services
market growth *n.* [U] an increase in demand within a particular country, area or group of people for a product or service
market research *n.* [U] a business activity that involves collecting information about what goods people in a particular area buy, why they buy them, etc.
market share *n.* [C, U] the percentage of sales in a market that a company or product has
market survey a study of the state of a particular market, showing competitors' sales, buyers' intentions, etc.

marketing *n.* [U] activities to design and sell a product or service by considering buyers' wants or needs, for example where and how they will buy it, how much they will be willing to pay, etc.
interactive marketing *n.* [U] the activity of deciding how to advertise and sell a product or service that is based on interactions (= occasions when someone talks to and listens to someone else) with customers, for example looking at a customer's internet searches, getting feedback from customers, etc.
marketing campaign *n.* [C] a planned series of actions that are intended to make people more aware of a product or idea, or to persuade people to buy a product or service
marketing channel *n.* [C] a way of sending out information about a product or service, for example social media, newspapers, television, etc.
street marketing *n.* [U] a way of advertising a product or service by doing something unusual in a public place

mentor *n.* [C] an experienced person who gives advice to less experienced people to help them in their work

merge *v.* [I, T] if two or more companies, organisations, etc. merge, or if they are merged, they join together

merger *n.* [C] an occasion when two or more companies, organisations, etc. join together to form a larger company, etc.

millennial *n.* [C] someone who was born in the 1980s or 1990s and became an adult during or after the year 2000

mindset *n.* [C] someone's general attitude, and the way in which they think about things and make decisions

m-learning *n.* [C] (**mobile learning**) learning that involves using smartphones and small computers that you carry with you

Glossary

multinational *n.* [C] a large company that has offices, factories and business activities in many different countries

negotiation *n.* [C usually plural, U] official discussions between groups who are trying to reach an agreement

negotiate *v.* [I, T] to discuss something in order to reach an agreement

negotiator *n.* [C] someone who takes part in official discussions, especially in business or politics, in order to try and reach an agreement

networking *n.* [U] an activity in which you meet with other people involved in the same kind of work in order to share information, help each other, etc.

neuroleadership *n.* [U] the use of studies of the brain to help improve people's ability to lead other people, especially in business

non-core business *n.* [C] businesses that are not considered the main or most important part of a company's business and that do not make the most income for the company (*see also* **core business**)

on-the-job *adj.* while working, or at work

operate *v.* [T] if a person or organisation operates a business, system, etc., they manage it and make it work

operations *n.* [plural] a company's normal activities related to providing services or producing goods, rather than other actions with financial effects, such as selling assets

operator *n.* [C] 1 someone who works a machine or piece of equipment
2 a person or company that operates a particular business

outcome *n.* [C] the final result of a process, meeting, discussion, etc. (= **result**)

outlet *n.* [C] a shop, company or organisation through which products are sold

outsell *v.* [T] to be sold in larger quantities than another product of the same type

own-brand *adj. BrE* own-brand products have on them the name of the shop that is selling them, rather than the producer's name (= **store-brand** *AmE*)

partner *n.* [C] 1 a company that works with another company in a particular activity, or invests in the same activity
2 someone who starts a new business with someone else by investing in it
3 someone you do a particular activity with

partnership *n.* 1 [C] a relationship between two people, organisations or countries that work together
2 [U] the situation of working together in business

perform *v.* 1 [I] if a product, business, etc. performs well or badly, it makes a lot of money or very little money
2 [T] to do work, carry out a duty, task, etc.
3 [I, T] to do something to entertain people, for example by acting a play or playing a piece of music

performance *n.* 1 [U] the way that someone does their job, and how well they do it
2 [C,U] the degree to which a company, investment, financial market, etc. is profitable

perk *n.* [C] something, in addition to money, that you get for doing your job, such as a car

PEST analysis *n.* [C] (**political, economic, social and technological analysis**) a careful examination of a market, in which political, economic, social and technological matters are considered

pilot *n.* [C] a test that is done to see if an idea, product, etc. will be successful

pitch¹ *v.* [I, T] to persuade someone to buy something, do something, or agree with a particular idea

pitch² *n.* [C] the things someone says in order to persuade someone to buy something, do something or agree with a particular idea

policy *n.* [C] a course of action that has been officially agreed and chosen by a political party, business, or other organisation
company policy *n.* [C, U] a course of action that has been officially agreed and chosen by a business or other organisation

portal *n.* [C] a website that helps you find other websites, or the website that you go to first in order to get to other content

position¹ *n.* [C] 1 *formal* a job (= **post**)
2 the place where someone or something is or should be, especially in relation to other objects and places

position² *v.* [T] if a company positions itself or a product in a particular way, it tries to get people to think about it in that way, especially in comparison to other businesses or products

post *n.* [C] *formal* a job, especially an important or well-paid one (= **position**)

PR *n.* [U] (**public relations**) the work of persuading people to have a good opinion of an organisation, company, etc.

predictive *adj.* relating to a system's ability to use information about what is likely to happen next

pricing *n.* [U] the prices of a company's products or services in relation to each other and in relation to those of their competitors, and the activity of setting them

prioritise (also **prioritize** *AmE*) *v.* [I, T] to put several tasks, problems, etc. in order of importance, so that the most important ones are done first

problem-solving *n.* [U] the activity of finding answers to problems or a good way of doing something difficult

procedure *n.* [C, U] a way of doing something, especially the correct or usual way

process *n.* [C] 1 a series of actions taken to perform a particular task or achieve a particular result
2 a method of making or producing goods

product *n.* 1 [C] something useful and intended to be sold that comes from nature or is made in a factory
2 [C] a service
product design *n.* [U] the work of planning and making a new product, including how it works, what it looks like, etc.
product innovation *n.* [C, U] when new or better products are designed and developed, or the new or better product itself
product line *n.* [C] a type of product that a company makes or sells that has several different sizes, models, etc. (= **range**)
product placement *n.* [C, U] a form of advertising in which a company arranges for one or more of its products to appear in a television programme or film

production *n.* 1 [U] the process of making or growing things to be sold as products, usually in large quantities
2 [U] an amount of something that is produced

productive *adj.* producing or achieving something

productivity *n.* [U] the rate at which goods are produced, and the amount produced in relation to the work, time and money needed to produce them

profile *n.* [C] a short description of someone or something, giving the most important details about them

profit¹ *n.* [C, U] money that you gain from selling something, or from doing business in a particular period of time, after taking away costs

profit² *v.* [I] to gain money from an event, selling something, etc.

profitable *adj.* producing a profit

project manager *n.* [C] the person whose job it is to plan how a particular piece of work will be done and organise all the people and tasks to do it

promote *v.* [T] 1 to help something develop, grow, become more successful, etc. or encourage something to happen
2 to try hard to sell a product or service by advertising it widely, reducing its price, etc.
3 to give someone a better-paid, more responsible job in a company or organisation

promotion *n.* [C, U] 1 a move to a more important job or position in a company or organisation
2 **sales promotion** an activity such as special advertisements or free gifts intended to sell a product or service

Glossary

promotional *adj.* relating to a sales promotion
    promotional event *n.* [C] an event (=occasion such as a party or meeting, etc.) that is intended to advertise a product, company, brand, etc.
    promotional offer *n.* [C] something a company is willing to give to someone or do for someone as a way of raising the sales of a product, service, etc.

proposal *n.* [C] a plan or idea which is suggested formally to an official person, or when this is done

propose *v.* [T] to suggest something such as a plan or course of action

publicise (*also* **publicize** *AmE*) *v.* [T] to give information about something to the public, so that they know about it

qualification *n.* **1** [C, usually plural] an examination that you have passed at school, university or in your profession
2 [C] a skill, personal quality or type of experience that makes you suitable for a particular job

quality control *n.* [U] the process of making sure that an organisation's goods and services are produced and sold as planned and designed, and are of the right quality

R and D (*also* **R&D**) *n.* [U] **1** (**research and development**) the part of a business concerned with studying new ideas and planning new products
2 (**research and development**) the department in a company responsible for developing new products, improving existing products, etc.

raise *v.* [T] **1** to make people consider a question, etc., for example by beginning to talk or write about it (=**bring up**)
2 raise your voice to speak or shout more loudly, especially because you are angry
3 increase the amount or level of something
4 to collect the money, capital, etc. that is needed to do something

range (*also* **product range**) *n.* [C] a set of similar products made by a particular company or available in a particular shop

recommend *v.* [T] **1** to advise someone to do something, especially because you have special knowledge of a situation or subject
2 to say that something or someone would be a good thing or person to choose

recommendation *n.* [C, U] **1** official advice given to someone about what to do
2 a suggestion that someone should choose a particular thing or person because they are very good or suitable

recruit *v.* [I, T] to find new people to work for an organisation, do a job, etc.

recruitment *n.* **1** [U] the process or the business of recruiting new people
2 [C] an occasion when someone is recruited

reference *n.* [C] **1** a letter written by someone who knows you well, usually to a new employer, giving information about your character, abilities or qualifications
2 a person who provides information about your character, abilities or qualifications when you are trying to get a job (= **referee**)

regulation *n.* [C] an official rule or order

remortgage *v.* [I, T] to borrow money by having a second or bigger mortgage (= loan) on your property, especially a house

report to *phr. v.* [T] to work under someone's authority, and to be managed by them

requirement *n.* [C] **1** something that an official organisation says a company or person must have or do
2 something that someone needs or wants

restructuring *n.* [U] the process in which a company or organisation changes the way it is organised or financed

retail *n.* [U] **1** the sale of goods to customers for their own use, rather than to shops, etc.
2 retail trade/market/business the selling of goods or services to members of the public, or companies involved in this
3 retail shop/outlet/store a shop, etc. that is open to members of the public

retailer *n.* [C] **1** a business that sells goods to members of the public, rather than to shops, etc.
2 someone who owns or runs a shop selling goods to members of the public

revenue (*also* **revenues** *plural*) *n.* [C] money that a business or organisation receives over a period of time, especially from selling goods or services

reward[1] *n.* **1** [C] something that you receive because you have done something good or helpful
2 [C, U] money that you earn for doing a job or providing a service

reward[2] *v.* [T] to give someone something, such as money, because they have done something good or helpful

rise *v.* (*past tense* **rose**; *past participle* **risen**) [I] to increase in number, amount or value

risk[1] *n.* [C, U] the possibility that something may be lost, harmed or damaged, or that something bad, unpleasant or dangerous may happen

risk[2] *v.* [T] put something in a situation in which it could be lost, destroyed or harmed

role *n.* [C] the way in which someone or something is involved in an activity or situation, and how much influence they have on it

run *v.* **1** [T] to control or be in charge of an organisation, company or system
2 be running late to be doing everything later than planned or expected
3 [T] to print something in a newspaper or magazine, or broadcast something on television

salary *n.* [C, U] money that you receive as payment from the organisation you work for, usually paid to you every month

sale *n.* **1** [C, U] the act of selling someone property, food or other goods
2 sales [plural] the total number of products that a company sells during a particular period of time
3 sales [U] the part of a company that deals with selling products
projected sales *n.* [plural] a calculation of how much of a product a company expects to sell in the future

sample *n.* [C] a small amount of a product that people can use or look at in order to find out what it is like

saving *n.* **1** [U] the act of keeping money to use later rather than spending it
2 [C, usually singular] an amount of something that you have not used or spent, especially compared with a larger amount that you could have used or spent
3 savings [plural] money that is kept in a bank to be used later or invested, rather than spent

sector *n.* [C] all the organisations or companies in a particular area of activity, industry, etc.

self starter *n.* [C] someone who is able to work successfully on their own without needing other people's help or a lot of instructions

service *n.* [C] a particular type of help or work that is provided by a business to customers, but not one that involves producing goods
after-sales service *n.* [U] repairs and advice given to a customer by a company after the customer has bought a product from the company
financial services *n.* [plural] the business activity of giving advice about investments and selling investments to people and organisations

share *n.* [C] one of the parts into which ownership of a company is divided
share price *n.* [C] the price of a particular company's shares at a particular time

skill *n.* [C, U] an ability to do something well, especially because you have learnt and practised it
communication skills *n.* [plural] the ability to express yourself in a way that other people will understand, including the words you use and the way you behave when you are speaking
digital skills *n.* [plural] the ability to use computers and the internet effectively
hard skill *n.* [C usually plural] an ability to do something practical that you have learnt and practised, for example reading, using a computer, or being able to do maths

Glossary

soft skill n. [C usually plural] an ability to get along with and talk to other people, understand and deal with your own emotions and tasks, or behave properly in many different situations

transferable skill n. [C usually plural] an ability to do something that can be used in many different situations, especially one that helps you do a job for which you have not been formally trained

slogan n. [C] a short phrase that is easy to remember and is used by an advertiser, organisation or other group

SME n. [C] (**small and medium enterprise**) a company that is not owned by another, larger company, and that has a small number of employees. In European countries, companies must have fewer than 250 employees to be called a medium-sized enterprise, and fewer than 50 employees to be called a small enterprise.

staff n. [U] the people who work for an organisation or business

start-up n. [C] a new small company or business, especially one that can grow quickly, and often one that involves using the internet in some way

strategic adj. relating to a strategy or strategies
    strategic planning n. [U] the plans a company makes about what it will do in the future. This involves deciding which products it should be making, which markets it should be in, and how profits can be increased (= **corporate planning**)

stretch v. [I, T] **stretch a brand** to use the same brand name for a different type of goods (see also **extend a brand**)

structure n. [C, U] the way an organisation, system, market, etc. is organised or put together
    flat structure n. [C] a way of organising a business in which there are no managers or only a few managers between the people who do most of the work in the organisation and the executives of the organisation
    management structure n. [C] the way that a company organises the people who manage the workers, which affects who is allowed to make decisions, who has responsibility for particular tasks, etc.
    tall structure n. [C] a way of organising a business in which there are many levels of managers between the people who do most of the work in the organisation and the executives of the organisation

subsidiary n. (plural **subsidiaries**) [C] a company that is at least half-owned by another company

supervise v. [I, T] to be in charge of a group of people or a particular area of work

supplier n. [C] a company that provides a particular type of product

supply¹ v. (past tense and past participle **supplied**) [T] **1** to provide goods or services to customers, especially regularly and over a long period of time
2 to give someone something they want or need

supply² n. (plural **supplies**) [C] an amount of something that is available to be sold, bought, used, etc.
    supply chain (also **distribution chain**, **chain of distribution**) n. [C] the series of organisations that are involved in passing products from manufacturers to the public

survey n. [C] a set of questions given to a group of people to find out about their opinions or behaviour
    market survey a study of the state of a particular market, showing competitors' sales, buyers' intentions, etc.

take over phr. v. (past tense **took over**; past participle **taken over**) [T] to take control of a company by buying more than 50 percent of its shares

takeover n. [C] the act of getting control of a company by buying over 50 percent of its shares
    takeover bid n. [C] an offer by one company to buy another, or the value of this offer

target¹ n. [C] **1** a result such as a total, an amount or a time which you aim to achieve
2 target market/customer/group the group of people that a product, service, idea, etc. is aimed at

target² v. [T] **1** to aim products, programmes of work, etc. at a particular area or group of people
2 to choose someone or something for a particular type of treatment

term n. [C] one of the statements of what must be done or is true in an agreement, contract or other legal document
    delivery terms n. [plural] an agreement in a contract between a buyer and seller about when goods will be delivered, how they will be paid for, etc.
    payment terms n. [plural] the conditions of a sales agreement that concern how the customer will pay, and especially how much time is allowed for payment
    terms and conditions n. [plural] all of the things that must be done as stated in a contract or agreement. If they are not done, the contract or agreement will end.

title (also **job title**) n. [C] a name that describes a person's job or position

timeline n. [C] a plan for when things will happen or how long you think something will take

track n. [C] **be on track** likely to achieve the result you want

track record n. [C, usually singular] all the things that a person or organisation has done in the past, which shows how good they are at doing their job, dealing with problems, etc.

transaction n. [C] **1** a payment, or the process of making one
2 a business deal

transition n. [C, U] the act or process of changing from one state or form to another

trend n. [C] the general way in which a particular situation is changing or developing

turnover n. [singular] **1** the amount of business done in a particular period, measured by the amount of money obtained from customers for goods or services that have been sold
2 (also **staff turnover**) the rate at which workers leave an organisation and are replaced by others

upmarket (also **upscale** AmE) adj. involving goods and services that are expensive and perhaps of good quality compared to other goods, etc. of the same type, or the people that buy them

vacancy n. (plural **vacancies**) [C] a job that is available for someone to start doing

values n. **1** [C, U] the amount of money something is worth
    good/excellent etc. value (for money) if something is good/excellent, etc. value, it is of good quality considering its price, or you get a large amount for the price
2 values [plural] the principles that a business or organisation thinks are important and which it tries to follow

venture into phr. v. [T] if a company or investor ventures into an area of business or investment, they become involved in it for the first time

volume n. [C, U] the total amount of something

warehouse n. [C] a large building used for storing goods in large quantities

workforce n. [singular] all the people who work in a particular country, industry or factory

workspace n. [C, U] the area in an office, house, etc. where you work at a desk

workshop n. [C] a meeting at which people discuss their experiences and do practical exercises, especially in order to find solutions to problems